DATE DUE

GAYLORD   PRINTED IN U.S.A.

Understanding
Jonathan Edwards

Understanding Jonathan Edwards

An Introduction to
America's Theologian

EDITED BY GERALD R. MCDERMOTT

OXFORD
UNIVERSITY PRESS

2009

OXFORD
UNIVERSITY PRESS

Oxford University Press, Inc., publishes works that further
Oxford University's objective of excellence
in research, scholarship, and education.

Oxford   New York
Auckland   Cape Town   Dar es Salaam   Hong Kong   Karachi
Kuala Lumpur   Madrid   Melbourne   Mexico City   Nairobi
New Delhi   Shanghai   Taipei   Toronto

With offices in
Argentina   Austria   Brazil   Chile   Czech Republic   France   Greece
Guatemala   Hungary   Italy   Japan   Poland   Portugal   Singapore
South Korea   Switzerland   Thailand   Turkey   Ukraine   Vietnam

Copyright © 2009 by Gerald R. McDermott

Published by Oxford University Press, Inc.
198 Madison Avenue, New York, New York 10016

www.oup.com

Oxford is a registered trademark of Oxford University Press

Library of Congress Cataloging-in-Publication Data
Understanding Jonathan Edwards: an introduction to America's
theologian / edited by Gerald R. McDermott.
    p. cm.
Includes bibliographical references and index.
ISBN 978-0-19-537343-1; 978-0-19-537344-8 (pbk.)
1. Edwards, Jonathan, 1703–1758.   I. McDermott, Gerald R.
(Gerald Robert)
BX7260.E3U53 2008
230'.58092—dc22   2008005336

9 8 7 6 5 4 3 2 1

Printed in the United States of America
on acid-free paper

*To Tibor Fabiny, a perspicacious scholar
with Edwardsian affections*

Acknowledgments

I am grateful for the many people who helped me gather these thinkers to present this book. Inspiration for this book came from thinking about getting Europeans to listen to Edwards experts talk in plain speech about "America's theologian." Thanks are due to Bishop István Szabó, bishop of the Dunamellék district of the Reformed Church of Hungary, and his assistant, Enikő Regéczy Nagy, for enabling me to connect those experts with ordinary folks and nonscholars in Europe. Tibor Fabiny was a critical intermediary in these discussions. Kenneth Minkema deserves special thanks for his generous ways, both scholarly and practical. The chronology is based on a much longer chronology compiled by Kenneth Minkema and used by permission of the author.

Finally, Jean—as always—was a constant and loving companion throughout the process.

In the cover illustration, Jonathan Edwards tries out a modern Wassily chair for his own purposes. The picture represents this volume's thesis—that Edwards uses modernity while challenging its presumptions.

Contents

Contributors

Chris Chun is a PhD candidate at the University of St. Andrews in Scotland, currently researching the theological influence of Jonathan Edwards on Andrew Fuller. His ThM thesis at Gordon-Conwell Theological Seminary examined the relationship between Edwardsian epistemology and pneumatology. Chris serves on the editorial committee of the critical edition of *The Works of Andrew Fuller* (forthcoming) and is editing one of its fifteen volumes. He is an ordained Baptist minister and a frequent speaker at churches, seminars, and retreats.

Tibor Fabiny is the chair of the Department of Hermeneutics at the Károli Gáspár University of the Reformed Church, Budapest, where he also teaches English Renaissance literature. He has had a long interest in interdisciplinary approaches to religion, the arts, and literature. He served as a Fulbright visiting scholar at Princeton Theological Seminary in 2004 and twice as Copenhaver scholar in residence at Roanoke College in Virginia. He is the author of a book on biblical typology, *The Lion and the Lamb,* and two other books in Hungarian, as well as numerous articles related to literature and theology. In May 2006 his home institution hosted the first international Jonathan Edwards Conference.

Katalin G. Kállay teaches American literature at Károli Gáspár University in Budapest and offers summer courses at the University of California in Santa Cruz. She took an MA at L. Eötvös University in

Budapest and her PhD at the Catholic University of Leuven, Belgium. Her first book on nineteenth-century American short stories, *Going Home through Seven Paths to Nowhere: Reading Short Stories by Hawthorne, Poe, Melville and James* was published in 2003 by the Hungarian Academy of Science. Her fields of research include nineteenth- and twentieth-century American fiction, literary responses to the Holocaust, and the relationship between philosophy and literature.

Wilson H. Kimnach is Emeritus Presidential Professor in the Humanities at the University of Bridgeport. A literary historian specializing in early American literature, the eighteenth-century sermon, and Jonathan Edwards, he has served as editor of sermons for the Yale edition of *The Works of Jonathan Edwards*. Professor Kimnach has published numerous articles and was recently joint editor of *The Sermons of Jonathan Edwards: A Reader*.

Sang Hyun Lee, K. C. Han Professor of Systematic Theology at Princeton Theological Seminary, received his MDiv and PhD degrees in systematic theology from Harvard University. His major publications are *The Philosophical Theology of Jonathan Edwards* and the *Princeton Companion to Jonathan Edwards* (editor). Professor Lee edited volume 21 of the Yale edition of *The Works of Jonathan Edwards* and is a member of the editorial board of the Works of Jonathan Edwards.

Gerald R. McDermott is professor of religion at Roanoke College, Virginia. He is the author of many articles and books, including *One Holy and Happy Society: The Public Theology of Jonathan Edwards; Jonathan Edwards Confronts the Gods: Christian Theology, Enlightenment Religion, and Non-Christian Faiths;* and *Seeing God: Jonathan Edwards and Spiritual Discernment*. He is currently working on a comprehensive survey of Edwards's theology.

Kenneth P. Minkema is director of the Jonathan Edwards Center, editor of *The Works of Jonathan Edwards* Online, assistant adjunct professor of American religious history at Yale Divinity School, and executive secretary of the American Society of Church History. Besides publishing numerous articles on Jonathan Edwards and related topics in professional journals, including the *Journal of American History*, the *William and Mary Quarterly*, the *New England Quarterly*, the *Massachusetts Historical Review*, and *Church History*, he has edited volume 14 in the Edwards *Works, Sermons and Discourses: 1723–1729*, and coedited *A Jonathan Edwards Reader, The Sermons of Jonathan Edwards: A Reader,* and *Jonathan Edwards at 300: Essays on the Tercentennial of His Birth*.

Wolter H. Rose teaches Semitic languages and history and culture of the ancient Near East at the Theological University of the Reformed Churches, Kampen, The Netherlands. He was awarded a DPhil in Old Testament studies from

Oxford University in 1997. His current interests include the morphology of the Hebrew verb and word order in the Hebrew clause. He has written on messianic expectations in the Old Testament, including a monograph, *Zemah and Zerubbabel: Messianic Expectations in the Early Postexilic Period*, and is now writing a commentary on the book of Zechariah.

Magdaléna Ševčíková took her PhD at Jan Commenius University in Bratislava (Slovakia) in 2005. Her dissertation was an analysis of *Communio Sanctorum*. Dr. Ševčíková has published articles on ecumenism and Lutheran dogmatics, including "Why the Virgin Mary Is a Paradigm for Men and Women in the Church" (Commenius University Publications). She has worked on women's issues for the Lutheran World Federation in Europe and currently pastors a Lutheran congregation outside Bratislava.

Harry S. Stout is the Jonathan Edwards Professor of American Religious History at Yale University. He received his PhD from Kent State University in 1974. He has been the recipient of multiple fellowships, including the National Endowment for the Humanities, the Guggenheim Foundation, and the Pew Charitable Trusts. He has written three prize-winning books: *The New England Soul*; *The Divine Dramatist*; and *Upon the Altar of the Nation*. He is the general editor of *The Works of Jonathan Edwards* and coeditor of a seventeen-volume collection on the religions of America for public high school libraries. He is presently chair of the Department of Religious Studies at Yale.

Anna Svetlikova is a PhD candidate in American literature at Charles University, Prague. Her project focuses on the literary aspects of the writings of Jonathan Edwards. Anna was awarded a Fulbright Fellowship to work at the Jonathan Edwards Center at Yale University in 2006–2007. She gave a guest lecture on Edwards's understanding of the imagination at Calvin College and holds a master's degree in Dutch and in English and American Studies from Charles University.

Douglas A. Sweeney is professor of church history and the history of Christian thought and director of the Carl F. H. Henry Center for Theological Understanding at Trinity Evangelical Divinity School. He is the author or editor of numerous books and articles about religious history and Jonathan Edwards, including *The Sermons of Jonathan Edwards: A Reader*; *Nathaniel Taylor, New Haven Theology, and the Legacy of Jonathan Edwards*; *Jonathan Edwards's "Miscellanies" Nos. 1153–1360*, volume 23 of *The Works of Jonathan Edwards*; *Jonathan Edwards at Home and Abroad: Historical Memories, Cultural Movements, Global Horizons*; *The American Evangelical Story: A History of the Movement*; and *The New England Theology: From Jonathan Edwards to Edwards Amasa Park*.

Michal Valco teaches theology at the University of Zilina and directs the Lutheran Bible School in Martin, Slovakia. An ordained Lutheran minister, Professor Valco did his master of divinity studies at Comenius University in Bratislava and Luther Theological Seminary in Gettysburg and was awarded his doctorate at Commenius University in 2005. His dissertation was on the sources and meaning of Chemnitz's Christology for his treatment of the Lord's Supper. Professor Valco's main theological interests are historical theology and Christian dogmatics. His first university textbook is currently being published under the title *From Creation to Redemption: Chapters from Lutheran Theology*.

Willem van Vlastuin is lector of systematic theology at Amsterdam Free University. He has published a monograph on Edwards: *De Geest van opwekking: Een onderzoek naar de leer van de Heilige Geest in de opwekkingstheologie van Jonathan Edwards (1703–1758)* (The Spirit of Revival: A Study in the Doctrine of the Holy Spirit in the Revival Theology of Jonathan Edwards [1703–58]). Professor van Vlastuin has written several other books, including *Revival*, which was translated into English and Russian. He is also part-time pastor at Katwijk aan Zee and chairman of the Bonisa mission to China.

Miklos Vetö, born in Budapest in 1936, participated in the Hungarian Revolution of 1956 and fled to France as a political refugee. With doctorates in philosophy (Oxford, Sorbonne, University of Nanterre) and Catholic theology (University of Strasbourg), he taught at Marquette, Yale, Poitiers, and universities in Africa and Canada. In 2007 he was named a member of the Hungarian Academy of Sciences. Professor Vetö has published more than twenty books, including *La Pensée de Jonathan Edwards*, an English translation of which will appear in the United States in 2009. He is currently preparing a treatise on metaphysics.

Important Dates in the Life of Edwards

1703   October 5: Born in East Windsor, Connecticut
1716   September: Begins undergraduate studies at Connecticut Collegiate School, Wethersfield (later known as Yale College)
1720   May: Completes baccalaureate degree
       September: Delivers Valedictory Oration
       October 3: Begins graduate studies at New Haven
1721   Summer: Conversion experience at East Windsor
       Writes "Of the Rainbow," "Of Light Rays"
       Begins "Natural Philosophy," "Of Atoms," "Of Being," "Prejudices of the Imagination"
1722   May: Completes graduate studies
       August 10: Arrives in New York City to begin preaching to English Presbyterian congregation
       Begins "Resolutions," "Diary," "Catalogue of Books," and "Miscellanies"
1723   October: Writes "Spider Letter," begins "Notes on the Apocalypse"
       Writes "Apostrophe to Sarah Pierpont"
1724   Elected tutor at Yale College
1726   Chosen to be assistant to Solomon Stoddard at Northampton church
1727   July 28: Marries Sarah Pierpont in New Haven
1729   Solomon Stoddard dies; Edwards becomes senior pastor

1731   Purchases "Negro girl named Venus" for £80 in Newport, Rhode Island
       Preaches Boston lecture, later published as *God Glorified in the Work of Redemption*

1734   Preaches *A Divine and Supernatural Light*, thereafter published
       December: Connecticut Valley revivals begin

1735   June 1: Joseph Hawley Sr. commits suicide by slitting his throat

1737   *A Faithful Narrative of the Surprising Work of God* published in London

1738   April–October: Preaches *Charity and Its Fruits* (published 1852)
       Corrected edition of *Faithful Narrative* published in Boston

1739   March–August: Preaches *History of the Work of Redemption* (published 1774)

1740   October 17–19: George Whitefield preaches in Northampton; Edwards accompanies him as far as East Windsor
       December: Writes "Personal Narrative" in reply to request from Rev. Aaron Burr

1741   July 8: Preaches *Sinners in the Hands of an Angry God* at Enfield, published shortly thereafter
       August–September: Awakening peaks in Northampton
       September 10: Delivers *Distinguishing Marks of the Work of the Spirit of God* at Yale commencement, published shortly thereafter

1742   January 19–February 4: Sarah Pierpont Edwards experiences series of religious ecstasies; afterward undergoes treatment for "hysterical original"
       Fall–winter: Writes *Some Thoughts Concerning the Present Revival of Religion in New England*
       Begins sermon series (apparently ending in 1743), eventually published as *Treatise Concerning Religious Affections*

1743   End of March: *Some Thoughts* published

1744   "Bad Book" episode

1745   July 15–17: Whitefield visits Northampton

1746   June: *Religious Affections* published
       August 19: French and Indians take Ft. Massachusetts; Edwards parsonage "forted in" and quartered with soldiers
       August 25: Indian raiding party attacks near Southampton
       September 19: Preaches ordination sermon of Samuel Buel at East Hampton, Long Island, published as *The Church's Marriage to Her Sons, and to Her God*

1747   May 28: David Brainerd arrives in Northampton
       October 9: Brainerd dies at Edwards parsonage
       October 12: Preaches Brainerd's funeral sermon, published (in December) as *True Saints, When Absent From the Body, Are Present With the Lord*

October: *An Humble Attempt to Promote Explicit Agreement and Visible Union of God's People in Extraordinary Prayer* published

Autumn: Begins work on *Life of David Brainerd*

1748   June 26: Preaches funeral sermon of John Stoddard at Northampton, published as *A Strong Rod Broken and Withered*

December: Completes *An Account of the Life of the Late Reverend Mr. David Brainerd*

1749   August: *An Humble Inquiry into the Rules of the Word of God* published

October 17: Treaty signed with eastern tribes, ending French and Indian War

December 26: Preliminary council meets to consider controversy between Edwards and Northampton church

1750   June 22: Dismissed as pastor of Northampton

July 2: Preaches *Farewell Sermon* (published 1751)

July–November: Preaches on supply basis at Northampton

1751   August 8: Formally installed as pastor to English and Indian congregations at Stockbridge

1752   Summer: *Misrepresentations Corrected, and Truth Vindicated* published

September 28: At Newark, preaches *True Grace, Distinguished From the Experience of Devils* (published 1753) to Presbyterian Synod of New York

1753   April: Completes first draft of *Freedom of the Will*

1754   Summer: Edwards parsonage fortified and quartered with soldiers against fears of Indian attacks

December: *Freedom of the Will* published

1755   February 11–13: Reads recently completed *End for Which God Created the World* to Bellamy and Hopkins; *The Nature of True Virtue* completed before February 1757 (published 1765)

July 9: Gen. Edward Braddock's forces defeated at Monongahela River in western Pennsylvania, with Braddock among the dead

September 1: Stockbridge attacked by Indians; four English killed

1757   May: Completes *Original Sin*

September 29: Trustees of College of New Jersey write to offer presidency

1758   February 16: Assumes office as president of College of New Jersey

February 23: Inoculated for smallpox

March 22: Dies of complications from inoculation

October 2: Sarah Pierpont Edwards dies of dysentery in Philadelphia

September: *Original Sin* published

1759   July 25: Estate inventoried and probated

August 4: Slaves Joseph and Sue, "lately the proper goods of . . . Jonathan Edwards, deceased," sold to John Owen of Simsbury, Connecticut, for £23, by executors Timothy Edwards and Timothy Dwight

Understanding
Jonathan Edwards

Introduction: How to Understand the American Theologian

Gerald R. McDermott

At one point toward the middle of my time in grad school, I was rummaging around for a dissertation topic. I had been planning, tentatively, to write about the intersection of religion and politics (which scholars then called "civil religion") in the antebellum period (the period before the Civil War). As I searched through the writings of pastors and theologians and other intellectuals during the period, I was struck by a common theme that seemed to pop up everywhere. Nearly everyone seemed to refer to "the great President Edwards" (he had been president of the College of New Jersey—the later Princeton), and many of the theologians insisted they were simply carrying on what President Edwards had started. Even when they weren't!

In other words, if you were a pastor or theologian back then and wanted to gain a hearing, you had to claim the mantle of Jonathan Edwards (1703–1758) to be considered legitimate. This wasn't true of everyone, or of every school of theology, but it was surprising to see that even those who clearly rejected important parts of Edwards's thinking, such as Charles Finney, nevertheless felt compelled to claim connections to Edwards and his theology.

So I decided that if I was to understand antebellum America, I would have to go back almost a century, to the mid-eighteenth century, to learn what this towering figure had to say. I imagined I could spend a week or two there, get control of Edwardsian basics, and then return to more interesting things in the nineteenth century.

Well, I went back and got stuck. Or, to put it more accurately, I became entranced by this deep and penetrating mind. Now, more than twenty years later, I am still attracted to its brilliance. Let me try to explain what has fascinated me and so many others over the centuries.

Why Edwards?

First, not everyone who reads Edwards is attracted to him. Harriet Beecher Stowe complained that Edwards's sermons on sin and suffering were "refined poetry of torture." After staying up one night reading Edwards's treatise on the will, Mark Twain reported, "Edwards's God shines red and hideous in the glow from the fires of hell, their only right and proper adornment. By God, I was ashamed to be in such company."

Generations of Americans have drawn similar conclusions after reading his "Sinners in the Hands of an Angry God" sermon in their high school and college literature classes. They would be surprised to learn that Edwards was obsessed by God's beauty, not wrath, and that, as historian Patrick Sherry recently argued, Edwards made beauty more central to theology than anyone else in the history of Christian thought, including Augustine and the twentieth-century Swiss Catholic Hans Urs von Balthasar.

They would also be surprised to learn that Edwards is widely regarded as America's greatest philosopher before the twentieth century, and arguably this continent's greatest theologian ever. One measure of his greatness is Yale University Press's critical edition of his works, which has twenty-six volumes—but even that represents only half of his written products. Another token of Edwards's importance is the three-volume *Encyclopedia of the American Religious Experience*, which contains far more references to Edwards than to any other single figure.

Although Edwards was revered for his piety and intellectual prowess in antebellum America, the Unitarians who gained cultural power after the Civil War dismissed him as an anachronistic symbol of the Puritanism that allegedly slowed America's advance to modernity. There were demurrals: Edwards was the hero of H. Richard Niebuhr's *Kingdom of God in America* (1937), and Ola Elizabeth Winslow's biography of Edwards won the Pulitzer Prize in 1940. But intellectuals generally did not take Edwards seriously again until 1949, when the Harvard historian Perry Miller published his acclaimed biography of the New England thinker, suggesting that only Edwards's unshrinking assessment of evil was capable of dispelling modernity's naïve utopianism.

Since the middle of the twentieth century Edwards scholarship has exploded, with the number of dissertations on his work doubling every decade.

The most prestigious university presses and journals have published hundreds of books and articles on his thought and influence.

Why such a profusion of interest? One reason is certainly, as William Sparkes Morris once put it, "because genius fascinates," but also because of the extraordinary range and depth of his thinking. For Miller, Edwards was a prophet of modernity. Miller said famously that Edwards stood so far above and ahead of his immediate culture that our own time is "barely catching up." Edwards's understanding of the human psyche was so advanced that "it would have taken him about an hour's reading in William James, and two hours in Freud, to catch up completely." Edwards scholars have concluded that Edwards's relationship to modernity was far more ambivalent, but Miller's comment shows the intrigue that Edwards has excited in many thinkers outside the bounds of the Christian churches.

Another reason for the breadth of Edwards's influence is the wide range of his work. Historians have studied Edwards's role as a pastor and the effect of his sermons and books on the Great Awakening, the American Revolution, the modern missionary movement, and the course of both American theology and philosophy; theologians appreciate his insights into the history of salvation (he relates sacred to secular history in his *Work of Redemption*), the Trinity (each Person in the Trinity has distinct roles), the relationship between divine sovereignty and human freedom (some say he did as well as anyone showing how the two are compatible), original sin (he linked our sin with Adam's, but not without showing our complicity in Adam's), typology (he believed all the world was filled with divinely implanted pointers to Christ and his kingdom), and spiritual discernment; ethicists profit from his writings on true virtue and Christian morality and his attack on Enlightenment ethics; literary critics are fascinated by his masterly employment of imagery and other literary strategies; students of aesthetics point out that he related God to beauty more than anyone else in the history of Christian thought; historians of American philosophy argue that he was America's premier philosopher before the great flowering of American philosophy at the turn of the twentieth century. Some scholars even suggest that Edwards offered the eighteenth century's most penetrating critique of the Enlightenment and has something to teach us about how Christians should think about non-Christian religions!

Perhaps most important for serious readers of religion and theology, Edwards is widely recognized as America's greatest theologian. Nearly twenty years ago Robert Jenson, the great American Lutheran theologian, published a monograph entitled *America's Theologian*. The nearest competitor to Edwards for that moniker, H. Richard Niebuhr, confessed that he was greatly indebted to Edwards and saw himself as extending the Edwardsian vision. Nineteenth-century

American theologians at Andover, Princeton, and Yale nearly universally claimed his mantle. But it wasn't only the theologians who were impressed: in large sections of antebellum America many homes contained two books—the Bible and a collection of Edwards's writings.

Those antebellum Americans were drawn to Edwards for some of the same reasons he attracts legions of followers today outside of academia. Many are captivated by what the prolific pastor and writer John Piper calls Edwards's "God-entranced vision of all things." Others desire personal renewal or corporate revival for their communities and find in Edwards a singular guide to spiritual renovation. J. I. Packer, the Oxford-trained theologian who has written enormously popular books for average Christians, thinks Edwards's theology of revival is the most important contribution Edwards makes to today's church. Others have considered his *Religious Affections* to be the most penetrating guide to spiritual discernment ever written. Still others are drawn to his rigorous pattern of spiritual discipline, his logical and compelling sermons, and the way he includes God's holiness and wrath in the larger picture of divine beauty.

Edwards's Theology

Edwards's theological project was gargantuan, addressing hosts of issues both parochial and perennial. Because his thought is so complex and multidimensional, a brief description such as this can easily distort. But one can say that much of his work was related to his lifelong battle with deism, the early modern rationalist movement that identified religion with morality and judged all religious expressions by what its thinkers deemed to be "common sense"—which was by no means common even to those in its own era.

Deists claimed that ordinary reason can determine what is true religion, so that the problem with bad religion and human relations generally was a failure to use reason properly. Edwards responded that this analysis of the human condition was too superficial. There is no such thing as "ordinary" or "naked" reason because the mind is darkened and disabled by indwelling sin. Hence reason is not neutral but conditioned by self-interest. It is no wonder, he remarked more than once, that intelligent people are responsible for great evil.

Deists assumed that all human action proceeded from good or bad thinking. But Edwards insisted that the springs of human motivation lie much deeper than the thoughts of the mind. In his famous formulation, he asserted that all human feeling and thinking and acting are rooted in the "affections," the underlying loves and dispositions that incline us toward or away from things. (These are not the emotions, as many scholars have erroneously reported, but something akin to what earlier traditions called the "soul," from which emotions arise.) This is the source of true religion as well as all other human perception and behavior. Hence true religion, Edwards wrote, must influence and spring from these deepest levels of the human psyche. The Scriptures, he said, confirm this. They place the heart of religion in the affections: fear, joy, hope, love, hatred, desire, sorrow, gratitude, compassion, and zeal.

On the one hand, then, Edwards defended the religion of the heart against the critics of revival who condemned emotionalism to the point that they were left with a religion of the head only. But Edwards also denounced religion that was merely emotion, devoid of cognitive understanding of basic Christian truth. In a manner unmatched by most other spiritual theologians, Edwards linked head and heart, experience and understanding.

Because true religion comes from sources much deeper than human thinking, Edwards insisted that we need a "divine and supernatural light." The Spirit must penetrate beneath the surface convictions of human reason to awaken a "sense of the heart" focused on the glory of the divine nature and the beauty of Jesus Christ.

Therefore, the essence of true religious experience is to be overwhelmed by a glimpse of the beauty of God, to be drawn to the glory of his perfections, and to sense his irresistible love. George Marsden once wrote that it is something like being overwhelmed by the beauty of a great work of art or music. We can become so enthralled by the beauty that we lose consciousness of self and self-interest and become absorbed by the magnificent object. So also we can become drawn out of self-absorption by the power of the beauty of a truly lovable person. Our hearts are changed by an irresistible power. But this power gently lures; it does not coerce. Edwards taught that our eyes are opened when we are captivated by the beautiful love and glory of God in Christ, when we see this love most powerfully demonstrated in Christ's sacrificial love for the undeserving. Then we feel forced to abandon love for self as the central principle of our lives and turn to the love of God.

Edwards describes our side of this experience as like being given a sixth sense: a sense of the beauty, glory, and love of God. He observes, "The Bible speaks of giving eyes to see, ears to hear, unstopping the ears of the deaf, and opening the eyes of them that were born blind, and turning from darkness to light." Therefore the spiritual knowledge gained in true conversion is a kind of "sensible" knowledge—as different from intellectual knowledge as the taste of honey is different from the mere intellectual understanding that honey is sweet.

True Christian experience, then, is sensible and affective. The Christian, says Edwards, does not "merely rationally believe that God is glorious, but he has a sense of the gloriousness of God in his heart. . . . For as God is infinitely the Greatest Being, so He is allowed to be infinitely the most beautiful and excellent: and all the beauty to be found throughout the whole creation is but the reflection of the diffused beams of that Being who hath an infinite fullness of brightness and glory; God . . . is the foundation and fountain of all being and all beauty."[1]

If Edwards challenged the religion of the Enlightenment (deism), he also took on Enlightenment ethics and cosmology. When nearly all eighteenth-century moralists were constructing ethical systems based on self-interest, presuming that human nature naturally seeks the good, Edwards countered that the affections are fallen. Therefore true virtue can come only from a heart spiritually transformed so that it sees God's glory and seeks his will and the public good rather than private interest.

Deists in the eighteenth century were also disconnecting the world from God's immediate control, positing a clockwork cosmos that runs on its own. The result was to objectify the universe, separating nature from the human and its feelings so that it could be used for technological purposes. But Edwards was relentlessly God-centered. He taught a kind of "panentheism" in which no part of the creation is ever independent of God, but all is sustained by God, moment by throbbing moment, as an emanation of his being.

Yet Edwards was no pantheist. God is not the same as the universe. Just as a sunbeam is sustained by the sun but is different from the sun, so the world is sustained by God as his emanation but is different from God. So while Enlightenment theorists said that the universe is a great machine that operates autonomously, Edwards said that God sustains it nanosecond to nanosecond. In fact, God's power is literally the binding force of atoms: the universe would collapse and disappear unless God upheld its existence from moment to moment (Col. 1.17: "In him all things consist"). As Avihu Zakai has recently put it, Edwards reenchanted a cosmos that had been stripped of the divine.[2]

This is one of the many ways Edwards was ahead of his time. He anticipated post-Newtonian physics, in which all matter is ultimately seen in terms of interacting fields of energy, with every part dependent on every other part, and the forces governing these rather mysterious. Physicists have been concluding for almost a century what Edwards declared two and a half centuries ago: there are no independent substances that can subsist on their own.

Why This Book?

The presses have been groaning under the weight of books on Edwards in the past fifty years. But this book is different.

Most books on Edwards have been one of two sorts. Many have been written by non–Edwards scholars. They have often been helpful, but they are largely unaware of the many new insights gained by Edwards scholars. And some in fact misrepresent this profound thinker.

Then there are the scholarly books on Edwards. Many of these are extremely insightful, but most are written by scholars and for scholars. They are full of academic jargon that is nearly impenetrable to nonspecialists and often address rather narrow and arcane subjects.

This is the first Edwards book that is written by a collection of Edwards scholars—some of the best in the world—but self-consciously addressed to nonspecialists. The chapters that follow go out of their way to use plain language and to define technical terms when they appear. The subjects of the chapters are broad and expansive and represent much of what Edwards considered central to his own concerns: revival, the Bible, beauty, literature, philosophy, typology, and even world religions. So rather than being a series of narrow and technical papers, these are expert essays on the broad themes of Edwards's thinking that will appeal to a wide range of readers.

Because this book treats the most important Edwardsian themes with accessible language from top Edwards scholars, it is perhaps the ideal introduction to the American theologian. It will serve well as both a personal guide to the interested reader and as an engaging textbook for classes on American religion or the American theologian.

At the same time, this volume offers a fresh approach to Edwards. Every essay is new and represents a new reflection on its subject by scholars who have been thinking through their topic for (often) decades.

This book provides yet another new feature. In keeping with its goal of reaching nonspecialists and nonscholars but bringing the best of scholarly insights to that audience, each chapter is followed by a response from a European scholar not previously familiar with Edwards.[3] These responses show the impact of Edwards on those outside of Edwards studies. They also show the relevance Edwards has for non-Americans—and some of the reasons why this eighteenth-century mind continues to attract so many readers and thinkers.

The Chapters That Follow

This book targets what we consider to be many of Edwards's chief interests. Edwards was concerned first and foremost for what he called "true religion" and worked zealously to bring it to life in his own and other churches. This was the motivating force behind his passion for revival. In chapter 2, Harry S.

Stout, the Jonathan Edwards Professor of American Religious History at Yale University, gives us an elegant overview of Edwards's work for revival—which the Massachusetts theologian believed is the key to all of history. Stout argues that Edwards used the history of revival to develop a whole new way of doing theology. Instead of writing a systematic theology, with its traditional list of theological topics, Edwards believed that history—especially the history of redemption that is driven by revival—provides the most penetrating and enjoyable access to divine mysteries. Stout compares Edwards's way of revival to that of the preeminent revivalist of the era, George Whitefield, and concludes that the (in)famous "Sinners in the Hands of an Angry God" is arguably America's greatest sermon.

Edwards also had a passion for the Bible. Far too little scholarly work has been done on his use of the Bible, which rivals in quantity and insight that of any in the history of Christianity. Douglas Sweeney, a church historian and the editor of one of the Yale volumes on Edwards's private notebooks, gives us a detailed survey of Edwards's approaches to the Bible in chapter 3. He explains that Edwards recommended church members to make the study of the Bible a habit of life because of his overwhelming conviction that the Bible is a supernatural revelation of the mind of the Creator. Yet a "divine and supernatural light" is essential, he said, to understand that mind. Edwards was fully aware of that era's historical criticism of the Bible, but he was not afraid—unlike many of today's Bible scholars—to interpret the text both historically and theologically. In other words, he boldly asserted not just what the text meant in the ancient world, but also what it means for today. He took a middle road on biblical allegory and typology, rejecting the extreme of seeing unbiblical allegory everywhere, but regarding the Bible as a unified book that is linked integrally between Old and New Testaments.

In his interpretation of the Bible, Edwards used typology (the science of symbols or signs that God has placed in the Bible and the world) extensively. In fact, this eighteenth-century Bible interpreter said we cannot make sense of how the Bible works unless we have a thoroughgoing knowledge of typology. This is why we enlisted the Hungarian expert on biblical typology, Tibor Fabiny, to write chapter 4. Fabiny lays out the contours of Edwards's biblical typology and proposes that the center of that system was the paradoxical nature of beauty, found most poignantly in Christ's dying sacrifice. For Fabiny, this was what Edwards thought to be the inner meaning of both the Bible and its typology. Fabiny then goes on to compare Edwards's typology to those of Shakespeare and Luther.

No book on Edwards can ignore his aesthetics, which is his understanding of beauty and its relation to God. As we have seen already, this was absolutely central to his view of reality. In chapter 5 Sang Hyun Lee, the Princeton theologian and author of one of the most influential analyses of Edwards of the past two decades, sketches Edwards's conception of beauty. Lee argues that for Edwards the fundamental nature of anything that exists is beauty, and the most distinctive characteristic of God is his divine beauty. To know and to love God, therefore, is to know and love the beauty of God, and to know the ultimate nature of the world is to know and love the world as an image of God's beauty. Lee's chapter contains perhaps the most incisive short treatment in print of the heart of Edwards's theological vision.

Readers of Edwards, even those who haven't liked his theology, have usually admired the tools he used: words that are connected in often lyrical fashion to sketch his vision of all that exists. He both loved language and was frustrated by its limits. He devoured most kinds of literature and believed he was a far better writer than speaker. Wilson Kimnach, a literary scholar who has edited all the sermons volumes in the Yale edition of *The Works of Jonathan Edwards*, provides in chapter 6 an exquisite overview of Edwards's interest in and production of literature. Kimnach argues that Edwards had literary ambitions even greater than his contemporary, Benjamin Franklin. His appetite for reading was almost unlimited, and he enjoyed not only the *Ladies Library* but also the novels of his day. His greatest contribution to literature was his perfection of the sermon genre, which focused on the essential heart of religion rather than doctrinal formulae. He strove to move his congregation by the application of the rhetorical lash and philosophical reasoning. He used the traditional Puritan "plain style" and the Ramist analytical method (dividing each thing simply and clearly into two parts), in contradistinction to the easy generalities and elegant fluency of Tillotsonian moralists (influenced by John Tillotson, Archbishop of Canterbury 1691–1694).

If Edwards wanted to use words to move the world's affections toward a vision of God's beauty, he also wanted to change the thinking of the intellectual elite. He therefore took philosophy very seriously and addressed a good part of his treatises to the philosophical world. The result was the most influential American philosophy before the Civil War and a system of thinking that, according to Miklos Vetö, is not only important in the history of philosophy but also has relevance today. Vetö is a distinguished philosopher in France and the author of a celebrated book on Edwards's philosophy. His chapter 7 gives us a lucid introduction to these philosophical breakthroughs. According to Vetö, Edwards employed philosophical reasoning in a far more profound and systematic way than his Puritan predecessors did, focusing on three themes or domains: being, knowledge, and the will. Vetö concludes that Edwards's theory of knowledge is the veritable culmination of the Western philosophical tradition's attempt to comprehend the metaphysical specificity of spiritual knowledge; that his understanding of the will is unprecedented before Kant in its incisive grasp of the autocratic nature of the will and its sui generis intelligibility; and that in his rethinking of dogma through philosophical argumentation, Edwards is comparable to Augustine and Aquinas.

Very few Edwards scholars and nonscholarly Edwards fans have known this, but Edwards became more and more fascinated by world religions the older he got. He knew that if he was to complete his magnum opus of Christian theology properly (which his untimely death prevented), he was going to have to place Christian faith within the context of the history of other religions. His massive private notebooks are filled with notes toward this end, showing that this was of huge interest to him. In chapter 8 I give a brief outline of how he came to understand non-Christian religions and their place in the history of redemption. I explain that a principal stimulus to his interest was the deists' use of other religions to attack Christian orthodoxy. Edwards used three approaches to counter deism and understand the religions: (1) the *prisca theologia* (literally, "ancient theology"), an ancient Jewish and Christian apologetic tradition that claimed other religions were derived indirectly from Christian revelation; (2) his conviction that God speaks through all of nature and history (typology); and (3) his thinking about the possibility of salvation for non-Christians (dispositional soteriology).

So what? Of what use is Edwards today? This introduction has hinted at a number of answers to this question, and each of the succeeding chapters suggests more. But in the conclusion I try to draw a number of these suggestions together and advance a few additional ones. Among other things, I argue that Edwards's religiophilosophical thought is especially helpful in a twenty-first-century world that is frightened by violent religion and confused by religious pluralism. Edwards shows that true religion at its heart is consumed with beauty and peace, and that Christian theology has a way of seeing truth and beauty in other religions while at the same time pointing to final truth. His vision of God as both joy and beauty, understood through both Scripture and reason, provides a bridge between the Reformed and Roman Catholic traditions and offers inspiration to every mind seeking God and beauty. Furthermore, Edwards has helpful things to say about shaping a social and political order that ensures both freedom and pluralism. I also comment on what he has to say about conversion and spiritual formation, missions, preaching, ethics and community, what it means to be human, and the Reformed tradition.

Last, and not least important, who was Edwards as a man? We cannot appreciate Edwards and his work without knowing something of his biography. For this we have called on Kenneth Minkema, the executive director of

The Works of Jonathan Edwards at Yale. In chapter 1 Minkema gives us a balanced (admiring but warts-and-all) introduction to the American theologian's life and career. There is no one else who can say, as Minkema can, that he has devoted the majority of his working weeks for more than twenty years to Edwards and his writings. In Minkema's informative overview of Edwards's life and career, we learn about his international and colonial worlds. For example, Minkema tells us that Edwards thought of himself as a British subject loyal to the Empire but was at the same time sensitive to his colony's grievances. He was ambivalent toward Indians (hating their religion but loving many of those he knew personally), a philosopher who picked and chose from the world's best thinkers, and a religious thinker whose theology sowed the seeds of the very democracy he feared. He defended slavery but opposed the slave trade and offered Janus-faced positions on gender. His spirituality was intense, his influence immense: four thousand books, dissertations, and articles have been distributed in the past half-century. And because of the worldwide expansion of evangelical Christianity, his star is rising around the world.

NOTES

1. Jonathan Edwards, "A Divine and Supernatural Light," in John E. Smith, Harry S. Stout, and Kenneth P. Minkema, eds., *A Jonathan Edwards Reader* (New Haven: Yale University Press, 1995), 111; Jonathan Edwards, *The Nature of True Virtue*, in *The Works of Jonathan Edwards*, ed. Paul Ramsey (New Haven: Yale University Press, 1957), 8: 550–51.

2. Avihu Zakai, *Jonathan Edwards's Philosophy of History: The Reenchantment of the World in the Age of Enlightenment* (Princeton, NJ: Princeton University Press, 2003).

3. The one exception is my response to the essay by Tibor Fabiny, a Hungarian expert on biblical typology.

I

Jonathan Edwards's Life and Career: Society and Self

Kenneth P. Minkema

Getting at the "personal" Edwards is a difficult task. We can ascertain his historical significance, the breadth of his thought, and the depth of his piety. But understanding Edwards as a person continues to intrigue specialists and nonspecialists alike. The following essay considers the personal Edwards from two vantage points: self and society. By "self" Dr. Minkema means what we can gather from what he said about himself, or what others who knew him said about him. This is of course a tricky affair, since autobiography can present different "selves" and contemporaries can be biased. "Society" comprehends the full round of engagement with others, including vocationally, economically, in family, and in community. These public networks, grounded in events of the time, also go far toward helping us know the private Edwards.

Jonathan Edwards, pastor, revivalist, Christian philosopher, missionary, and college president, is widely regarded as one of the most significant figures in Christian history. Many scholars put him on a par with Augustine, Aquinas, Luther, and Calvin for original theological reflection. A brilliant defender and innovator of Protestant Reformed and Puritan thought, Edwards exerted a lasting influence on Christianity worldwide. Born in Connecticut in 1703, Edwards attended Yale College and served as a tutor before becoming the pastor of Northampton, Massachusetts. There, Edwards established himself internationally as a revivalist, overseeing "awakenings" during 1734–1735 and again in the "Great Awakening" of the early 1740s. But his relationship with his congregation became strained until, in 1750, following a bitter dispute about the qualifications for church membership, he was dismissed. He went on to serve as a missionary to the Mahicans and Mohawks at Stockbridge, Massachusetts, where he also wrote many of the treatises that would secure his fame. In late 1757 he was called to be the president of the College of New Jersey, but he served at this post only a few months before he died in March 1758 following a smallpox inoculation . . .

That's the snapshot of the person we are examining in this book. Unless I'm prepared to uncover some previously unknown, dramatic fact about Edwards's "life and career," merely presenting an extended summary of his biography could get us off to a rather dull start. But, since I'm not at liberty to propose that Edwards was an embedded Jesuit, or a card-carrying member of the David Hume Fan Club, or the author of a lost gospel, I want to approach his life and career by addressing the themes of society and self, moving from the external to the internal. In that way, I hope at once to introduce him to the uninitiated and to give those more acquainted with him some material for contextualization and for better understanding the chapters that follow. To conclude, I will bring Edwards's "career" to the present time by briefly describing the recent surge of interest in him on a global basis.

Society

I begin with Society, defined very broadly, to situate Edwards temporally within international, colonial, regional, and local contexts. This is not to explain him away as a product of time and circumstance, but rather to provide something of a foundation as we subsequently consider various important themes in his thought.

We ugly Americans are quick to claim Edwards as one of us, as *America's* most significant religious figure, but our European colleagues, and especially those from the United Kingdom, are right to point out that he was a *British* subject, and saw himself as such. In his early twenties, Edwards reminded himself, in his "Notes on Style," "Before I venture to publish in London, to make some experiment in my own country; to play at small games first, that I may gain some experience in writing."[1] That statement opens up a world of difference to parochial claims of Americans "owning" Edwards.

Edwards's ancestors fled England in the early seventeenth century as part of the Puritan exodus to escape persecution at the hands of Archbishop Laud. In the New World, the Puritans established a "Bible commonwealth" with the goal of duplicating the purity of the early New Testament churches. Through a system of social and sacred covenants, individual, town, and commonwealth were bound together in a venture to create a godly, puritan society. Early on, the town and church were nearly coterminous. Only those who were full church members could partake in the Lord's Supper and have their children baptized, and there were other incentives for full church membership, such as the power to vote and the ability to hold office. New Englanders saw themselves as the New World Israel and the protectors of true religion. In ways like this, the secular and the sacred spheres in Edwards's world were closely linked.

But it is important to recall that, if the New England Way was not originally intended by the settlers to provide a theological model for Europe to emulate, it did become so in the minds and hearts of succeeding generations. John Winthrop's portrait of a "city on a hill," as annunciated in his sermon aboard the *Arbella* in 1629, was given a privileged status as the premier statement of the "errand into the wilderness." As presumptuous as this vision of world redemption was, it was nonetheless a prime motive undergirding New England society.[2]

The perspective of the home government was something yet again. The colonization of the eastern seaboard of North America, the islands of the Caribbean, and beyond was part of the process of nation- and empire-building that characterized the seventeenth and eighteenth centuries. Spain, Britain, and France sought the resources of the New World—minerals, animal pelts, lumber, food, and slave labor—and to establish ports to support trade that would bring those resources and profits into national coffers. So, while the events occurring in England during the early seventeenth century—Civil War and Interregnum—conspired to keep attention away from New England and the other English colonies, with the Restoration in 1660 the climate changed. Agents of the monarchy, Parliament, and the Board of Trade sought to assert more direct control over the colonies through closer political, military, and economic regulation and scrutiny. The Puritan political experiment effectually ended in 1684, with the revocation of the Massachusetts Bay charter; the entity to replace it was the Dominion of New England, and, though Puritan *religious* culture endured, this was the beginning of a process by which the colonists came more and more to conform to the sociopolitical ways and means of the mother country.

This is the colonial world into which Edwards was born, at the very western rim of the fitfully expanding English empire. It was early in the reign of Queen Anne, the last of the Stuarts before the Hanoverian dynasty took the throne in 1714. The ascension of George I clinched the identity of the British monarchy as Protestant, an important development in the struggle between Catholics and Protestants in that country, and one that Edwards and his contemporaries counted as one of the blessings of "English liberty."

The connection between religion and empire was a vital one. The religious wars of the seventeenth century, especially the Thirty Years' War, exacerbated Catholic-Protestant hostilities stemming from the Reformation. One aspect of the colonial period that has only recently been receiving its due attention is the extent to which colonists were engaged in warfare and religious violence— a theme that resonates today.[3] These conflicts were, more often than not, an extension of the European theater. During the eighteenth century, before the American Revolution, English colonists were engaged in four imperial conflicts that were extensions of European struggles over royal successions and alliances. Edwards lived to be fifty-five years old, but for only eighteen of those years was New England at peace—and even during peacetime, there were still occasional Indian raids or rumors of invasion by the French or Spanish.

During Edwards's life, the successive wars brought death to his kin and disruption to himself and his family. The War of Spanish Succession, known in America as Queen Anne's War and fought from 1703 to 1712, during which Jonathan's father, Timothy, served as a chaplain, saw bitter fighting along the Connecticut River. In 1704, while maneuvering in Europe was leading up to the Battle of Blenheim, in far-off Massachusetts the frontier ran with blood. The western hamlet of Northampton called Pascommuck was set on by a party of French soldiers and Penobscot Indians, in which relatives of the Edwardses were tomahawked and scalped. That same year, French and Indians also attacked Deerfield, slightly north of Northampton, decimating the town and taking dozens captive, including Edwards's cousin Eunice Williams, who became the famous "unredeemed captive."[4]

With such familial and community memories, Edwards's own activities were enmeshed in the ongoing martial conflicts. In 1746, during the War of Austrian Succession, he was completing his famous *Treatise Concerning Religious Affections* as watchtowers went up around Northampton to guard against attacks by the French and Iroquois. In the spring and summer of 1754, at the beginning of the Seven Years' War, Stockbridge suffered several Indian raids in which colonists were killed and taken captive, and Edwards's house was "forted in" with a stockade and quartered by soldiers; Edwards lived in daily fear of attack and made preparations to evacuate his family. Yet at the very time these things were happening, Edwards was writing what is probably his most renowned work, *Freedom of the Will.* The urgent circumstances explain why he wrote this lengthy and complex treatise in such haste: less than half a year's time. He saw his writings as salvos in the mental fight against the forces of false religion that were gathering even at the very gates of his town.

Through the series of wars, Edwards's strident anti-Catholicism gave content to his view of sacred history and his millennialism.[5] He interpreted the Antichrist as the Catholic Church (or, one of the twin Antichrists, the other being Islam) and counted setbacks to the French, Spanish, and other Catholic powers as signs of the coming final overthrow of Christ's enemies. Scholars and modern believers have often puzzled at the martial tone of Edwards's writings and his often vitriolic hatred of cultural "others" such as Indians and Catholics. But the atmosphere of wars and rumors of war in which he constantly lived may help to explain the millennial, apocalyptic meanings that such conflicts took on for him and his contemporaries.

The American Indians were viewed with great ambivalence, as potentially both close friends and cruel foes. Missions, however, constituted a potential bridge. Edwards is recognized as one of the great fountainheads out of which the modern mission movement flows by virtue of his own work as an Indian missionary and his publication of *The Life of David Brainerd*, which became a standard text for domestic and foreign missionaries since its publication in 1749. There were also the *History of the Work of Redemption* (1774), which traced the history of and suggested the future of missions, and the *Humble Attempt* (1748), which taught the necessity of prayer for revival and mission work. But we must recognize that Edwards also saw christianizing native Americans, in part, as a function of empire. In letters to provincial officials, he laid out the importance of allying with Indians, such as the Mahicans and Mohawks, so that they could provide buffers between the English populations and French-allied tribes and so they could act as conveyors of information from interior tribes.

Edwards's politics were of a Tory, or pro-royalist, bent. His civic sermons abound with words of support for the king and his ministers and, more to the point, with condemnations of those who question authority and ordained power. He explained how factions in New England mirrored, writ small, the parties in England: a Court, or pro-monarchy, interest, and a Country interest, which was advancing the ascending Whig ideology restricting the arbitrary rights of rulers. Edwards read the major Whig writers such as Steele and Gordon and magazines such as the *Guardian*, reflecting the pervasiveness of Whig thought in the colonies. In this vein, he criticized rulers who followed self-interest more than the common good. In the end, Edwards was committed to the perpetuation of communitarian, commonwealth values over against an emerging proto-capitalist, individualistic ethos.[6]

As his political views were a hybrid, so was his philosophy. His intellectual selectivity in approaching Enlightenment philosophy is striking. To be sure, Edwards had a base in Reformed, Puritan, Dissenting, and Continental scholastic authors, but he also read as widely in the "New Learning" as his isolated position would allow. His earliest writings show the influence of Newton, Locke, the Cambridge Platonists, and the British empiricists, as well as Malebranche, Pascal, and other continental figures.[7] From the start, he employed a critical, targeted adoption of traditional and current thought. He was surprisingly eclectic, using ideas and evidence from writers he would otherwise oppose for his larger purpose: the defense of a Reformed, neo-Calvinist worldview, in which human reason operates within the limits of the higher reason of revelation. Though, as Perry Miller pointed out, Edwards came on the basic features of his thought "preternaturally early," he played with ideas and was willing to nuance and adapt them to new discoveries in science and philosophy.[8]

Edwards lived in a society that was decidedly dependent on class, on the "due subjection of inferiors to superiors," as John Winthrop had stated in his *Model of Christian Charity*. Edwards based his conception of life itself on a divinely ordained hierarchy: God, angels, humankind, animals, and so on down. Within human society, there were those who were naturally meant to lead and those who were naturally meant to follow. The Edwardses were among New England's version of aristocracy. Their extended clan boasted some of the most powerful clergyman, politicians, and military figures in the British American colonies. Ever conscious and defensive of his place on the social ladder, Edwards expected deference from those below him, even as he deferred, sometimes grudgingly, to those above him. His immersion in this hierarchical culture extended to the inner capacities of the saints, among whom he spoke of an "aristocracy of grace," and even to heaven itself, in which there were "degrees of glory." His was no democratic paradise, just as Dante's Hell was no place of egalitarian suffering.

Yet Edwards, as can be argued for Puritan theology, sowed the seeds of the democratic ethos that he feared. He taught that divine knowledge was as open to the "humble cottager" as to the most learned professor, that God was no respecter of persons in bestowing grace. The awakenings themselves, historians have noted, upset attitudes of deference and introduced anti-authoritarianism. In 1744, several young Northampton men were discovered reading "bad books" (midwives' manuals) and verbally harassing young women. The culprits, who had supposedly been converted under Edwards, rebelled against Edwards and the august church committee after being charged with contempt of authority. Their leader, Timothy Root, focused his scorn on the symbol of authority: Edwards's wig. "I won't worship a wig," Root declared, upon which, after a few more insulting words, he led his companions off to the nearest tavern for a mug of flip (a molasses-sweetened concoction of beer and rum). Significantly, Root and his cronies got off with only the feeblest of apologies.[9]

Edwards's sense of status extended to issues surrounding race. Owning slaves was a symbol of social rank, and during his lifetime he owned a succession of African slaves. In fact, Edwards defended the institution of slavery as ordained by God in Scripture. However, he came to oppose the slave trade as an impediment to spreading the gospel in Africa, thereby providing a basis for the abolitionism espoused by his son Jonathan Jr. and disciples such as Samuel Hopkins. For Edwards, just as white society was ordered vertically, there were racial hierarchies as well. For much of his life, he adhered to the accepted wisdom of the time that Africans, Indians, and Jews were culturally inferior to white Christian Europeans. However, his daily exposure to Indians at Stockbridge caused him to reevaluate his views of human nature to some degree; he came to see that Europeans and Indians differ, in the end, not innately but only in circumstance and providence. He came to respect many of the natives he served and considered them better Christians than some of the English inhabitants.[10]

In addition to the issue of race, Edwards offered some intriguingly Janus-faced positions on issues of gender. One of the distinctive aspects of his family was the preponderance of women in it. Jonathan grew up the only son in a family of eleven (his father quipped that he had "sixty feet" of daughters), and he and his wife, Sarah Pierpont, raised eight daughters, all of whom were highly educated and erudite. Members of Edwards's family were quite cosmopolitan in their views of gender and marriage, though they did not refute the received wisdom of early modern European culture that, in the order of nature, women were the "weaker vessels." Even so, Edwards felt that, within their relative and proper spheres, men and women were equal and that marriage was a companionate relation. We are only beginning to appreciate Edwards's part in gender history. He was a traditional patriarch, but no misogynist. He sought to curtail women's public speech but allowed that they were more spiritual than men. The majority of his supporters in Northampton were women. The persons he chose as exemplars of true sainthood were all women—Abigail Hutchinson, Phebe Bartlett, his wife, Sarah—with the exception of the decidedly nonmasculine David Brainerd. And Edwards's so-called feminized spirituality, with its emphasis on affections and the expression of emotions, wielded a great influence in the literature of sentimentality that emerged in female writers during the American antebellum period.[11]

Edwards and his extended family were part of what has been called "the refinement of America," in which eighteenth-century British colonists sought to emulate the latest English fashions and tastes.[12] The inventory of the Edwards's household goods reveals mostly utilitarian devices, but the family's relatively refined tastes show through in certain items. Edwards himself sported a beaver hat, a fine calamanco (Flanders wool woven with a satin twill) vest, silver knee buckles, spectacles, and a cane. His wife owned a small silver engraved patch-box that contained, not items for mending, but round felt beauty marks, resembling moles, that were adhered to the face. Even in the wilds of Stockbridge, then, she retained the literal markings of high European culture. The family had a tea service and ate on china plates with damask tablecloths and napkins, and the walls were decorated with "looking glasses," or mirrors, and "small pictures," framed prints or possibly even watercolors painted by Sarah or her daughters—a version of provincially genteel, though unostentatious, living.

Self

I realize the peril in attempting to describe Edwards's self, since scholars have argued either that Edwards does not reveal an essential self—even his *Personal Narrative* is not all that personal[13]—or that he assumes different "selves" or voices depending on occasion. Nonetheless, I shall try to sketch some of the features of Edwards's faith and personality that provide helpful connections to his wider thought and significance.[14]

As a young man, Edwards composed a series of "Resolutions" by which to govern his life that partook of Puritan-like self-discipline and self-abasement. The first "Resolution" set the tone:

> Resolved, that I will do whatsoever I think to be most to God's glory,
> and my own good, profit and pleasure, in the whole of my duration,
> without any consideration of the time, whether now, or never so
> many myriads of ages hence. Resolved to do whatever I think to be
> my duty, and most for the good and advantage of mankind in gen-
> eral. Resolved to do this, whatever difficulties I meet with, how many
> and how great soever.[15]

This statement sets earthly life in clear perspective. As the rest of the "Resolutions" make clear, "my own good," for Edwards, meant the salvation of his soul rather than temporal happiness apart from God.

New England's religious culture placed great emphasis on spiritual discipline—what scholars call the "precisianist" strain—because Puritans tried to live their lives with precision based on God's word.[16] Central to this was a ceaseless examination of one's spiritual life by the use of diaries. The Puritans were tireless diary keepers, Edwards not least among them. This precisianist discipline extended to daily habits and the body. Thus, Edwards self-consciously tried to regulate his diet, his speech, his habits; he "improved" time, or made the best possible use of every minute—he was an eighteenth-century spiritual multitasker.

If this wasn't ambitious enough, Edwards resolved to be, as much as was possible through God's help, "a complete Christian." Living to God in every thought, word, and deed, modeling himself after and "venturing" his soul upon Christ, were essential. "Resolved, to live with all my might, while I do live," he declared. This meant living every moment as if it were "the last hour of my life" and committing every act as if he were about to "hear the last trump." Edwards's piety was Puritan in its existentialism, with its dictum, *Memento mori*, "Remember death": "Resolved, to think much on all occasions of my own dying, and of the common circumstances which attend death."[17] Remembering death, however, did not lead to fatalism. Instead, it was a spur to activism, to dedicate himself to religion and to God.

Puritanism has been satirically defined as "the haunting fear that someone, somewhere may be happy." Perhaps so far I've only given an impression of Edwards that justifies that definition. But all of this self-regulation was done not for its own sake, nor because Edwards had no pleasure in life. Rather, we have to understand his higher goal: the complete surrender of self for the glory of God, which for Edwards was the be-all and end-all of his existence, not to mention all existence. Much of Edwards's personal faith, as well as his formal theology, can be understood through this rubric: God's purpose in creating and redeeming the world is God's own glory, the communication of God's essence.[18]

Edwards's concerns were ultimate, his commitments intense. As a young man, he sensed an important difference between himself and the religious culture in which he was raised: he had not "experience[d] regeneration, exactly in those steps, in which divines say it is generally wrought."[19] By "steps," he referred to the teaching among New England divines that conversion occurred in stages in which one utilized the "means of grace"—reading, worship, and prayer—to help "prepare" for regeneration. He decided "never to leave searching" until he had solved this problem. This was an important moment for Edwards. As he later came to realize, his experience of grace upset accepted conventions. This deviation from the norm opened him up to reconceiving how God acts in the soul and the role that believers have in that relationship. Eventually, Edwards came to emphasize the totality of one's religious experience in judging whether one had true grace—possessing divine light and exhibiting divine living—not the order, or length of time, or other unscriptural prescriptions.

Edwards's devotional life warrants attention. Though his sermons were not extemporaneous, his prayers were. Prayers during regular worship were as long as the sermon, an hour or more. The Edwards family engaged in daily worship, featuring prayer, and Edwards was remembered as one of the great pray-ers of his day. Singing, too, was a central component in worship; Edwards introduced Watts's hymns to his church, and his wife, Sarah, quoted hymns by the Erskines. In addition, *nature* was of great importance to Edwards's private worship. Consider his catalogue of natural types (symbols in nature of Christ's kingdom) in "Images of Divine Things,"[20] or his *Personal Narrative*, in which he describes his meditations on the palisades above New York City, his walks in pastures "for contemplation," or seating himself outside to watch approaching thunderstorms, all the while singing and chanting his praises, or even weeping (which seems to have been an important part of his devotional life). These are further elements of Edwards the mystic that need to be taken into account to better understand him.

Finally, we have yet to assess the degree to which Edwards's spiritual life was influenced by Pietism, a European religious movement characterized by mystical piety, holy living, ecumenism, millennialism, and proselytizing. His exposure to Pietism was indirect, through interlocutors such as Cotton Mather, but also direct through his reading of formative figures such as Johan Arndt. Edwards was an admirer of August Francke and his evangelical center at Halle (Germany), and Edwards's plan for tutoring Indian boys and girls bears some similarity to Francke's educational system. Finally, Edwards's later emphasis on practical Christian behavior, after the awakenings, partakes of the spirit of Pietism.

In the end, what is important to stress is that Edwards's spiritual search led him to become involved with European and American religious leaders, German Pietists, French Huguenots, English Dissenters, Scottish Presbyterians, and others, through which he was drawn into a transdenominational, pan-Protestant revival movement that enabled him to transcend his provincial experience and to conceive a larger vision of the church. This new religious impulse, for which Edwards was a formative figure, gave birth to modern evangelicalism, the influence of which has been felt across the globe.

Edwards Today

Edwards's influence on the course of nineteenth- and twentieth-century theology is the source of much study, taking in revivalism, world missions, philosophical and theological debate, ethics, and more. Edwards's star has waxed and waned with the times, and persistent secularism in some academic circles remains a challenge to making Edwards and Christian thinkers like him known and appreciated. However, the past twenty years or so have witnessed a resurgence of interest in Edwards not seen since before the Civil War. Publications of his writings from secular, academic, and religious presses abound; scholarship on him is fast approaching four thousand books, dissertations, articles, and other secondary literature; and Edwards's online presence is burgeoning through a variety of websites and blogs, including those of the Jonathan Edwards Center.[21]

We find a surprise among readers of Edwards: scholars actually account for only a small fraction. Far and away, those who come back to Edwards again and again are pastors, religious leaders and practitioners, and interested laity from around the world.[22] This is the audience the Jonathan Edwards Center is trying to serve, all the while realizing that we have to make Edwards accessible to the widest possible readership.

As Christianity expands across the globe and evolves into new Christianities, Edwards is increasingly consulted. Translations of his revival writings have appeared in the past decade or so in Russian, Transylvanian, Korean, and Chinese, joining those already in Welsh, Arabic, Choctaw, and French. Our Center hosts a website of Edwards's writings, and since its inception two years ago we have had visits from people in 120 countries. After the United States and the United Kingdom, users are most numerous in Brazil, Poland, Australia, South Korea, the Philippines, and Japan. A recent development is a Hungarian translation of Edwards's *Nature of True Virtue* and *Religious Affections* and a Czech translation of *Nature of True Virtue*. Developments of this sort show how religious leaders around the world are encouraging the use of Edwards, in diverse ways and for diverse motives, for the nurture of intellectual and spiritual life within their academic and faith communities.

Conclusion

Many readers of Edwards today, scholars and nonscholars alike, consult Edwards to see what they can appropriate for their personal and church life. Edwards has much to offer for people of faith today. In situating Edwards within a particular social world, my goal is certainly not to discourage that approach. However, certain aspects of his life and thought are understandable only within an eighteenth-century context, and it is essential to come to terms with that context. These obsolete and unappealing aspects make Edwards a man of his time, but they do not render his thought irrelevant for ours.

Edwards has been studied and praised as an inspiration for piety and personal spirituality, as a pastor, husband, and father, and as a Christian thinker who sought to reconcile his inherited Reformed worldview to the religious, intellectual, and scientific advances of his day. Edwards was a multifaceted, complex individual, but these features of his character and thought have led to a wide range of opinion on him. Yet I will venture to say that nearly every person who seriously studies Edwards will take away something that is of interest or that is useful, in some way or other, to their own experiences or interests.

NOTES

1. Jonathan Edwards, "Cover Leaf Memoranda," in *The Works of Jonathan Edwards*, ed. Wallace E. Anderson (New Haven: Yale University Press, 1980), 6: 194.

2. For different interpretations of New England's origins, see Perry Miller's classic essay, "Errand into the Wilderness," in *Errand into the Wilderness* (New York: Harper & Row, 1956), 1–15, as well as his two-volume study of *The New England Mind* (Cambridge, MA: Harvard University Press, 1939, 1953); and Theodore D.Bozeman, *To Live Ancient Lives: The Primitivist Dimension in Puritanism* (Chapel Hill: University of North Carolina Press, 1988). For the text of John Winthrop's *Model of Christian Charity*, see Alan Heimert and Andrew Delbanco, eds., *The Puritans in America: A Narrative Anthology* (Cambridge, MA: Harvard University Press, 1985), 82–92.

3. See, for example, Jill Lepore, *The Name of War: King Philip's War and the Origins of American Identity* (New York: Knopf, 1998); Fred Anderson, *Crucible of War: The Seven Years' War and the Fate of Empire in British North America, 1754–1766* (New York: Knopf, 2000); Mary Beth Norton, *In the Devil's Snare: The Salem Witchcraft Crisis of 1692* (New York: Knopf, 2002); and Evan Haefeli and Kevin Sweeney, *Captors and Captives: The 1704 French and Indian Raid on Deerfield* (Amherst: University of Massachusetts Press, 2003).

4. John Demos, *The Unredeemed Captive: A Family Story from Early America* (New York: Vintage Books, 1995).

5. See Avihu Zakai, *Jonathan Edwards's Philosophy of History: The Reenchantment of the World in the Age of Enlightenment* (Princeton, NJ: Princeton University Press, 2003).

6. Gerald R. McDermott, *One Holy and Happy Society: The Public Theology of Jonathan Edwards* (University Park: Pennsylvania State University Press, 1992).

7. On Edwards's influences, see Perry Miller, *Jonathan Edwards* (New York: Sloan, 1949); Norman Fiering, *Jonathan Edwards's Moral Thought and Its British Context* (Chapel Hill: University of North Carolina Press, 1981); and William S. Morris, *The Young Jonathan Edwards: A Reconstruction* (Brooklyn, NY: Carlson, 1991; reprinted Eugene, OR: Wipf & Stock 2005).

8. Important studies in this vein include Roland A. Delattre, *Beauty and Sensibility in the Thought of Jonathan Edwards* (New Haven: Yale University Press, 1968); Stephen H. Daniel, *The Philosophy of Jonathan Edwards* (Bloomington: Indiana University Press, 1994); Gerald R. McDermott, *Jonathan Edwards Confronts the Gods: Christian Theology,*

Enlightenment Religion, and Non-Christian Faiths (New York: Oxford University Press, 2000); and Robert E. Brown, *Jonathan Edwards and the Bible* (Bloomington: Indiana University Press, 2002).

9. See Patricia J. Tracy, *Jonathan Edwards, Pastor: Religion and Society in Eighteenth-Century Northampton* (New York: Hill &Wang, 1980; reprinted Eugene, OR: Wipf & Stock, 2006); Ava Chamberlain, "Bad Books and Bad Boys: The Transformation of Gender in Eighteenth-Century Northampton, Massachusetts," *New England Quarterly* 76 (June 2002): 179–203.

10. For Edwards and the New Divinity on slavery and abolition, see Joseph Conforti, *Samuel Hopkins and the New Divinity Movement* (Grand Rapids, MI: Eerdmans, 1981); Kenneth P. Minkema, "Jonathan Edwards's Defense of Slavery," *Massachusetts Historical Review* 4 (2002): 23–60; and Kenneth P. Minkema and Harry S. Stout, "The Edwardsean Tradition and the Antislavery Debate, 1740–1865," *Journal of American History* 92 (June 2005): 47–74. On Indians, see Gerald R. McDermott, "Jonathan Edwards and American Indians: The Devil Sucks Their Blood," *New England Quarterly* 72 (Dec. 1999): 539–57; Rachel Wheeler, " 'Friends to Your Souls': Jonathan Edwards' Indian Pastorate and the Doctrine of Original Sin," *Church History* 72 (Dec. 2003): 736–65.

11. Amanda Porterfield, *Feminine Spirituality in America: From Sarah Edwards to Martha Graham* (Philadelphia: Temple University Press, 1980); Sandra Gustafson, *Eloquence Is Power: Oratory and Performance in Early America* (Chapel Hill: University of North Carolina Press, 2000); Philip F. Gura, "Lost and Found: Recovering Edwards for American Literature," in *Jonathan Edwards at 300: Essays on the Tercentenary of His Birth*, ed. Harry S. Stout, Kenneth P. Minkema, and Caleb J. D. Maskell (Lanham, MD: University Press of America, 2005), 86–97.

12. Richard L. Bushman, *The Refinement of America: Persons, Houses, Cities* (New York: Knopf, 1992).

13. Published in *The Works of Jonathan Edwards* [hereafter, *WJE*], ed. George S. Claghorn (New Haven: Yale University Press, 1998), 16: 790–804.

14. For an exploration of related themes, see Kenneth P. Minkema, "Personal Writings," in *Cambridge Companion to Jonathan Edwards*, ed. Stephen J. Stein (Cambridge, UK: Cambridge University Press, 2007), 39–60.

15. "Resolutions," in *WJE* 16: 753.

16. Theodore D. Bozeman, *The Precisianist Strain: Disciplinary Religion and Antinomian Backlash in Puritanism to 1638* (Chapel Hill: University of North Carolina Press, 2004).

17. *WJE* 16: 753.

18. See Sang Hyun Lee, *The Philosophical Theology of Jonathan Edwards* (Princeton, NJ: Princeton University Press, 1989); Stephen R. Holmes, *God of Grace and God of Glory: An Account of the Theology of Jonathan Edwards* (Grand Rapids, MI: Eerdmans, 2000).

19. "Diary," in *WJE* 16: 759.

20. *WJE* 11: 50–142.

21. M. X. Lesser, *Jonathan Edwards: A Reference Guide* (Boston: G. K. Hall, 1981), and *Jonathan Edwards: An Annotated Bibliography, 1979–1993* (Westport, CT: Greenwood

Press, 1994); Jonathan Edwards Center website, http://edwards.yale.edu, and blog, http://jonathanedwardscenter.blogspot.com.

22. Prominent among American religious leaders who use Edwards in their ministries are John Piper, *God's Passion for His Glory: Living the Vision of Jonathan Edwards* (Wheaton, IL: Crossways, 1998); Samuel Storms, *Signs of the Spirit: An Inerpretation of Jonathan Edwards's "Religious Affections"* (Wheaton, IL: Crossways, 2007); and Josh Moody, *The God-Centered Life: Insights from Jonathan Edwards for Today* (Vancouver, Canada: Regent, 2006).

2

Alternative Viewpoint: Jonathan Edwards's Life and Career

Chris Chun

Since Ken Minkema did not uncover any long-hidden secret about Edwards, such as his being "an embedded Jesuit, or a card-carrying member of the David Hume Fan Club," or worse, "the author of a lost gospel," there is little with which I can disagree. But I can offer my own "humble attempt" to supplement Minkema's presentation.

Let me first discuss the influence of Edwards on British religious thinkers and particularly the English Dissenters and Scottish evangelicals.[1] Minkema is not alone in recognizing Edwards as "one of the great fountainheads out of which the modern mission movement flows" and in identifying *The Life of David Brainerd* as "a standard text for domestic and foreign missionaries."[2] Although this statement is certainly not incorrect, it is, in my view, incomplete. *The Life of David Brainerd* was rightly celebrated as an exemplary pietistic manual for many missionaries from the late eighteenth century through the nineteenth and twentieth centuries. However, there are two other significant works that are often overlooked in this context: *Freedom of the Will* and *Humble Attempt*.

Freedom of the Will

William Carey (1761–1834) was one of the most significant early leaders of the modern missionary movement and is often called the "father of modern missions,"[3] but he was not alone. One of his friends and colleagues was Andrew Fuller (1754–1815).[4] If Carey's *An Enquiry into the Obligations of Christians to Use Means for the Conversion of the Heathens* (1792) was the ethical catalyst for the missionary awakening, Fuller's *Gospel Worthy of All Acceptation* (1785) was its theological stimulus. In other words, Fuller was the theologian and Carey the activist and visionary of the mission movement. In the midst of a rapid decline among Baptist denominations in England—due largely to Hyper-Calvinism among Particular Baptists and Unitarians as well as deistic tendencies among General Baptists[5]—Fuller's *Gospel Worthy of All Acceptation* "fell like a bombshell on the playground of theologians, [and] Fuller was pilloried by Arminians and Hyper-Calvinists alike."[6] Fuller's theological ammunition for this dispute relied largely on the distinction made by Edwards in *Freedom of the Will* between "natural and moral inability."[7]

Both Hyper-Calvinists and Arminians maintained that unregenerate sinners ought not to be required to perform that which they are incapable of doing. Hyper-Calvinists said they needed to first look for those who have the inner warrant (a Scripture text in their mind) to come to Christ for their salvation and then preach to them exclusively, whereas Arminians maintained that sinners should not be required to respond to the gospel unless they had the ability to do so. Fuller used Edwardsian thinking to resolve this difficulty and argued the distinction between natural and moral ability.[8] As a Particular Baptist, Fuller believed that without the grace of "unconditional election" unregenerate "heathens" could not respond positively to the gospel.[9] Yet this helplessness was not due to a defect of any natural human faculty. Rather, their inability was of a "moral" or "criminal" type.[10] In other words, there are no natural, physical, external factors that would restrain unbelievers from choosing or rejecting the gospel. In this sense, they are "free" to accept and are therefore morally responsible for their choices. If they reject the gospel, they are choosing to do so in accordance with their own desires. The choices simply reveal who they are as individuals—whether or not they are reprobate or elect.[11] This is why natural ability became for Fuller the basis on which heathens had the "duty" to respond in faith and repentance, regardless of their eternal status.

Fuller did not usually give a detailed philosophical account of natural and moral inability, as did Edwards. Instead, Fuller's distinctions are more inclined to the implications for salvation. It is as if the results of the complex mathematical formula solved by Edwards were taken to their maximum potential by Fuller and applied to the formulation of a precise theology, which became the basis for what was to become known as the Modern Missionary Movement. It is therefore no wonder that among many evaluations of the impact of Edwards in England, the historian David Bebbington concludes that "probably most important in the reception of Edwards by the English Baptists was the impact on Andrew Fuller."[12]

The Humble Attempt

Due largely to the ecclesiastical division caused by the aftermath of the Great Awakening, there were few reasons to be optimistic about the religious climate in New England. In the face of these divisions, Edwards's encouragement came from his transatlantic correspondence, which included an invitation to participate in the ecumenical movement known as the "Concert of Prayer" in Scotland. Through these organized, regular prayer meetings, the Scottish evangelicals had implemented the "means" of advancing the revival. Prompted by the invitation, Edwards accepted the challenge of promoting such prayer meetings in colonial America. In February 1747 he began a series of sermons based on Zechariah 7:20–22. The result of this effort was later expanded into a book, *An Humble Attempt to Promote Explicit Agreement and Visible Union of God's People in Extraordinary Prayer for the Revival of Religion and the Advancement of Christ's Kingdom on Earth, Pursuant to Scripture-Promises and Prophecies of concerning the last Time* (1748).

Humble Attempt helped spark the modern missions movement when the Baptist pastor John Ryland Jr. received a parcel of books including the *Humble Attempt* from John Erskine in 1784. Ryland, fully aware of the esteem in which Fuller and John Sutcliff held Edwards, wasted no time in sending them the books and thereby changed missiological history. The reading of *Humble Attempt* by Fuller, Sutcliff, and other Northamptonshire members revived the Concert of Prayer that had begun in the 1740s in Scotland and New England but had subsided, and forty years later produced the "Prayer Call of 1784" in England.

The Prayer Call established the practice of using the first Monday of each month for prayer for the advancement of Christ's Kingdom. These Concerts, plus the 1789 republication of *Humble Attempt*, have been directly linked by historians to both Carey's historic ministry and the formation of the Baptist Missionary Society in 1792 and the London Missionary Society in 1795.[13] These events, taken together, were the genesis of the Protestant missionary movement.

Edwards's Optimism and Modern Missions

If historians have recognized the influence of *Humble Attempt* on the Prayer Call of 1784, few if any have seen the role that Edwards's eschatological optimism played in driving the modern missionary enterprise. Edwards's thinking about the end of the world depended on his interpretation of the slaying of the witnesses in Revelation 11. Some thought this implied a coming catastrophe for the church, but Edwards argued for the exact opposite to promote the Concert of Prayer. He feared that if the slaying of the witnesses was a future event yet to be fulfilled, it would be a great "hindrance" for the Concert. People should not merely wait for a time when the church is "almost extinguished, and blotted out from under heaven. . . . It will tend to damp, deaden and keep down, life, hope, and joyful expectation in prayer . . . before it is actually fulfilled." Edwards exhorted his readers instead to "expect that God will answer their prayers by speedily bringing on the promised glorious day."[14] For Edwards, the slaying of the witnesses took place in an epoch under the oppression of the Antichrist (the papacy). But because in the Reformation the "Antichrist hath fallen, at least, halfway to the ground, from that height of power,"[15] readers could be assured that that event lay safely in the past. Although there would be setbacks, the true church was on the rise. There would be an unprecedented outpouring of the spirit of God and a time when the whole world would embrace the light of the gospel, with Christ's kingdom victorious against the dark world.

Fuller also saw the ransacked days of the church as a thing of the past, for he interpreted the French Revolution as a crucial sign that that shook the "papal world to its centre."[16] The fact that *Humble Attempt* was reprinted in 1789, when the Revolution began, seemed to confirm the optimistic Edwardsian eschatology that Fuller adopted.

Although Fuller did not stress immediacy in the way Edwards did, both believed the latter days would be publicly discernible, and that the current ascendancy of Protestantism, coupled with diminishing papal authority in Europe and America, were evidence of fulfillment of apocalyptic forecasts in the Book of Revelation. Hence, if Edwards drew no "sharp lines between the spiritual and the political,"[17] neither did Fuller. In hindsight, we might conclude that both Edwards and Fuller misinterpreted the biblical prophecies. But there is little doubt that Edwards's eschatology inspired Fuller to promote missionary work so vigorously.

In conclusion, Minkema and other historians are right to say that Brainerd's piety functioned as a model for missionaries of the nineteenth century. They are also justified in saying that Edwards was a fountainhead of modern missions.[18] However, because of the evangelistic restraint of Hyper-Calvinism, the modern Anglo-American missionary movement might never have gotten off the ground—if it hadn't been for the metaphysics of "natural and moral inability" found in *Freedom of the Will*.

We could speak similarly of the *Humble Attempt*. Had it not been for Edwards's optimistic outlook and exhortation to communal prayer, the fuel needed for the rigors of foreign missions might well have been depleted.[19] Therefore, Edwards's missiological legacy is far greater than that of simply writing *The Life of David Brainerd*. As Stuart Piggin has written, Edwards lived "too long" before Carey and "too far" away from London, and had "too many non-missionary-specific thoughts" to have been the "father of modern missions."

Nevertheless, "Edwards deserves the title 'grandfather of modern Protestant missions,' on both sides of the Atlantic."[20] And from a British perspective, we can add that in addition to being "America's theologian" in the eighteenth century,[21] Edwards had significant impact on England and Scotland. In fact, his influence on the modern missionary movement alone would make him an important figure in the history of modern Christianity.

NOTES

1. In Britain, Edwards had substantial impact. His impact in the eighteenth century can be viewed in two stages: (1) during Edwards's lifetime in the 1740s and 1750s in Scotland and (2) his posthumous influence in the 1780s and 1790s in England. The latter has much to do with Andrew Fuller and the Northamptonshire Association.

2. See Joseph Conforti, "David Brainerd and the Nineteenth-Century Missionary Movement," *Journal of the Early Republic* 5 (Fall 1985): 309–29; "Jonathan Edwards's Most Popular Work: 'The Life of David Brainerd' and Nineteenth-Century Evangelical Culture," *Church History* 54 (June 1985): 188–201. See also Norman Pettit, "Prelude to Mission: Brainerd's Expulsion from Yale," *New England Quarterly* 59 (March 1986): 28–50; Andrew Walls, "Missions and Historical Memory: Jonathan Edwards and David Brainerd," in *Jonathan Edwards at Home and Abroad: Historical Cultural Movements, Global Horizons*, ed. David Kling and Douglas Sweeney (Columbia: University of South Carolina Press, 2003).

3. Of course, Jesuits were conducting missions long before the Protestant missionary movement. Moreover, before Carey's time the Moravians were also very active with missions. Yet mainstream Protestant involvement, with the new emphasis on Bible translation in missionary enterprise, was pioneered by Carey.

4. For a recent study of Fuller's life and thought, see Peter Morden, *Offering Christ to the World: Andrew Fuller (1754–1815) and the Revival of Eighteenth Century Particular Baptist Life*, in vol. 8 of *Studies in Baptist History and Thought* (Carlisle, PA: Paternoster, 2003); see also Michael Haykin, ed., *"At the Pure Fountain of Thy Word": Andrew Fuller as an Apologist*, in vol. 8 of *Studies in Baptist History and Thought* (Carlisle, PA: Paternoster, 2004). Moreover, modeled after the Yale edition of *The Works of Jonathan Edwards* [hereafter, *WJE*], there is a current undertaking to produce a modern critical edition of the entire corpus of Andrew Fuller's work through Paternoster Press. The project, estimated to be completed in 2015, is expected to comprise at least fifteen volumes.

5. "Particular" or Calvinistic Baptists held to a limited atonement, a belief that Christ's death and salvation were specifically designed for the elect. Hyper-Calvinists, however, believed that the call to repent and believe should not be universal, since reprobates do not have the ability to do so. "General" or Arminian Baptists believed in a general atonement, the belief that Christ died for the whole world, elect and nonelect alike. Thus, the efficacy of Christ's death is available to anyone who voluntarily exercises faith in Christ. In the context of the Enlightenment, the Unitarians (in opposition to the Trinitarians) argued for a single personality of God as the reason for their rule and denied the deity of Christ. Deists believed that God did not interfere with the laws of the universe, including human affairs, and usually rejected supernatural events and divine revelation. In Britain, Unitarianism and deism were prevalent in the thinking of eighteenth-century General Baptists.

6. Timothy George, *Faithful Witness: The Life and Mission of William Carey* (Birmingham, AL: New Hope, 1991), 56.

7. While Edwards's original intention for the natural and moral distinction was to argue against the "prevailing notion" of Arminianism, Fuller used the distinction to fight on two fronts, against both Hyper-Calvinists and Arminians. For more on this dispute, see Chris Chun, "A Mainspring of Missionary Thought: Andrew Fuller on Natural and Moral Inability," *American Baptist Quarterly*, 25, no. 4 (winter 2006): 335–55.

8. Fuller defined natural ability as "the enjoyment of rational faculties, bodily powers, and external advantages." See Andrew Fuller, *The Gospel of Christ Worthy of All Acceptation* (Northampton, England: T. Dicey, 1785), 185, in *Eighteenth Century Collections Online* at http://galenet.galegroup.com. In Fuller's view moral ability is closely related to the inclination or "sense of the heart." Because sinners don't have this, they cannot use their natural ability to right purpose.

9. See Philip Schaff and Henry B. Smith, eds., Articles XIII–XVIII, *The Canons of Synod of Dort,* in *The Creeds of the Evangelical Protestant Churches* (London: Hodder and Stoughton, 1877), 2: 582–85. For Fuller's commitment to five-point Calvinism (TULIP), see Thomas Nettles, "On the Road Again," in *By His Grace and for His Glory: A Historical, Theological and Practical Study of the Doctrines of Grace in Baptist Life* (Grand Rapids, MI: Baker Books, 1986), 108–30.

10. Having already "considered as well as I could" on *Freedom of the Will,* Fuller writes, "I have frequently been enquiring into the *nature* of that inability so plentifully ascribed in the scriptures to [the] fall of men. I found this to be chiefly of the *moral* kind; a *voluntary,* and therefore *criminal* and *punishable* inability." See Fuller, *Gospel of Christ Worthy,* v.

11. Fuller insists that free agency is in "the power of being what they are!" In Edwardsian fashion, Fuller states that free agency is "in the power of following the inclination." Andrew Fuller, *The Complete Works of the Rev. Andrew Fuller: With a Memoir of His Life by the Rev. Andrew Gunton Fuller* (Harrisonburg, VA: Sprinkle Publications, 1988), 2: 521, 656. Hence for both Edwards and Fuller, freedom is the ability of the individual to be the person that he or she is, as was the case for Judas Iscariot (Fuller, *Works,* 2: 520; see *Freedom of the Will,* in *WJE* 1: 296). However, this "free action" is utterly determined by the condition of a person, which in turn can be traced to personality, character, upbring-

ing, genetic inheritance, external and internal circumstances of life experience, and so forth.

12. David Bebbington, "Remembered around the World: The International Scope of Edwards' Legacy," in Kling and Sweeney, *Jonathan Edwards at Home and Abroad*, 184. For supplementary discussions, see Mark Noll, "Jonathan Edwards's Freedom of the Will Abroad," in *Jonathan Edwards at 300: Essays on the Tercentenary of His Birth*, ed. Harry Stout, Kenneth Minkema, and Caleb Maskell (Lanham, MD: University Press of America, 2005), 89–108.

13. The Call was critical to the beginnings of Carey's ministry. According to Thornton Elwyn, "Northamptonshire Association prayer call was one of the most decisive events in the life of that period, and probably for all Christendom." Thornton Elwyn, "Particular Baptist of the Northamptonshire Baptist Association as Reflected in the Circular Letters," *Baptist Quarterly*, 37, no.1 (Jan. 1997): 380. In 1789, for the purpose of wider circulation, this prayer movement republished the "pocket-size" edition of *Humble Attempt*. In describing the significance of the new edition, Murray states, "It is arguable that no such tract on the hidden source of all true evangelistic success, namely prayer for the Spirit of God, has ever been so widely used as this one." Iain Murray, *Jonathan Edwards: A New Biography* (Carlisle, PA: Banner of Truth, 1987), 299. Even if Elwyn and Murray have overstated the significance of these events, it is arguable that the Prayer Call, together with the republication of *Humble Attempt*, paved the way for the formation of the Baptist Missionary Society and the London Missionary Society.

14. Jonathan Edwards, *Humble Attempt*, in *WJE* 5: 378–79.

15. Ibid., 5: 381.

16. See, Fuller, *Works*, 3: 252–53.

17. George Marsden, *Jonathan Edwards: A Life* (New Haven: Yale University Press, 2003), 338.

18. Bebbington also notes that it was Edwards who stood at the "headwaters of Evangelicalism." David Bebbington, *Evangelicalism in Modern Britain: A History from the 1730s to the 1980s* (London: Unwin Hyman, 1989), 5.

19. Perhaps it was the Edwardsian optimism that helped Carey coin his famous challenge, "Attempt great things for God; Expect great things from God." The sermon in which this was first articulated was based on Isaiah 54:2–3 and initially delivered on May 30, 1792, at Nottingham.

20. In quoting the work of Ronald Davies, Piggin has argued this point. See Stuart Piggin, "The Expanding Knowledge of God: Jonathan Edwards' Influence on Missionary Thinking and Promotion," in Kling and Sweeney, *Jonathan Edwards at Home and Abroad*, 266, 287 n. 2. See also Ronald E. Davies, "Jonathan Edwards: Missionary Biographer, Theologian, Strategist, Administrator, Advocate, and Missionary," *International Bulletin of Missionary Research* 21, no.2 (Apr. 1997): 60–67.

21. Robert Jenson, *America's Theologian: A Recommendation of Jonathan Edwards* (New York: Oxford University Press, 1988).

3

Edwards and Revival

Harry S. Stout

This essay explores the cultural and intellectual context for Edwards's revival sermons preached during the "Great Awakening" of the early 1740s. The essay concentrates on the theme of redemption in Edwards's thought and preaching, with a special focus on its implications for revival preaching. Most central here is Edwards's use of hell and terror as rhetorical goads to promote the "New Birth" in his hearers. The centerpiece of this preaching, indeed the apotheosis, is "Sinners in the Hands of an Angry God," which the author explores theologically and rhetorically. In addition to examining the printed text of "Sinners," Professor Stout also discusses the rhetorical significance of Edwards's brief, handwritten notes, which compelled a more extemporaneous delivery. Finally, he looks at the clerical opposition of "Old Lights" to Edwards and Revival as the context for Edwards's theological treatises.

No eighteenth-century figure thought more about revivals than Jonathan Edwards. Whether promoting them in his own congregation and region or defending them against archcritics such as Boston's Charles Chauncy, there never was a day that he did not write, work, and preach to promote revival. At the center of Edwards's thoughts on revival was supernatural conversion. That event marked the beginnings of a "new creation" (one of Edwards's favorite terms), conceived through the work of the Holy Spirit and carried out through the "affections" of the heart rather than the enlightenment of the mind. Conversion was the "end" of revivals,

Edwards argued, and for Chauncy and other Old Lights to complain about "enthusiastic means" was to miss the whole point: "We need not be sorry for breaking the [usual] order of means, by obtaining the end to which the order is directed."[1]

Edwards and History

In a profound sense, revivals were in Edwards's genes. Were there to be a spiritual genome, "revival" and "Jonathan Edwards" would make a perfect match. From his father, Timothy Edwards, he would acquire the tools and ambition to be America's greatest preacher and theologian. And from his maternal grandfather, Solomon Stoddard, he would inherit a revivalist role model without peer. When Edwards succeeded Stoddard in the wealthy and powerful Northampton, Massachusetts, pulpit, he succeeded an evangelistic legend. Under Stoddard's impassioned and terrifying preaching, Northampton residents went through five "harvests" of mass conversions, marked by sudden jumps in church membership. The challenge for young Edwards would be to replicate his grandfather's achievement.

Like his grandfather, Edwards would strategize for revival, and always at the center of that strategizing would be the young people. In April 1734, the death of a young person in the congregation set off a general concern among the youth, and in the months that followed Edwards saw "soul concerns" spread through the town. Soon revivals spread from the youth to the adults. In all, Edwards noted, over three hundred people were savingly converted; well over two hundred were admitted into church membership in the two-year period—at one point as many as one hundred in one day. Equally pleasing to Edwards was the atmosphere of harmony and Christian behavior that prevailed in notoriously contentious Northampton. Even more encouraging were reports from nearly thirty communities up and down the Connecticut River Valley attesting to the revival spirit in their churches.

As reports of the revivals in Northampton spread, religious leaders throughout Anglo-America began to inquire into the truth and nature of the phenomena. To satisfy their curiosity, Edwards wrote what would become a best seller: *A Faithful Narrative of the Surprising Work of God in the Conversion of Many Hundred Souls in Northampton*. The pamphlet was published in London in 1737 and in Boston a year later. Subsequent translations soon appeared in German and Dutch, putting Edwards and his church before the eyes of an international audience.

Like the incipient scientist he was, Edwards presented readers with an astute social and demographic profile of the town of Northampton, followed by a sophisticated portrait of the religious psychology that he observed among his parishioners. In particular, he made famous two of his converts, the dying Abigail Hutchinson and the four-year-old Phebe Bartlett, whose religious experience he described almost clinically in psychological terms. A Faithful Narrative became nothing less than the model for conducting and monitoring future revivals worldwide.

In A Faithful Narrative, Edwards introduced the theme of Arminianism that would engage his career as a polemicist and energize his enemies in the New England pulpit. Noting a "great noise" over the threat of Arminianism, Edwards observed, "The friends of vital piety trembled for fear of the issue, but it seemed, contrary to their fear, strongly to be overruled for the promoting of religion."[2] Sadly, for Edwards, the victory over Arminianism would not last, and the enemies of revival would only grow stronger.

At the very time Edwards's triumphalist account appeared in print, his "Little Awakening" was coming to an ignominious end. In June 1735, Edwards's uncle Joseph Hawley, certain that he was damned and incapable of conversion, killed himself by slitting his throat. The tragedy cast a pall over the town, and from that point on the revival waned precipitously. A disconsolate Edwards watched as his congregation, including many of those who were supposedly converted, returned to their "vicious habits" and general indifference to religion.

Though disappointed in the failure of his revival to promote lasting peace and piety, Edwards never gave up hope. The reason is to be found in a sermon series of no fewer than thirty installments preached in 1739 and later published as A History of the Work of Redemption. Though primarily concerned with critical historical problems regarding the biblical narratives, the original sermon series, which Edwards intended (but did not live long enough) to turn into a major treatise, had as its immediate inspiration the Northampton revivals he shepherded five years earlier. In these sermons, Edwards depicted revivals as the operational vehicle that God would employ to accomplish his magisterial plan of cosmic redemption.

In seeking a form to describe God's plan of redemption, and the revival's central place in it, Edwards bypassed systematic theology in favor of cosmic narrative. For Christian faith to survive and lead the way into a new heaven and a new earth, it would need to don new garments. By 1739, and even earlier, Edwards began to suspect that "history" was, in fact, larger than the antiquarian terms by which it was then known; indeed, it was larger than theology itself. In his evolving thought, carefully recorded and organized in reams of notebooks, commentaries, and sermons, history was emerging as nothing less than a container for the synthetic whole of theology, and indeed of God's innermost self-revelation.[3] Gone were parochial notions of history as genealogy or the simple chronicle of human achievements and sequential events. Gone, even, the larger but still theologically restrained notion, familiar to Puritans always, of history as the chronicle of "God's Wonder-Working Providence" on earth. Edwards had an even grander conception of history, capacious enough to contain all these ideas—and more.

Earlier Protestant thinkers such as Philip Melanchthon, John Calvin, and William Ames had thought of theology as the ultimate canvas on which to record the being of God and His relationship to His creation. Whatever distance the Reformers may have traveled from Rome, they still retained a medieval sense of systematic theology as the queen of the sciences. Edwards would substitute history. His history was not the history of William Bradford or Cotton Mather, a mere recording of New England towns and their ministers under the nationalistic gloss of *Magnalia Christi Americana*. Nor was it history in the emerging "Enlightenment" sense, the "scientific" history of politics and great men based strictly on empirical observation with no recourse to supernatural revelation.

Alongside these modern senses of history, however, lies another, more mythic sense of history that is best labeled "metanarrative." The modern model of history, which we might label "ordinary" or "historiographical" or, in Edwards's term, "actual" time, is simple chronology: history measured in minutes and years and recorded in written records. But as anthropologists and biblical scholars remind us, it is also possible to order and understand history in what we might term mythic or, in Edwards's terms, "divine" or "virtual" time: history as seen from God's time-transcending eternal perspective. Central to this model would be separate but overlapping senses of time, as in the creation myths common to all religions. But, as we shall see, Edwards had an even larger story in mind: a narrative of "redemption." To frame the metanarrative of redemption Edwards would employ historiographical time from every source he could lay his hands on, both sacred and profane. But he would also subject it to the most important time in the narrative: divine time. For all of his piety, perhaps *because* of his piety, Edwards was not afraid to see time from God's vantage point. He would take his narrative where others before him were afraid to tread. If a majestic enough story could be constructed, Edwards speculated, it could contain all the doctrines and philosophical underpinnings of systematic theology in a more compelling—and popularly accessible—format. In other words, a metanarrative method could do all that systematic theology, and for that matter historiography, could do and more.

Edwards's history incorporated philosophy, theology, and narrative as a synthetic whole. Earlier he had established the proposition that "heaven is a world of love," a metaphysical state infused with the innermost being and character of the Trinity. So too, he proposed, earth was a world of pulsating divine energy, and hell a perversion of love that set in motion the intergalactic super-natural conflict between God and Satan, with earth as the prize. What if the his-tory of all three—heaven, earth, and hell—were integrated into one narrative, a narrative superior to systematic theology for its drama, and to earthbound historiography for its prophetic inspiration?

At the same time that Edwards discovered his true artistic genre, he located the organizing theme for this history as "salvation," or "redemption," the most sublime theme of all, grander even than creation. If Edwards's vision bore a close similarity to Scripture itself, that should not be surprising to modern scholars. Scripture narratives, as Erich Auerbach and Hans Frei have shown, represented a new literary form, a "realistic narrative."[4]

Edwards's doctrine of redemption as the central thread of his great project would not have been well suited to a systematic theology. To be grasped in all its completeness, it had to move out of the polemical confines of the schoolmen and theologians and present itself as a narrative story. Indeed, the greatest story ever told. It is precisely the epic quality of *History of Redemption*, in its post-humously printed form in the nineteenth century, that gave it its "enormous influence" on "popular culture."[5]

Heaven, Earth, and Hell

The "scheme" of redemption perfectly fit Edwards's ambitions to move through two times with the overt goal of promoting revivals worldwide. At the outset he observed that "the work [of redemption] itself and all that pertained to it, was virtually done [i.e., in divine time] and finished [before creation], but not actu-ally [in historiographical time]." In "virtual" time—God's time—an indivisible divine "present" engulfs earthly past and future. God's time—and only God's time—is eternal. Even heaven, though world without end, is finite. In *A His-tory of Heaven*, Jeffrey Burton Russell makes this important distinction: "End-less life is one thing, but God's ability to comprehend and embrace all time in one moment is another. Endlessness is perpetual, but only the existence of the entire space and time of the cosmos in one moment is eternal."[6] In similar terms, Edwards pointed out that in God's time, every event merges with every other event, not in successive chronological sequence, but "several parts of one scheme . . . in which all the persons of the Trinity do conspire and all the vari-ous dispensations that belong to it are united, as the several wheels in one ma-chine, to answer an end, and produce one effect."[7]

Conscious of heaven and eternity, Edwards made clear that redemption *required* the fact of sin to generate the need for salvation (and hence the fall, and not creation, marked the starting point for his narrative in "actual" time); the "scheme" or divine plan was in fact eternal and "virtual." Before creation, "the persons of the Trinity were as it were confederated in a design and covenant of redemption." Indeed, "the world itself seems to have been created in order to it."[8] With the historical metanarrative in mind, he prompted his congregation to expect a personally riveting narrative of what God created them for. It was, Edwards stated, a far more important history than creation, for creation was the means to a greater end. Since God created the world as His stage to dramatize redemption, the "end" of creation could not possibly be, say, the happiness of his creatures, as "rationalists" and "deists" were claiming. It had to be God's own self-glorification.[9]

Because redemption and revival lay at the center of actual history, the hinge dates of earth's history were not tied to the rise and fall of the great empires but to the outworking of redemption: in individuals such as Abraham, David, Christ, the Apostles, and Constantine; in movements such as the Reformation, and the Puritan migration, and—quite soon, again—in places such as Northampton. In like manner, the triggering mechanism for these turning points in actual history would not be wars and conquests, but revivals of true religion.

Although modern-day critics have exaggerated the extent of "hellfire and damnation" in Edwards's typical Sunday sermons, the theme was not ignored and would become especially important in the revivals.

Throughout the history of fallen mankind, interaction among heaven, hell, and earth never ceased, according to Edwards, although it varied in intensity and immediacy. The form of that interaction he frequently likened to a journey or progress. In the artistic manner of Bunyan, Dante, Milton, and, later, C. S. Lewis, Edwards's history portrayed a dramatic contest between good and evil, with confederations within the Trinity itself playing the triumphant role.

Edwards divided his earth history into three major epochs: from the Fall of humankind to the Incarnation of Christ, the god-man; from the Incarnation to the bodily Resurrection of Christ; and from the Resurrection to the end of time. The briefest, yet most important period of interaction between heaven, hell, and earth came during the life, death, and resurrection of Christ. At Christ's birth, the minions of Satan trembled even as the response in heaven was ecstatic: "This appears by their joyful songs on this occasion, heard by the shepherds in the night. This was the greatest event of providence that ever the angels beheld."[10]

Following the resurrection, "Christ entered into heaven in order to the obtaining the success of his purchase. . . . And as he ascended into heaven, God the Father did in a visible manner set him on the throne as king of the universe. He then put the angels all under him, and he subjected heaven and earth under him, that he might govern them for the good of the people that he had died for."[11] Throughout his preaching Edwards drew on church history and profane history to integrate the postresurrection history of earth into one divine "conspiracy."

In contrast to modern avoidance of hell, seventeenth- and eighteenth-century religious culture and art were more attuned to hell than to heaven.[12] If Edwards was more balanced in his preaching, hell was hardly neglected; it formed a central component in his redemption narrative, especially in times of revival. Nor was it limited to the adults in his congregation. Edwards did not hesitate to introduce young hearers to the horrors of hell at the earliest moments. In a 1740 sermon directed to young children, he spared no detail in describing the evils of hell and Satan, but then went on to assure them that they were safe in Christ:

> If you love Christ, you will be safe from the devil, that roaring lion
> that goes about seeking whom he may devour. He will not be able
> to hurt; you shall be out of his reach. If the devil should appear to
> you, you need not be afraid of him, but might triumph over him.
> The devil knows that Christ will subdue him under the feet of such
> as love him. Christ will bring down that dreadful giant and cause all
> holy children that love him to come and set their feet upon his neck.[13]

Satan's kingdom was hell, a place without goodness or God: a physicality of pain and suffering where flames licked at sinners with relentless ferocity. Where many medieval writers favored images of hell that played on infinite darkness, Edwards preferred images of furnaces and fire. In a *Miscellanies* entry he wrote, "Hell is represented by fire and brimstone. . . . Lightning is a string of brimstone; and if that stream of brimstone which we are told kindles hell be as hot as streams of lightning, it will be vehement beyond conception."[14] What made this infinite stream of fire even more agonizing was the fact that God permitted the damned to view the alternative paradise of the saints in heaven. And, like Calvin, Edwards's God would allow for no second chances after death. Hell was eternal and irreversible. With relentless logic Edwards would insist that because God hates sin "it is suitable that he should execute an infinite punishment."[15] Soon, Edwards would discover that nothing would promote revival better than the haunting specter of "infinite punishment."

Like heaven's, hell's history was intimately connected to earth's, and necessary to engage the drama of redemption. In a *Miscellanies* entry dating from 1740, Edwards noted, "God hath so ordered it that all the great concerns and events of the universe should be some way concerning of this work [of redemption], that the occasion of the fall of some of the angels should be something about this." Indeed, he continued, redemption was "why the fall of man was so soon permitted." When the Israelites were enslaved in Egypt, "Hell was as much and much more engaged [than Egypt]. The pride and cruelty of Satan, that old serpent was more concerned in it than Pharaoh's."[16] With deliverance, Israel enjoyed a victory as much over hell as over Egypt.

When earth history, at last, was come to an end in the final climactic battles with Antichrist and Satan, all three worlds would come together, with heaven especially enlisted for the conflict: "At the day of judgment, the Sun of righteousness shall appear in its greatest glory; Christ shall then come in the glory of the Father, and all the holy angels with him." In a sermon on "Millennial Glory" Edwards cautioned that the destructions to accompany this day would exceed the persecutions of the Jews at Christ's death:

> Soon after [the resurrection] he brought the amazing destruction of
> the unbelieving Jews, terribly destroying their city and country by the
> Romans. So when he will come in a spiritual sense at the beginning
> of the expected glorious times of the church, he will come [not only]
> for the deliverance and healing and rejoicing of his church, but for the
> amazing destruction of Antichrist and other enemies of his church.[17]

With the toppling of Antichrist, Satan's earthly kingdoms would be utterly abolished. Satan would be banished from earth as he was from heaven. There would be a "new heaven" no less than a "new earth." Indeed, from *Miscellanies* entries it is clear that Edwards believed the "new heavens and new earth" would strictly be located in heaven: "The NEW HEAVENS AND NEW EARTH, so far as a place of habitation, is meant by 'em, are heaven and not the lower world." While the old heaven was corruptible, as evidenced by Satan's fall, the new heaven would be pure and incorruptible, a paradise without end. With Christ's Second Coming, the saints already in heaven and those joining them would see glories that were previously unavailable even in heaven. Human minds would see universes inside an atom: "'Tis only for want of sufficient accurateness, strength and comprehension of mind, that from the motion of any one particular atom we can't tell all that ever has been, [all] that now is in the whole extent of creation . . . and everything that ever shall be. Corol. [Corollary] What room for improvement of reason is there [in heaven] for angels and glorified minds."[18]

Revivals as Millennial Harbingers

In seeking signs of the triumph of Christ the redeemer, revivals assumed central importance. They were simultaneously tangible events, prophetic signs, and portents of coming triumphs. Even as he read voraciously in the history of heaven, earth, and hell and sketched their interconnected histories, Edwards eagerly scanned the horizons of his own world for signs of revival and regeneration that would presage the new heavens and the new earth. In a letter to Josiah Willard, a widely connected evangelical and the secretary of the Massachusetts Province, Edwards inquired after the state of revivals worldwide. Familiar with the itinerant phenomenon George Whitefield in the British Isles, he extended his inquiry to Prussia, and in particular to the city of Halle, where a Dr. August Hermann Francke was rumored to have promoted revivals. He also expressed curiosity about the East Indies and Moscovy, adding, "I cannot hope that God is about to accomplish glorious things for his church, which makes me the more desirous of knowing as fully as may be the present state of religion in the world."[19]

From his reading and correspondence, Edwards was able to apprise his congregation of recent events and set them in historical context. At a "private meeting" in December 1739 he reported on "God's Grace in Other Places." In particular he singled out "a remarkable work of God's grace that has of late appeared in some parts of the British denominations." Even more surprising was the fact that this movement grew out of the Church of England, which, though "sound in its principles in the beginning of the Reformation," fell prey to heresy and corruption, "especially during King Charles the Second's reign." With mounting excitement, recalling Northampton's great revival of 1734, he informed his listeners that "God has raised up in England a number of younger ministers . . . called, by way of derision, the New Methodists."[20] Soon, this British revival would land on colonial shores with hurricane force.

On October 17, Whitefield arrived in Northampton and preached to Edwards's congregation and in the parsonage later that evening. The next day he preached twice more. All correspondents agreed that something dramatic had happened. Whitefield himself reported great movings, including "Mr. Edwards," who "wept during the whole time of the exercise."[21] Edwards reported that "the congregation was extraordinarily melted by each sermon, almost the whole assembly being in tears for a great part of the time."[22]

Northampton after Whitefield

Following Whitefield's visit, Edwards sought to fan the flames by preaching a sermon series on the parable of the sower, enjoining his listeners to be planted in the Word. Though pleased that a revival spirit seemed to be thriving, Edwards was careful not to gloat. Recalling the earlier revival, he asked, "Was there too much of an appearance of a public pride, if I may so call it? Were we not lifted up with the honor that God had put upon us as a people, beyond most other people?"[23]

In December, Edwards wrote to Whitefield describing the state of religion in Northampton as having "been gradually reviving and prevailing more and more, ever since you was here." He noted of special importance "a considerable number of our young people, some of them children, having already been savingly brought home to Christ." Among these young converts was "one, if not more, of my children." In a later account, first written as a letter to Boston's Thomas Prince and later published in Prince's magazine, *Christian History*, Edwards happily reported, "In about a month there was a great alteration in the town, both as to the revival of professors, and awakening of others. . . . By the middle of December a very considerable work of God appeared among those that were very young, and the revival of religion continued to increase; so that in the spring, an engagedness of spirit about things of religion was become very general amongst young people and children."[24]

Edwards had good reason to focus on the young people. From a demographic analysis of Northampton church membership lists, the historian Kenneth Minkema has shown how large a majority of the recalcitrant members who criticized Edwards and eventually dismissed him were older members who had entered the church under the ministry of his grandfather and predecessor, Solomon Stoddard. Many of these members resented Edwards's fame at the expense of their beloved Mr. Stoddard and his criticism of Stoddard's lax admission policies. But by then, Edwards was not innocent. In retaliation he berated the aged as too old for conversion and held the youth up as role models of faith.[25]

The youth were Edwards's best hope and the ones he would especially cultivate for conversion. Signs of "young people" and even "children" converting appeared as a special providence throughout his reports. Following the drowning of a young man named Billy Shelden in February 1741, Edwards pressed home the mortality of youth. The lesson he enjoined was familiar: "Don't set your heart on youthful pleasures and other vain enjoyments of this world." Instead, prepare for eternity. Even now, Edwards warned, another youth was presently dying of consumption and "on the brink of eternity . . . therefore lose no more time."[26]

In another sermon, delivered in July 1740, Edwards again directed his young listeners' attention to a different world, but this time to heaven rather than hell. He was particularly concerned about the consequences of conversion in respect to youthful conversation. In place of mundane or vulgar conversation he enjoined his young listeners to move their thoughts and communications toward "the great things of another world." Such subject matter would be infinitely rewarding and encouraging in contrast to the sorrows of life in this world. Young people everywhere, but especially in Northampton, "should be much in speaking of the saints' happiness and glory in heaven, where they will be perfectly holy and happy in the full enjoyment of God and Christ, and in perfect love and friendship one with another, forever and ever."[27]

At about the same time that Edwards wrote to Whitefield in December, he penned his *Personal Narrative.* In reading it, one sees how the revivals buoyed his sagging spirits and uplifted his soul. He recalled his earlier yearnings with startling immediacy. He now recalled, "My mind was much taken up with contemplations on heaven, and the enjoyments of those there; and living there in perfect holiness, humility, and love."[28] How much of this description pertained to Edwards's youthful experience and how much to his renewed hope in 1739 is unclear, but certainly these words expressed Edwards's present state.

Edwards the Awakener

Given Edwards's perspective on earth, heaven, and hell, we can see why Whitefield's revivals loomed large in his thinking. Indeed, Edwards was obsessed with Whitefield. In his own way he would imitate him. By December 1740, unmistakable evidence appears in Edwards's manuscript sermons that he had begun to experiment and perfect his own revival rhetoric in Whitefield-like directions. If Edwards's greatest growth as a preacher occurred earlier in the 1730s, his growth as a revivalist specializing in the New Birth came now. His sermon Notebook 45, begun in 1739, is the largest of three and marks a shift in style that reflects both the effect of Whitefield's revivals and his own turbulent relationship with his congregation.[29] By this time Edwards had adopted the duodecimo (7 to 8 inches high) sermon books that could be "palmed" in the pulpit, allowing for greater freedom and the appearance of extemporaneity.

Edwards knew he was no orator. His voice, gestures, and memory could not equal Whitefield's dramaturgical style. But he also knew he had one advantage that he intended to exploit for his own glory and the glory of God: rhetoric. Edwards was a genius with words, and he set himself to compose the "perfect idea" of an awakening sermon. To aid in that process he would modify not only his delivery and gestures, but the balance of ideas and the very structure of the composition in ways that are easily uncovered.

Besides altering the form of his manuscript notes, Edwards shifted his content decisively from heaven to hell. Whereas the history of heaven communicated love, the essence of "the new sense of the heart," Edwards believed, for a moment anyway, that one could get to life eternal only after first being scared to death.[30] This rhetorical need demanded the change in emphasis from the history of heaven to the history of hell. In earlier years, sermonic invocations of heaven had easily surpassed hell. But in the 1740s, hell, in all its fury and torture, would have to be enlisted if heaven was ever to be gained. Edwards knew that the indispensable emotional appeal in an awakening sermon was fear, even terror, and it knew no age limits. Children needed to absorb horror no less than adults. Just as children must be taught to fear fire at the earliest age, so also must they be taught to fear the fires of hell. In a later defense of revival preaching, Edwards would observe, "'Tis no argument that a work is not from the Spirit of God, that it seems to be promoted by ministers insisting very much on the terrors of God's holy law, and that with a great deal of pathos and earnestness."[31]

Edwards's first deliberate attempt to shape a new awakening sermon appeared in his sermon entitled "Sinners in Zion" (December 1740). In examining its composition it becomes clear that Edwards was already at work perfecting the style for a Whitefield-like revival sermon. The form would have to promote and encourage extemporaneous delivery, and the content must shift from heaven to hell, from the joys of redemption to the horrors of the damned. In a further step toward freeing up his speech, Edwards began to include large white space breaks in his notes as a signal to extemporize. In place of fully written-out sentences, he began supplying rhetorical cues:

> You are warned by it.
> You are invited by it.

A Second "Sinners"

Two weeks after preaching "Sinners in Zion," Edwards preached another "Sinners" sermon: "Sinners in the Hands of an Angry God." It is not clear what effect this sermon had on his own congregation. Probably not much. After all, they had heard its substance only two weeks before. Awakening sermons require unfamiliar audiences and spontaneous delivery. Certainly no reports exist of exceptional responses. But in one of his repreachings at Enfield, Connecticut, on July 8, the effects were extraordinary. The Reverend Stephen Williams of nearby Longmeadow attended and recorded the event in his diary:

> Went over to Enfield, where we met Dear Mr. Edwards of New Haven
> who preached a most awakening Sermon from those words Deut
> 32:35—and before ye Sermon was done there was a great moaning and
> crying out throughout ye whole House. What shall I do to be saved—oh
> I am going to Hell—oh what shall I do for a christ etc. etc.—so that ye

minister was obliged to desist. [The] shrieks and crys were piercing and Amazing. After some time of waiting the congregation were still so that a prayer was made by Mr. W—and after that we descended from the pulpit and discoursed with the people—some in one place and some in another. And Amazing and Astonishing [was] ye power. God was seen and severall souls were hopefully wrought upon that night and oh ye cheerfulness and pleasantness of their countenances—that received comfort. Oh that God would strengthen and confirm etc. We sung an hymn and prayed and despersed ye Assembly.

Such was the power—and the fear—generated by this sermon that Edwards apparently never finished preaching it, possibly the only time this had happened. Reflecting on the sermon, Williams wrote that Edwards "seemed affected and moved ready to dissolve in Tears etc., but cant well tell why."[32]

"Sinners in the Hands of an Angry God" is arguably America's greatest sermon. It has been analyzed extensively both in the Yale edition and in other works.[33] But what is interesting for our purposes here is not the final text as it appeared in print, or even the handwritten, fully written text preserved in Yale's Beinecke Library, but an accompanying two-page outline that Edwards prepared at the time of composition for multiple deliveries with minimal notes or prompts.[34] The outline would compel him to preach extemporaneously and connect personally with his listeners. When reading the fragment text as opposed to the fully written-out text, one can discern an almost perfect awakening sermon:

> [Humankind] alwaies exposed to fall
> suddenly fall
> noting that tis G. that holds em up
> no want of power in G.
> > They deserve it.
> > They are Condemned to it [hell]
> > Tis the place they belong to
> > God is angry with them.
> > The devil if not Restrained would Immediately fly upon them
> and seize them as his own
> > They have those Hellish principles in them that if G. should take
> off his Restrains
> > Tis no security that there are no visible means of death at hand.
> > Their own care and prudence to preserve their own lives. (no. 21)

For all the attention paid to "Sinners," no one has appreciated the significance of this fragment version. It confirms the novelty of the sermon, not only on the level of content and rhetoric in print, but of its extemporaneous abbreviation. Assuming that Edwards delivered this sermon on more than two occasions, we can see this two-page fragment text as the *real* "Sinners" sermon, the highly portable and powerful cue card allowing multiple deliveries—and unprecedented terror. Contained in these two pages was rhetorical dynamite.

Conclusion

As effective as Edwards's notes were in conveying the reality of hell's torments, and as powerful as they were in putting terrified listeners in grave concern for their souls, revival would once again disappoint Edwards. Ruefully, he recognized that unrelenting terror could not work indefinitely, nor would his parishioners respond with the "affections" he demanded.

Beyond apathy, Edwards faced an invigorated clerical opposition led by "Old Light" Arminians who were convinced that his highly touted "affections" were nothing more than blind "enthusiasm" and base passion. In his classic treatise on *Seasonable Thoughts on the State of Religion in New-England*, Boston's Charles Chauncy attacked both Edwards and the "vulgar" audiences who endorsed him: "Nay, what Engine has the Devil himself ever made Use of, to more fatal Purposes, in all Ages, than the Passions of the Vulgar heightened to such a Degree, as to put them upon acting without Thought and Understanding?" He continued, "The plain truth is, an enlightened Mind, and no raised affections, ought always to be the Guide of those who call themselves Men."[35] These were fighting words to Edwards, and even as the fires of revivals waned, he would dedicate the remainder of his life to producing major philosophical treatises aimed to respond to the Arminian threat and uphold the Calvinism of his forefathers.

By 1745, the evangelical campaign for the transatlantic world became derailed in the face of renewed war with France, and Edwards would become derailed by his own congregation, who dismissed him with rancor on both sides. Edwards would not live to see another awakening and went to his grave disappointed and a failure.

But as a chronicle of revivals, Edwards's words would outlive him and elevate him to center stage in the now long Anglo-American history of revivals, awakenings, and "crusades." Even the great Whitefield would fade, as Edwards's imprint remained fixed in the "evangelical" tradition. Would Edwards have been surprised to know that he was the premier American revivalist? Probably not. To the end, he believed passionately that he had history on his side, and with it, the certainty that God would make his manual for revival the engine of cosmic transformation and millennial triumph.

NOTES

1. Jonathan Edwards, *Some Thoughts Concerning the Present Revival* (Boston, 1742), 294.

2. John E. Smith, Harry S. Stout, and Kenneth P. Minkema, eds., *A Jonathan Edwards Reader* (New Haven: Yale University Press, 1995), 61.

3. Based on his reading of Edwards's "regulatory notebooks," composed in the 1720s, Wilson Kimnach concludes that Edwards "conceived of his life's work at a fairly early age." Wilson H. Kimnach, "General Introduction to the Sermons: Jonathan Edwards' Art of Prophesying," in *Works of Jonathan Edwards* [hereafter *WJE*] (New Haven: Yale University Press, 1992), 10: 10, 56.

4. Erich Auerbach, *Mimesis: The Representation of Reality in Western Literature*, trans. Willard R. Trask (Princeton, NJ: Princeton University Press, 1953); and Hans W. Frei, *The Eclipse of Biblical Narrative* (New Haven: Yale University Press, 1974).

5. *WJE* 10: 10, 82.

6. Jeffrey Burton Russell, *A History of Heaven: The Singing Silence* (Princeton, NJ: Princeton University Press, 1997), 10–11.

7. *WJE* 9: 118.

8. Ibid.

9. Edwards treated this theme most fully in his *Dissertation Concerning the End for which God Created the World* in *WJE* 8: 401–536.

10. *WJE* 9: 301.

11. Ibid., 361.

12. Like that of other Puritan preachers, Edwards's thinking about hell and Satan was influenced heavily by medieval glosses on Scripture as well as Scripture itself. See Edward K. Trefz, "Satan as the Prince of Evil: The Preaching of the New England Puritans," *Boston Public Library Quarterly* 7 (1955): 3. On the gradual minimalization of hell and Satan outside of the Puritans, see D. P. Walker, *The Decline of Hell: Seventeenth-Century Discussions of Eternal Torment* (Chicago: University of Chicago Press, 1964).

13. See *WJE* 22: 169.

14. Jonathan Edwards, *Miscellanies*, in *WJE* 13: 275.

15. For a fuller elaboration of Edwards's sense of hell, see Norman Fiering, *Jonathan Edwards's Moral Thought and Its British Context* (Williamsburg, VA: Institute of Early American History and Culture, 1981), 61–62; and Philip C. Hammond, *Heaven and Hell in Enlightenment England* (Cambridge, UK: Cambridge University Press, 1994), 98, 151.

16. *Miscellanies*, in *WJE* 13: no. 176.

17. See *WJE* 22: 77.

18. *Miscellanies*, in *WJE* 18 : nos. 809, 710.

19. *WJE* 16: 83.

20. See *WJE* 22: 106.

21. Quoted in Arnold A. Dallimore, *George Whitefield: The Life and Times of the Great Evangelist of the Eighteenth-Century Revival*, (Westchester, IL: Cornerstone Books, 1980), 1: 539.

22. Letter of Edwards to the Reverend Thomas Prince, dated December 12, 1743. *WJE* 16: 116.

23. See *WJE* 22: 248.

24. *WJE* 16: 87, 116–17.

25. Kenneth Minkema, "Old Age and Religion in the Writings and Life of Jonathan Edwards," unpublished paper, March 2000.

26. See *WJE* 22: 323. In fact, Edwards exaggerated the numbers of youthful converts. See Minkema, "Old Age and Religion."

27. See *WJE* 22: 161.

28. *WJE* 16: 795. The case for dating the *Narrative* to December 1740 is made by George Claghorn (747).

29. Wilson Kimnach describes these shifts in *WJE* 10: 62–63.

30. The best treatment of Edwards and hell appears in Fiering, *Jonathan Edwards's Moral Thought*, 200–216.

31. *WJE* 4: 246.

32. Stephen Williams, "Diary," entry for July 8, 1741, typescript, Storrs Library, Longmeadow, MA, vol. III, p. 174.

33. See *WJE* 10: 113–15, 175–78; J. O. Leo Lemay, "Rhetorical Strategies in 'Sinners in the Hands of an Angry God' and *Narrative of the Late Massacres in Lancaster County*," in *Benjamin Franklin, Jonathan Edwards, and the Representation of American Culture*, ed. Barbara B. Oberg and Harry S. Stout (New York: Oxford University Press, 1993), 186–203; and Edward J. Gallagher, "'Sinners in the Hands of an Angry God': Some Unfinished Business," *New England Quarterly* 73 (2000): 202–21.

34. The dating of the fragment is uncertain; see Kimnach, "General Introduction," in *WJE* 10: 145. But whatever the date, it is clear that this outline was intended to promote "spontaneous" rhetoric, leading Kimnach to speculate, "The thought arises that JE, under the influence of Whitefield, might have made an outline of his Northampton sermon for the Enfield performance" (145).

35. Charles Chauncy, *Seasonable Thoughts on the State of Religion in New-England* (Boston, 1743), 23.

4

Alternative Viewpoint: Edwards and Revival

Willem van Vlastuin

We are indebted to Harry Stout for pointing out that Edwards's theology has a historic structure: all aspects of theology are related to history, and history is one great history of redemption.[1]

For Edwards history was much greater than the history of politics and scientific developments. The sacred and profane alike, he believed, belong to the overarching story of redemption. In this way theology is subordinated to history. Stout comes to the conclusion that history is God's innermost self-revelation.[2] From a Puritan point of view this is astonishing, because Puritans made a distinction between the revelation of God in nature and the revelation of God in scripture. Edwards went further. God did not only gave an impression of his existence in history, but he revealed his inner self.

Revivals are at the heart of this history.[3] This is because they are the operational vehicle that God uses to accomplish his magisterial plan of cosmic redemption. Every revival is a step forward in the great plan of God. From this conviction of Edwards we can understand his extensive correspondence with people in different parts of the world. He wanted to be in contact with the developments related to the fulfillment of the kingdom of God.

Every revival was a prophecy and a guarantee of the climax of revivals, the millennium. Furthermore, the revivals in his own congregation gave Edwards hope. By them he was reassured that the Spirit will indeed be poured out and the whole world will bow to Jesus.

There will indeed be a glorious time within the bounds of history to accomplish the conclusion of history.

I will evaluate Stout's remarks from four perspectives (spiritual, historic, Reformed, and systematic) and end with a conclusion.

Edwards's Theology of History from a Spiritual Perspective

We can better understand the life and labors of Edwards if we see his passion for revival and the millennium.[4] His deeply earnest sermons were meant to awaken sinners. To that end, he preached God's absolute sovereignty, the sinfulness of sin, and eternal punishment in hell. Throughout, he made a sharp distinction between the real work of God and counterfeit conversion. There was nothing he feared so much as superficial conversions. These heavy themes were intended to bring sinners back to the feet of a gracious God.

Edwards is best known for his hellfire sermons, but in fact he preached more about sanctification and our need for holiness.[5] He believed in the power of the Spirit to renew hearts, characters, families, churches, and societies. Hence the need for Christians to strive after conformity to Jesus. Their lives will then be adorned with the fruit of the Spirit, such as love, self-denial, patience, temperance, and meekness. This means that it is not enough to be revived once in our lives. Children of God must continually seek to be revived in order to overcome the recurring inroads of sin and to glorify God.

Edwards detailed what he found to be marks of a revived state. Revival will produce holy affections for God, and the most important affection is love. When the Spirit is poured out in our souls, the love of God is poured out. The hypocrite loves his own experience, but the real Christian has love for God. By the power of the Spirit Christians love God above all things and all other persons. God becomes great for us and we are humbled. Against our old nature we love the holiness of God. There is a "new sense" (something like a new vision) of God and his salvation. The believer is happy in God and experiences a foretaste of heaven.

This spirituality is at the heart of Edwards's theology. His *Humble Attempt* (1748) and *Religious Affections* (1746) are not two isolated books, but belong to one framework of living and thinking. In *Religious Affections* he described the real Christian life, which, according to his convictions, consisted of holy affections. In his *Humble Attempt* he explained why he expected the millennium. The millennium would be more glorious than a time of worldwide revival in which the Christian life is extended in breadth and depth. With his description of this expectation, Jonathan Edwards tried to stir up affectionate longings for

God's kingdom in history. So *Humble Attempt* was intended to promote the spiritual life.

What Stout calls a metanarrative of history is a spiritual history. We cannot understand Edwards's view of history without understanding the spiritual affections of his heart. The great works of God that would be visible are the works of the Holy Spirit, recognizable from holy affections. Edwards had a passion for God and therefore a passion for his works in history.

This focus on the great and glorious works of the Spirit is concentrated on the millennium, as described in *An Humble Attempt.* In the millennium the glory of God would be revealed within the bounds of this history. There is a self-revelation of God in his historical works.

Edwards's Theology of History from a Historical Perspective

During his life Edwards was obsessed with the history swirling around him. It was a hopeful sign that his *Faithful Narrative* (1736), which provided a model for revival, was reprinted many times and translated in different languages. He read all the newspapers and journals he could find, not only about the war with Spain and France, but also about revivals and the preaching tours of Whitefield and others.

Edwards expected that the Great Awakening would lead, eventually, to the millennium.[6] His expectations were great, and his disappointments were as big as his expectations. The Great Awakening waned, and he was dismissed from his revived (!) congregation in Northampton and went to live in the wilderness among the Indians. But he continued to work at his historical theology, full of expectations of the great works of God.

Then Edwards was called to Princeton, where he died just after his arrival in the spring of 1758. If Edwards had died during the climax of the Great Awakening, newspapers would have written about the death of this great man of God. Now a single sentence was enough. At that point his critics could say that it looked as if he had deceived himself with a rational and theoretical vision—a scholar with a pale face in an isolated study with little contact with reality.

The seeds of his insights, however, bore fruit. The rise of the modern Protestant missionary movement is inconceivable without the Great Awakening in general and the eschatological views of Jonathan Edwards in particular.[7] Edwards's *Humble Attempt* was especially important. The paradigm of this book was the progressive unfolding of the plan of redemption in history. Edwards believed that there were many unfulfilled prophecies in Scripture.

These unfulfilled prophecies gave hope for the worldwide extension of God's kingdom and were to be brought to reality by prayer.

As Chris Chun pointed out earlier in this book, *An Humble Attempt* and its vision inspired a group of English Baptist ministers, including William Carey and his friends.[8] In 1784 they started to pray for the work of the mission and in 1789 reprinted *An Humble Attempt*. Andrew Fuller belonged to this group of ministers. In 1785 he published his *Gospel Worthy of All Acceptation*. His message had an Edwardsian color. In this book he explained that God's sovereign election and our obligation to accept the gospel are consistent. Because the obligation to accept the gospel was universal, there was a responsibility to evangelize worldwide. To give concrete form to this responsibility, William Carey published *An Enquiry into the Obligation of Christians to use Means for the Conversion of the Heathen* (1792). In this book the reader could perceive the influence of Jonathan Edwards.

These were the beginnings of the modern Protestant missionary movement. A group of Baptist ministers formed the Baptist Missionary Society in 1792. Some three years later the London Missionary Society was founded. For all these Christians, the vision of *Humble Attempt* was decisive. The Scots started their own organization in 1796. It is not too much to say that the missiological vision of these organizations originated with Edwards.

We know the history. Carey himself went out to India. Many others would follow. On their journeys the missionaries were encouraged by Edwards's biography of David Brainerd.[9] Edwards confirmed this message by his own example as a missionary in Stockbridge.[10]

We can see, then, that Edwards's view of history was not simply academic musing, but has had continuing impact on the real world to this day. We might even say that his theology of history was strong enough to move people, extend the kingdom of God, and influence the course of history.

Edwards's Theology of History from a Reformed Perspective

Because Jonathan Edwards belonged to the Reformed tradition, it would be helpful to compare his theology of history to Calvin's. Both preachers believed history was controlled by the eternal and unchangeable plan of God. As biblical theologians, their narrative framework was creation-fall-redemption. They stressed the necessity of reconciliation between God and human by the blood and cross of Jesus Christ, applied to the heart by the irresistible work of the Holy Spirit.

But there are some interesting and important differences. Take their understanding of prophetic texts in Scripture. Calvin believed they were already fulfilled in principle.[11] For example, every promised victory is in principle already present in the victory of Jesus Christ. Christians live by faith in this fulfillment and experience a measure of this victory in history. But it will not be until the end of history, at the second coming of Christ, that Christians will see the complete fulfillment of the promised victories.

Calvin applied this hermeneutic to the promise of the new heaven and the new earth. This promise, he wrote, has some meaning for the distant future, but was also already fulfilled in Jesus Christ.[12] The Reformer did not apply Isaiah 11:9 ("The earth shall be full of the knowledge of the Lord, as the waters cover the sea") to the future, but understood that this prophecy was fulfilled in the time of the New Testament.[13] In the time of the New Testament the knowledge of God was much richer than during the period of the Old Testament. The spiritual knowledge during the old covenant could be compared with the knowledge of a little child. Under the new covenant the full light of wisdom had come.

Calvin went one step further and applied this understanding to the church. Because of the union between Christ and his church, the church shares in the fulfillment of the promises and prophesies. Biblical prophecies of the second coming of Christ were already fulfilled in Christ, and therefore for the Christian believer. In Christ the believer is already a new creature. The old things are passed away and all things are become new (2 Corinthians 5:17). In Christ the saints are the rulers of the world. Christians can be persecuted, but they are in Christ more than conquerors. The kingdom of Christ is not visible for the carnal men, but only approvable by faith.[14]

Much more can be said about Calvin's understanding of history and biblical prophecies. But these remarks are enough to see a central difference with Edwards. Occasionally Edwards took the prophecies of a new heaven and the new earth to refer to New Testament times.[15] But more commonly he applied them to the millennium.[16] Sometimes he can even speak about the triumphant state of the church when speaking about the millennium.[17]

While Calvin stressed that the kingdom of Christ is concealed, Edwards emphasized that the kingdom of the Lord will be visible within history. The continental theologian insisted that faith itself is evidence of the unseen glory of the kingdom, but his later colleague was convinced of the visible and recognizable glory of God's kingdom in the millennium. Calvin tried to seek a balance between the "already" and the "not yet" of the kingdom, placing more stress on the "already" than the "not yet." Edwards took the opposite tack and underscored the "not yet" of the glory of Christ.

Far more could be made of this difference, especially concerning the different theological frameworks, but in the interest of space I will move on.

Edwards's Theology of History from a Systematic Perspective

Edwards made history the main structure for his theological system. In his *History of Redemption* he suggested an outline for the structure of such a work of divinity, dividing history into three major periods: the time before Christ, the time of Christ, and the time of the Spirit after Christ. The first period is for preparation, the second for foundation, and the third for the building of the church.

In making history the central theme of his theological system, Edwards took a very important decision with far-reaching consequences. All theological questions, convictions, and dogmas had to be placed in the order of history. This leads to some questions.

What is the meaning of Pentecost? Edwards spoke about the continued outpourings of the Holy Spirit in both the Old and New Testaments and then throughout church history. What difference, then, did Pentecost really make? There are some places in his works that suggest that Pentecost made a qualitative difference, but these places look like remarks in the margin that do not have a fundamental influence on the system of his theology. On the whole we get the impression that Pentecost had a more quantitative than qualitative meaning for Edwards.

How can a cessationist also talk about continued outpourings of the Spirit? We know that Edwards was a strict cessationist: he believed the special gifts of the Spirit (tongues, prophecy, etc.) ceased after the canonization of the New Testament, and he firmly denied the possibility of any new revelation. He was not happy with impressions and dreams about heavenly or godly subjects, although in his later years he showed some acceptance of these phenomena. He stressed that the possession of certain gifts of the Spirit was totally different from possessing the Spirit himself. Non-Christians such as Balaam and King Saul may prophesy by the Spirit but still be wicked men. We can have the clothes of the gifts of the Spirit without having the new character of a reborn Christian. But my question is whether it is possible to stress so strongly the cessation of gifts and at the same time speak about the outpourings of the Spirit. Edwards may not have considered this problem.

How can biblical revelation still be special if placed within the largest framework of history? In Reformed theology it is customary to make a sharp distinction between the history of biblical revelation on the one hand, and secular and church history on the other. But in his historical scheme, Edwards placed both the history of biblical revelation and the history of salvation in the broader context of history in general. We cannot deny that it is an intelligent design and an impressive structure. But is it possible that by this way of doing theology, the special place of biblical revelation is underestimated? Is it thinkable that the history of biblical revelation becomes only a phase in a history in which the unique and exclusive place of biblical history disappears? Will biblical history remain special in this scheme or will general history become special?

In this "theology as history," does the work of the Spirit become more important than the work of Christ? The great design of Edwards placed a heavy weight upon history. Redemption has to be accomplished by the Spirit working in history. Most of the great fight has yet to take place, before and during the millennium. Hence some of the most important redemptive work of God has yet to be done. The "not yet" of the kingdom of God seems more realistic than the "already." Edwards seemed to live more for the kingdom of God that is yet to come than for the King who has already come. It gives theology a burdensome sense if the "not yet" is stressed more than the "already." Christians experience the heavy load of the war that is still to be fought.

This calls into question the relation between Christ and the Spirit. In Reformed theology the work of the Spirit is seen to be the application of the work of Christ, and it is routine in this tradition to say that the Spirit will not add anything to the work of Christ. The Spirit applies Christ and His work to the hearts and lives of people, brings sinners back to the cross to find eternal life in the death of Christ, and thereby shows the glory of Christ in the "theology of the cross."

But making history the central theme of the theological system can have the effect of making the work of the Spirit more central than the work of Christ.[18] In theological terms, the order of salvation then becomes more important than the history of salvation. The experience of holy affections replaces faith in the unseen reconciliation of Christ—thus my concern that Edwards's emphasis on history has loosened the connection between Christ and the Spirit.

Conclusion

Edwards's theology of history was at the heart of his theological vision. His emphasis on warm affections was also integral to this vision. It has been these perspectives that have influenced so much of both the modern church and important lines of its thinking.

Edwards was an original theologian in the Reformed tradition. He was not a slavish follower of his predecessors, and we should not slavishly follow all of his theological leads. If we are to be true to his larger purpose of seeing God rightly, we must think through the problems that Edwards's theology poses. Then Edwards will be all the more a theologian for today.

NOTES

1. Much academic work has been done on Edwards in relation to history. For a recent study, see Avihu Zakai, *Jonathan Edwards's Philosophy of History: The Reenchantment of the World in the Age of Enlightenment* (Princeton, NJ: Princeton University Press, 2003), 182–271.

2. For the relationship between God's inner self and history, see Sang Hyun Lee, "Editor's Introduction," in *The Works of Jonathan Edwards* [hereafter, *WJE*] (New Haven: Yale University Press, 2003), 21: 1–106.

3. The importance of Edwards for revival is generally acknowledged. See Perry Miller, *Jonathan Edwards* (New York: William Sloane, 1949), 137; Ian Murray, *Jonathan Edwards; A New Biography* (Carlisle, PA: Banner of Truth Trust, 1987), 457–72.

4. For Edwards on the millennium, see J. F. Wilson, "History, Redemption, and the Millennium," in *Jonathan Edwards and the American Experience*, ed. Nathan Hatch and Harry Stout (New York: Oxford University Press, 1988), 131–41.

5. See John Gerstner, *The Rational Biblical Theology of Jonathan Edwards*, 3 vols. (Powhatan, VA: Berea Publications, 1991), 1: 623.

6. Gerald McDermott has shown that Edwards put the millennium off for 250 years: *One Holy and Happy Society: The Public Theology of Jonathan Edwards* (University Park: Pennsylvania State University Press, 1992), 49–60, 78–79.

7. These aspects were seen by early scholars of Edwards. See E. A. Payne, "The Evangelical Revival and the Beginnings of the Modern Missionary Movement," *Congregational Quarterly* 21 (July 1943): 223–36; J. Foster, "The Bicentenary of Jonathan Edwards' Humble Attempt," *International Review of Missions* 37 (1948): 375–81. The influence of Edwards on missions also attracted Dutch scholars. See J. van den Berg, *Constrained by Jesus' Love: An Enquiry into the Motives of the Missionary Awakening in Great Britain in the Period between 1698 and 1815* (Kampen, Netherlands: J. H. Kok, 1956), 83–93, 103–5, 120, 129, 161, 180–87, 207–10; J. A. de Jong, *As the Waters Cover the Sea: Millennial Expectations in the Rise of Anglo-American Mission 1640–181* (Kampen, Netherlands: J. H. Kok, 1970).

8. A. H. Oussoren, *William Carey, Especially His Missionary Principles* (Leiden: A. W. Sijthoff's Uitgeversmaatschappij, 1945), 23, 128.

9. Stuart Piggin has given many examples of the great value of the biography of Brainerd for missionaries: "'The Expanding Knowledge of God': Jonathan Edwards's Influence on Missionary Thinking and Promotion," in *Jonathan Edwards at Home and Abroad*, ed. David W. Kling and Douglas A. Sweeney (Columbia: University of South Carolina Press, 2003), 273–74.

10. S. H. Rooy, *The Theology of Missions in the Puritan Tradition: A Study of Representative Puritans: Richard Sibbes, Richard Baxter, John Eliot, Cotton Mather, and Jonathan Edwards*, (Delft: W. D. Meinema, 1965), 286.

11. Calvin explains this in his exegesis of Daniel 7:27 in *Calvini Opera quae supersunt omnia*, ed. G. Baum, E. Cunitz, and E. Reuss (Brunsvigae, Germany: C. A. Schwetschke et filium, 1863–1900), 41: 81–86 [hereafter *CO*]; see also D. E. Holwerda, "Eschatology and History: A Look at Calvin's Eschatological Vision," in *Readings in Calvin's Theology*, ed. Donald McKim (Grand Rapids, MI: Baker Book House, 1984), 311–42, especially 327–30.

12. Calvin, *CO* 37: 453 (comm. Is. 66:22).

13. Calvin, *CO* 36: 244.

14. *CO* 23: 598–603 (Comm. Gen. 49:10); 36: 242 (Comm. Is. 11:6).

15. See Edwards's sermon, "The Perpetuity and Change of the Sabbath on 1 Corinthians 16:1–2," part II. 2, in *WJE* 15: 233–34.

16. See Edwards's well-known sermon "True Saints, when absent from the Body, are present with the Lord" for the funeral of David Brainerd, part III. 2, in E. Hickman, ed., *The Works of Jonathan Edwards* (Carlisle, PA: Banner of Truth Trust 1974), 2: 31.

17. See Edwards, *Notes on the Bible*, on Matt. 24:21ff, part 7, in *WJE* 15: 254–55.

18. See W. van Vlastuin, *De Geest van opwekking: Een onderzoek naar de leer van de Heilige Geest in de opwekkingstheologie van Jonathan Edwards (1703–1758)* (Heerenveen, the Netherlands: Groen, 2001), 319–44. There is an English summary on pages 345–56.

5

Edwards and the Bible

Douglas A. Sweeney

In this chapter Douglas Sweeney emphasizes the importance of the Bible in Edwards's life, thought, and work. He catalogues the wide range of Edwards's biblical writings and details Edwards's theological understanding of Scripture. He explains Edwards's doctrine of divine revelation, and he outlines Edwards's methods of interpreting the Bible, examining them in light of the long history of exegesis and commending them in revised form to readers of Scripture today.

Search the scriptures; for in them ye think ye have eternal life: and they are they which testify of me. . . . Had ye believed Moses, ye would have believed me: for he wrote of me. But if ye believe not his writings, how shall ye believe my words?

—John 5: 39, 46–47 (KJV)

Jonathan Edwards devoted most of his life to meditating on Scripture, delving deeply into its contents, reading biblical commentaries, and praying fervently for the Spirit's help interpreting and applying the Bible faithfully to life. Notwithstanding his reputation as a literary artist, natural scientist, philosopher, and psychologist of religion, he was chiefly a biblical thinker, a minister of the Word. As his disciple Samuel Hopkins once remarked of his priorities: "He studied the Bible more than all other Books, and more than most other Divines do. . . . He took his religious Principles from the Bible, and not from any human System or Body of Divinity."[1]

Edwards loved to study Scripture. As he vowed in his "Resolutions" while a boy in his late teens, he sought "to study the Scriptures so steadily, constantly and frequently, as that I may find, and plainly perceive myself to grow in the knowledge of the same." And as he wrote in the "Personal Narrative" of his early spiritual life, he took "the greatest delight in the holy Scriptures, of any book whatsoever."

> Oftentimes in reading it, every word seemed to touch my heart. I felt an harmony between something in my heart, and those sweet and powerful words. I seemed often to see so much light, exhibited by every sentence, and such a refreshing ravishing food communicated, that I could not get along in reading. Used oftentimes to dwell long on one sentence, to see the wonders contained in it; and yet almost every sentence seemed to be full of wonders.[2]

Edwards shared this fascination with parishioners frequently, inculcating a passion for the wonders of the Word. In one beloved Edwards sermon, preached in 1739, he promised his flock that "things of divinity," or things revealed in the Bible, "are things of superlative excellency." Nothing is "so worthy to be known as these things." They "are as much above those things which are treated of in other sciences, as heaven is above . . . earth." They have preoccupied the attention of the "patriarchs, prophets, and apostles, and the most excellent men that ever were in the world." And if such mundane testimony were not enough to compel investment by his people in the Word, Edwards reminded them that the Bible is also "the subject of the study of the angels in heaven; I Pet. 1:10–12."[3]

Edwards emphasized that life-long biblical learning was for all—not just clergy and "men of learning, but . . . persons of every character." God calls everyone to hunt the treasure hid in holy writ, both the "learned and unlearned, young and old, men and women." Not even the brightest Bible scholar will ever begin to find it all. In fact, the ones who "studied the longest, and have made the greatest attainments . . . know but little of what is to be known." The Bible's "subject is inexhaustible," for God "is infinite, and there is no end to the glory of his perfections." In Edwards's estimation, this reality leveled the playing field somewhat for simple readers while inspiring nobler efforts from sophisticated scholars. No matter how gifted the student, Scripture "contains enough" within it "to employ us to the end," indeed "to employ the . . . saints and angels to all eternity." Consequently, all of us should apply our hearts and minds to Holy Scripture, making the study of its books "a great part of the business of our lives." Edwards drove this point home by recommending that his people devote as much of their time to seeking the things of God as seeking Mammon.

Content not yourselves with having so much knowledge as is thrown in your way, and as you receive in some sense unavoidably by the frequent . . . preaching of the word, of which you are obliged to be hearers, or as you accidentally gain in conversation; but let it be very much your business to search for it, and that with the same diligence and labor with which men are wont to dig in mines of . . . gold.[4]

Edwards's manuscripts attest to his great reverence for the Bible. His more than twelve hundred sermons, of course, confirm his love for Scripture, full as they are of meaty, biblical exposition. But many of Edwards's private notebooks also feature exegesis, revealing the vast extent of his Scriptural portfolio.

Edwards's best-known biblical manuscripts are called his "Notes on Scripture," four volumes of miscellaneous remarks on Scripture texts. Begun in 1724, they were kept throughout his life and cross-referenced with his other private notebooks. His most bulky biblical manuscript is called the "Blank Bible," technically known as "Miscellaneous Observations on the Holy Scriptures." It is a large, blank book, given to Edwards by his brother-in-law, the Reverend Benjamin Pierpont, interleaved with the pages of a smaller King James Bible. Beginning late in 1730, Edwards filled the ample margins that surrounded its biblical leaves with a commentary, or gloss, on the whole of sacred Scripture. Thus from Genesis to Malachi and Matthew to Revelation, he left a record of his engagement with the Bible. There are other manuscripts, too, in which he wrote about the Bible. His "Notes on the Apocalypse" comprise a large volume on the book of Revelation. "Images of Divine Things" and "Types" contain remarks on much of the imagery—or types—of Christ, the church, and human redemption that he found in Scripture and nature (especially in the Old Testament). He kept a booklet on "Hebrew Idioms," even a notebook in "Defense of the Authenticity of the Pentateuch as a Work of Moses and the Historicity of the Old Testament Narratives." He drafted hundreds of sheets on sundry doctrines of the Bible. Altogether, this material fills thousands of manuscript pages in the extant Edwards corpus. It is an understudied treasure trove of biblical exegesis.[5]

Edwards died before he could publish two enormous biblical projects, both of which had engrossed his mind for years. As he explained in a letter written late in 1757 in response to an invitation to become the next president of the College of New Jersey (later Princeton University), he was loathe to take the job, for he was hoping to complete them and suspected that a presidency would only get in the way.

The first of these two works was to be built upon the longest sermon series he ever preached, a thirty-sermon exposition of the history of redemption (preached in 1739). It would be a great [i.e., large] work, which I call *A History of the Work of Redemption*, a body of divinity in an entire new method, being thrown into the form of an history, considering the affair of Christian theology, as the whole of it, in each part, stands in reference to the great work of redemption by Jesus Christ; which I suppose is to be the grand design of all God's designs, and the *summum* and *ultimum* of all the divine operations and decrees; particularly considering all parts of the grand scheme in their historical order.[6]

By the time he wrote this letter, Edwards had filled three notebooks with ideas on how to expand his sermon series into a book. If completed, this magnum opus would have secured his reputation as the Anglo-American world's leading biblical theologian.[7]

The second of these two works was even more exegetical. Edwards titled it *The Harmony of the Old and New Testament*.

The first [part] considering the prophecies of the Messiah, his redemption and kingdom; the evidences of their references to the Messiah, etc. comparing them all one with another, demonstrating their agreement and true scope and sense; also considering all the various particulars wherein these prophecies have their exact fulfillment; showing the universal, precise, and admirable correspondence between predictions and events. The second part: considering the types of the Old Testament, showing the evidence of their being intended as representations of the great things of the gospel of Christ: and the agreement of the type with the antitype. The third and great [largest] part, considering the harmony of the Old and New Testament, as to doctrine and precept.

Edwards hoped that this work would offer "occasion for an explanation of a very great part of the holy Scripture . . . in a method, which to me seems the most entertaining and profitable, best tending to lead the mind to a view of the true spirit, design, life and soul of the Scriptures, as well as to their proper use and improvement."[8]

He drafted hundreds of manuscript pages for inclusion in this book. For part 1, on biblical prophecy, he penned four entries in his "Miscellanies" notebooks, all treating what he labeled either "Prophecies of the Messiah" (mainly in the Old Testament) or "Fulfillment of the Prophecies of the Messiah" (in the New). Two of these entries proved so large that they consumed a whole book.[9] For part 2, on the wealth of biblical types of the Messiah, Edwards drafted another entry in a "Miscellanies" notebook: "That the Things of the Old Testament

Are Types of Things Appertaining to the Messiah and His Kingdom and Salvation, Made Manifest from the Old Testament Itself." In published form, this miscellany exceeds a hundred pages in length. Edwards wrote it in addition to his "Images of Divine Things" and "Types" mentioned above.[10] For part 3, on the theological harmony of Scripture, Edwards kept a separate notebook on "The Harmony of the Genius, Spirit, Doctrines, & Rules of the Old Testament & the New." Most of this book is ordered canonically (Edwards made it through the Psalms). Several entries appear topically. All attest to his interest in the doctrinal integrity, or "harmony," of the Bible.[11]

Edwards worked so hard on Scripture because he thought it was from God, a supernatural revelation of the mind of the Creator that unfolded his intentions for the redemption of the world. He considered it "divine." He thought it "full of wondrous things." He said that its contents were the "most excellent things in the world." He routinely extolled the privileges of those who owned a Bible, employing language such as this, preached on the eve of the Great Awakening:

> What a precious treasure God has committed into our hands in
> that he has given us the Bible. How little do most persons consider
> how much they enjoy in that they have the possession of that holy
> book. . . . What an excellent book is this, and how far exceeding all
> human writings. . . . He that has a Bible, and don't observe what is
> contained [in] it, is like a man that has a box full of silver and gold,
> and don't know it.

Edwards taught that "most . . . are to blame" for their "inattentive, unobservant way of reading" this gift of heaven. "The word of God contains the most noble, and worthy, and entertaining objects . . . , the most excellent things that man can exercise his thoughts about." Those who had truly "tasted the sweetness" of God's Scriptural divinity ought to live out their days, he said, in "longing for more and more of it."[12]

Edwards often spoke of Scripture as the very "Word of God." He also called it "the word of Christ" or, as he described it in Manhattan as a teenage parish pastor, "the epistle of Christ that he has written to us." The Bible thus functioned for Edwards as a vital "word of life; as the light of life; a sweet . . . life-giving word." He called it "a perfect rule," a reliable "guide to true happiness." And he held an exceptionally high view of its method of inspiration. He taught that God "indited" the Scriptures (i.e., proclaimed, pronounced, or composed them) through the Bible's human authors, thus imbuing the biblical narratives with "a strange and unaccountable kind of enchantment." Not surprisingly, then, he thought the Bible to be "an infallible guide, a sure rule which if we follow we cannot err."[13]

According to Edwards, the best posture for those who would understand the divine was "to sit at Jesus' feet and hear his word." We must "go to him whose Word it is and beg of him to teach," for "he has reserved to himself this work of enlightening the mind with spiritual knowledge, and there is no other can do it; there is none teaches like God." Like Mary of Bethany in the gospels, the sister of Lazarus and Martha, who took "a pound of ointment of spikenard, very costly, and anointed the feet of Jesus, and wiped his feet with her hair" (John 12:3), we should know better than to busy ourselves with "[trouble] about many things." Rather, as Jesus said to Martha, only "one thing is needful: and Mary hath chosen that good part" (Luke 10:41–42), for she had clung to Christ and hung on His every word. Similarly, we should cling to every word that comes from the mouth of God, for "the word of God is the great means of our eternal good. . . . 'Tis the most necessary means, and without which our souls must famish." It is like "MILK," Edwards proposed, flowing "from the breasts of the church." It is like rain, for which God's people have "a great and earnest thirsting."[14]

Edwards spoke often of the need to study "what reason *and* Scripture declare." He echoed the common Calvinist dictum that those who would understand the world and its relationship to God need the "book of nature" *and* the "book of Scripture."[15] But he emphasized consistently the priority of the Bible. As he wrote in *Distinguishing Marks of a Work of the Spirit of God* (1741), "All that is visible to the eye is unintelligible and vain, without the Word of God to instruct and guide the mind." And as he had preached in a crucial sermon on this theme a few years earlier:

> We make a distinction between the things that we know by reason,
> and things we know by revelation. But alas we scarce know what we
> say: we know not what we should have known . . . had it not been for
> revelation. . . . Many of the principles of morality and religion that we
> have always been brought up in the knowledge of, appear so rational
> that we are ready to think we could have found 'em out by our own
> natural reason. . . . [But] all the learning, yea, all the common civil-
> ity that there is in the world, seems to be either directly or indirectly
> from revelation, whether men are sensible of it or no. . . . Everything
> that is good and useful in this fallen world, is from supernatural help.

This became a central theme in his response to the English deists. In opposition to their call for a modern religion of nature and reason, Edwards insisted late in his life on the necessity of transcendent, supernatural revelation—even for the maintenance of a healthy civic virtue. This was also a major theme in Edwards's early preaching and writing. As he drafted in his "Miscellanies" in 1728, "Were it not for divine revelation, I am persuaded that there is no one doctrine of that which we call natural religion [but] would, notwithstanding all philosophy and learning, forever be involved in darkness, doubts, endless disputes and dreadful confusion." And as he preached to his congregation near the end of the 1730s, human reason can tell us a lot about the works of God in nature, but "there is nothing else that informs us what [the] scheme and design of God in his works is but only the holy Scriptures."[16]

Supernatural revelation and the spiritual light it provides were, for Edwards, essential for clarifying the nature of reality. It was not that the world could not be known at all without the Bible, or that the Bible served as a textbook in natural history, science or reason. Rather, for Edwards, God's Word and Spirit illuminate our worldly wisdom, rendering our knowledge more clear, beautiful, and real than ever before. In a remarkable notebook entry dating from 1729, Edwards depicted this point so vividly that I quote him here at length:

> A mind not spiritually enlightened [by means of the Bible and God's Spirit] beholds spiritual things faintly, like fainting, fading shadows that make no lively impression on his mind, like a man that beholds the trees and things abroad in the night: the ideas ben't strong and lively, and [are] very faint; and therefore he has but a little notion of the beauty of the face of the earth. But when the light comes to shine upon them, then the ideas appear with strength and distinctness; and he has that sense of the beauty of the trees and fields given him in a moment, which he would not have obtained by going about amongst them in the dark in a long time. A man that sets himself to reason without divine light is like a man that goes into the dark into a garden full of the most beautiful plants, and most artfully ordered, and compares things together by going from one thing to another, to feel of them and to measure the distances; but he that sees by divine light is like a man that views the garden when the sun shines upon it. There is . . . a light cast upon the ideas of spiritual things in the mind of the believer, which makes them appear clear and real, which before were but faint, obscure representations.[17]

Edwards wrote scores of pages about this "divine and supernatural light," as well as its role in the production of a "spiritual understanding" (I Corinthians 2). He taught that revelation elucidates the harmony of the cosmos, grants a teleological glimpse of the world's relationship to God, that spiritual knowledge of its contents constitutes a greater blessing "than any other privilege that ever God bestowed." He went so far, in fact, as to say that those who "hear the Word . . . and keep it . . . bring forth Christ" himself in their hearts; that Christ is truly "formed in them"; that spiritual knowledge of the Bible intensifies our vital union with the living Word of God, the one through whom the world was created and for whom it is preserved; and that this union is "more blessed" than "to have Christ" within one's "arms, or at the breast, as the virgin Mary had." Spiritual knowledge even grants what Edwards referred to in one sermon as "an earnest" or "the dawnings" of the beatific vision. It enables the people of God to share in the very life of God (II Peter 1:4). For the new principle in the souls of those who enjoy this special blessing "is not only from the Spirit, but it also partakes of the nature of that Spirit."[18]

In keeping with this view of supernatural revelation, Edwards interpreted the Bible with a reverence for its character, faith in its coherence, and conviction that the Spirit continues to use it powerfully. In an era characterized by the rapid spread of biblical criticism, theological skepticism, and religious minimalism, Edwards demonstrated a robust faith in Scripture's credibility, expounding it with confidence in traditional Christian methods.

During the age of the Enlightenment, to an extent unprecedented earlier in history, experts on the Bible focused attention on the diversity of its ancient life settings (*Sitze im Leben*) and thus the *differences* in context, purpose, style, and even meaning across its roughly fifteen hundred years of human composition. These "higher" biblical critics often thought of themselves as historians.[19] The leading question they asked of any text in the Bible was how it would have been understood by its original recipients. They investigated the Bible much as they would any other compilation of classical materials. They did not presume its unity. They bracketed, or denied, older views of its inspiration. They disassembled the canon, examined its contents separately, and used them principally to reconstruct the life of ancient Israel.

Edwards devoured their writings. He cherished biblical history and labored over the findings of the biblical avant-garde. Despite his reputation as a "precritical" reader or "premodern" thinker, he was fully apprised of recent trends in modern critical thought.[20] He disliked the trends that seemed to hinder the progress of the gospel. He spent a lot of time defending Protestant orthodoxy in the face of new attacks against its moral viability. But this involved him deeply in the problems of historicism. It guaranteed that he would engage the critics on their turf.

Still, Edwards tried to interpret the Bible theologically. He handled it not as a collection of antiquarian artifacts, but as the living Word of the God who calls Himself "I Am." Thus he studied it both as scholars study sets of primary sources (to understand the lives of those for whom they were first put to writing) *and*—in a manner more important to his daily pastoral ministry—as priestly theologians study the oracles of God (to understand his will for those who still have ears to hear). This sets him apart from many modern Western biblical scholars, whether Christian or non-Christian. For higher criticism has ruled the roost in modern biblical studies, shaping the ways that even pastors think of preaching Sunday sermons.

For several generations, learned preachers have been taught to think primarily as historians, explaining sermon texts by reference to their ancient, social contexts. Only later, if at all, have they been taught to expound their sermon texts in light of the whole canon, or the history of redemption, no matter how far apart the Bible's human authors stood. There are notable exceptions to this homiletical rule. But most of the time, when modern preachers have made theological moves they have become rather nervous. Scholars caution them to scrutinize the structural viability of the bridges that they build between the ancient worlds of Scripture and the worlds of their parishioners. Historians know better than to make great leaps of faith without sufficient natural evidence that one can survive the fall. Better to keep one's sermon fixed upon the lessons of the past than attempt to unite—awkwardly—such patently different worlds.

But Edwards rarely worried about the bridges that he built. He spent a great deal of time doing historical exegesis. He knew the Bible's contents better than most scholars, past or present. He knew the bulk of them by heart, in fact, as evidenced by the constant use of Scripture in his speech as well as the blanks pervading his sermon notes where Bible verses should be. (Rather than take the time to copy Bible verses into his manuscripts, Edwards frequently substituted long, squiggly lines, trusting his memory to provide the missing text while he was preaching.) Nonetheless, he spent the lion's share of his time—every week—interpreting Scripture theologically, preaching it doctrinally (with trust in its transcendence and an unapologetically synthetic methodology), and applying it explicitly to the lives of those around him. He has often been depicted as a "spiritual" interpreter, a trait that may require explanation.[21]

Protestants typically pride themselves on literal exegesis, by which we usually mean discussion of the meaning of the Bible based on study in the grammar of and history behind its parts. Ever since the Reformation, we have distanced this method from the so-called allegorical, or spiritual, exegesis often used by Roman Catholics to authenticate teaching that is not clearly supported by a "plain" reading of Scripture. Our strategy has been to slice through the many centuries of exegetical excess—overwrought renderings and outright fabrication of symbolic biblical meanings—repristinating a simpler, apostolic reading of Scripture and the faith that it commends. This has involved a refutation of most traditional exegesis. But many other moderns, whether Protestant or not, have helped us cope with the destruction caused by such a critical method by affirming a dim view of the Catholic "dark ages" (i.e., the "Middle Ages," those between the more enlightened classical and modern periods of history) and their spiritual, and exegetical, barbarism.

Even early church fathers, though, advocated allegory. Origen, for example, spoke of three senses of Scripture—body, soul, and spirit—suggesting that God had arranged for errors in the Bible's bodily sense (i.e., historical sense) in order to elevate our minds to its much "higher," spiritual sense.[22] Augustine proved more cautious, teaching that those interpreting Scripture must be sure to base their readings on the literal sense of the text, or "the intention of the writer through whom the Holy Spirit" spoke. Even he, though, thought that biblical texts could harbor multiple meanings and rejoiced that God revealed himself in multidimensional ways. "Could God have built into the divine eloquence a more generous or bountiful gift," he asked, "than the possibility of understanding the same words in several ways, all of them deriving confirmation from other no less divinely inspired passages [of Scripture]?"[23]

Through most of the Middle Ages, a moderated form of Origen's spiritual exegesis held sway within the world of serious Bible scholarship.[24] By the ninth century, in fact, most scholars had agreed that every passage in the Bible held *four* different senses: (1) a literal sense, conveyed by the "letter" of the text (from the Latin word *littera*); (2) an allegorical sense (from the Greek word ἀλληγορέω, "to speak figuratively"), also called the doctrinal, mystical, or Christological sense, symbolized by the objects of the Bible's literal sense; (3) a moral sense, referred to as the tropological sense (from the Greek word τροπολογέω, "to speak in tropes or figures of speech"), found when looking for the ethical or legal drift of the text; and (4) a heavenly sense, referred to as the anagogical sense (from ἀνάγω, "to lead up"), found when contemplating the eschatological import of the text.[25] This "four-horse chariot" (*quadriga*) of medieval exegesis found its ultimate codification in the work of Thomas Aquinas.[26] It was memorized in schools with the help of a popular ditty:

> The letter shows us what God and our Fathers did;
> The allegory shows us where our faith is hid;
> The moral meaning gives us rules of daily life;
> The anagogy shows us where we end our strife.[27]

During the time of the Reformation, biblical learning was transformed. Great strides were made in the study of the ancient biblical languages, textual scholars emended scribal errors in the Bible (by making use of older, more reliable biblical manuscripts), and printing presses expedited the distribution of Bibles, biblical commentaries, and other Christian treatises. Protestants, especially, touted improvements in the study of the Scriptures and their meaning. And most Protestant Reformers followed Luther's lead in emphasizing literal exegesis.[28] In his well-known commentary on the epistle to the Galatians, when discussing chapter 4, the *locus classicus* for those defending allegorical readings (Paul himself says there that his discussion of Hagar, Sarah, Ishmael, and Isaac is "an allegory"),[29] Luther vouched for the usefulness of spiritual exegesis but insisted forcefully on the precedence of the literal.

> There are usually held to be four senses of Scripture. They are called the literal sense, the tropological, the allegorical, and the anagogical, so that Jerusalem, according to the literal sense, is the capital city of Judea; tropologically, a pure conscience or faith; allegorically, the church of Christ; and anagogically, the heavenly fatherland. Thus in this passage [Galatians 4:24ff] Isaac and Ishmael are, in the literal sense, the two sons of Abraham; allegorically, the two covenants, or the synagog and the church, the Law and grace; tropologically, the flesh and the spirit, or virtue and vice, grace and sin; anagogically, glory and punishment, heaven and hell, yes, according to others, the angels and the demons, the blessed and the damned. This kind of game may, of course, be permitted to those who want it, provided they do not accustom themselves to the rashness of some, who tear the Scriptures to pieces as they please and make them uncertain. On the contrary, these interpretations add extra ornamentation, so to speak, to the main and legitimate sense, so that a topic may be more richly adorned by them, or—in keeping with Paul's example—so that those who are not well instructed may be nurtured in gentler fashion with milky teaching, as it were. But these interpretations should not be brought forward with a view to establishing a doctrine of faith. For that four-horse team (even though I do not disapprove of it) is not sufficiently supported by the authority of Scripture, by the custom of the fathers, or by grammatical principles.[30]

By Edwards's day, the literal sense had come to prevail throughout the West, among both Protestants and others who now favored historical methods (and suspected the superfluity of Catholic exegesis). For the Puritans and their heirs, the reasons were largely pastoral. If the study of the Word was ever to captivate the laity, "learned and unlearned, young and old, men and women," then its meanings must be plain, in the main, to simple minds. As confessed by the divines who assembled at Westminster, "All things in Scripture are not alike plain in themselves, nor alike clear unto all: yet those things which are necessary to be known, believed, and observed for salvation, are so clearly propounded, and opened in some place of Scripture or other, that not only the learned, but the unlearned, in a due use of the ordinary means, may attain unto a sufficient understanding of them."[31] A "sufficient understanding" would require earnest effort. Some passages might not be understood by everyone. But the Bible's main story line was given for all to read. Indeed, its message of redemption carried the power of God to save even the humblest of believers. Scholars should seek to clarify this message for the laity rather than dizzy them on learned flights of fancy.

Despite this stated Protestant preference for the literal sense of Scripture, spiritual exegesis did survive the Reformation. Luther himself often interpreted the Bible allegorically. Calvin came to master the art of biblical typology. The Puritans, as well, resorted to spiritual exegesis, particularly in places such as the Song of Solomon. Like many other early Protestants, then, Edwards practiced literal *and* spiritual exegesis. He majored in the literal sense. Scholars sometimes overwork his spiritualizing tendencies. He served as a parish pastor, though, a minister of the Word. He was called by God to preach the Bible whole, for the church. So he took advantage of *all* the tools that helped him make its contents come alive for those in his care. He sought to help them find their place in the grand story of redemption, which began in the Garden of Eden and is yet to be fulfilled.

Edwards's best-known form of spiritual exegesis was typology. He trusted that God had filled the Bible with types, or vivid symbols, of the Messiah, human redemption, and the coming kingdom of heaven—types that adumbrate and enrich our understanding of their antitypes, or things that God intended them to signify. As he penned in one of his notebooks during the mid-1740s, Scripture itself seemed to suggest "that it has ever been God's manner from the beginning of the world to exhibit and reveal future things by symbolical representations, which were no other than types of the future things revealed." He rarely publicized his theories about these images and shadows, but his notes effervesced with typological analysis. It helped him to discern the divine nature of reality, purposes in history, and harmony of Scripture. According to Edwards, Adam, Abraham, and David were types of Christ, as each shadowed forth an aspect of his Messianic role. The prophet Jonah was a type of Christ's death and resurrection, as he emerged from three days in the belly of a whale. The "future struggling of the two nations of the Israelites and Edomites was typified by Jacob's and Esau's struggling . . . in the womb." And in another, fairly representative typological comment, Edwards mused in one of his notebooks, "By Moses' being wonderfully preserved in the midst of . . . waters, though but a little helpless infant, . . . seems apparently to be typified the preservation and deliverance of his people."[32]

Edwards granted that "some types . . . are much more lively" than the others.[33] Compared to many medieval Christians, he discussed them with restraint. He warned that "persons ought to be exceeding careful in interpreting of types, that they don't give way to a wild fancy; not to fix an interpretation unless warranted by some hint in the New Testament of its being the true interpretation, or a lively figure and representation contained or warranted by an analogy to other types that we interpret on sure grounds." He tried to show, in fact, that such restraint can yield a faithfully Protestant approach to biblical types. He sought a sound, golden mean "between those that cry down all types, and those that are for turning all into nothing but allegory and not having it to be true history; and also the way of the rabbis that find so many mysteries in letters."[34]

Still, Edwards had a fulsome, typological view of reality, one that gave his thought a unique, and rather striking, spiritual focus. Not content to restrict typology to the contents of the canon, he taught that *all the world* was laden with the emblems of the divine. To say that God created the universe ex nihilo (out of nothing), he thought, was to say that God created out of nothing but himself. It was to say that the universe reflected—on purpose—the inner-Trinitarian life of God. Human sin clouds our vision of the vestiges of God that remain outside the realm of supernatural revelation. The spectacles of Scripture and the Spirit are required to correct our view of the world's divine design. And yet for those who are given eyes to see, the world is full of signs, yea intentional reminders, of our origin and destiny in the providence of God. To those forgetful of their Maker, for example, there are signs given to warn them of the fearsome consequences of their sin. The "extreme fierceness and extraordinary power of the heat of lightning is an intimation of the exceeding power and terribleness of the wrath of God." For those who need a glimpse of the promise of the gospel, on the other hand, God provides a host of hopeful signs. "The silkworm is a remarkable type of Christ," Edwards wrote, "which, when it dies, yields us that of which we make such glorious clothing. Christ became a worm for our sakes," he continued, "and by his death finished that righteousness with which believers are clothed, and thereby procured that we should be clothed with robes of glory."[35]

Reality was grounded in the mighty acts of God. Salvation history gave the universe its purpose and coherence. And the gospel tied together all the contents of the Bible, transcending their diverse social contexts. Edwards knew that these convictions would not score him many points in the enlightened world of modern biblical scholarship. He expected, on the contrary, "by . . . ridicule and contempt to be called a man of a very fruitful brain and copious fancy." Nonetheless, he persisted on his typological path. As he once proclaimed defiantly, "I am not ashamed to own that I believe that the whole universe, heaven and earth, air and seas, and the divine constitution and history of the holy Scriptures, be full of images of divine things, as full as a language is of words; and that the multitude of those things that I have mentioned are but a very small part of what is really intended to be signified and typified by these things."[36]

Edwards's God was real and powerful. His Word could not be relativized by modern unbelief, torn apart by biblical criticism, or tamed by those too dull to see its spiritual signs and wonders. It was alive. It was active. And it testified to Christ—from the Pentateuch to the Apocalypse. "Had ye believed Moses," Jesus preached once in Jerusalem, "ye would have believed me: for he wrote of me" (John 5:46). Shortly after the resurrection, walking along the road to Emmaus, Jesus explained to two of his friends how the Scriptures spoke of him, making clear their gospel focus and thrilling the hearts of his companions: "Beginning at Moses and all the prophets, he expounded unto them in all the scriptures the things concerning himself. . . . And they said one to another, Did not our heart burn within us, while he talked with us by the way, and while he opened to us the scriptures?" (Luke 24:27, 32).

In one of his early published sermons, entitled "The Excellency of Christ," Edwards reinforced this notion of the Bible's Christocentrism, using all of Scripture to support his thesis statement: "There is an admirable conjunction of diverse excellencies in Jesus Christ." After a brief introduction to the context of his Scripture text, from Revelation 5, in which Jesus is depicted both as a mighty "Lion" of Judah and a lowly "Lamb" who was slain for the salvation of the world, Edwards devoted the rest of the sermon to a canonical orchestration of this Christological paradox. Using scores of Scripture references, from every part of the Bible, he showed his people that the Messiah had always been characterized this way. He was both a divine person, who is strong and mighty to save, as well as a humble Son of Man, who condescended to befriend us. Edwards applied his doctrine boldly to the lives of those who listened, inviting all to "close" with a Savior who fulfills our every need:

> And thus is the affair of our redemption ordered, that thereby we
> are brought to an immensely more exalted kind of union with God,
> and enjoyment of him, both the Father and the Son, than otherwise
> could have been. For Christ being united to the human nature, we
> have advantage for a more free and full enjoyment of him, than we
> could have had if he had remained only in the divine nature. So
> again, we being united to a divine person, as his members, can have
> a more intimate union and intercourse with God the Father . . . than
> otherwise could be. Christ who is a divine person, by taking on him
> our nature, descends from the infinite distance and height above us,

and is brought nigh to us; whereby we have advantage for the full enjoyment of him. And, on the other hand, we, by being in Christ a divine person, do as it were ascend up to God, through the infinite distance, and have hereby advantage for the full enjoyment of him also. . . . Christ has brought it to pass, that those that the Father had given him, should be brought into the household of God; that he, and his Father, and his people should be as it were one society, one family; that the church should be as it were admitted into the society of the blessed Trinity.[37]

Edwards did things with the Bible that few would do with it today. His exuberant, canonical, Christological exegesis was clearly not as controlled as many modern scholars would like. Edwards knew much less than students today about the Bible's background in the history of ancient Israel and its Middle Eastern neighbors, the forms of classical literature, and the faiths of those who shared the world of the Bible's leading characters—so, of course, he spent less time explaining its texts in light of these things. Moreover, as Stephen Stein has emphasized, "Edwards frequently celebrated the violence at the heart of the biblical accounts," interpreting them in ways that offend more liberal, peaceable Christians. Edwards cheered the spread of the gospel through the rise and fall of nations. He believed that God is glorified in the reprobation of sinners. And he viewed New England's history through the lens of eschatology, praying and preaching against the French forces of the "antichrist" (the Roman Catholic Church) during the French and Indian wars.[38] Few today would want to interpret Scripture just as Edwards did.

Still, Edwards's exegetical work contains a wealth of resources for those who preach, teach, and study the history of Christianity. He knew how to tread traditional *and* modern paths to meaning. He employed *multiple* methods of interpreting the Bible. He offers a prime example of the so-called theological interpretation of Scripture shaped by the best historical research of his day. His work was up-to-date and traditional, critical and canonical, historical and profoundly theological. Those who seek to recover a form of theological exegesis that does not abandon the best of modern, critical biblical scholarship could learn a thing or two from Edwards's eighteenth-century efforts.[39]

NOTES

1. Samuel Hopkins, *The Life and Character of the Late Reverend Mr. Jonathan Edwards* (Boston: S. Kneeland, 1765), 40–41.

2. Jonathan Edwards, "Resolutions" No. 28, in *The Works of Jonathan Edwards* [hereafter *WJE*] (New Haven: Yale University Press, 1998), 16: 755; and Jonathan Edwards,

"Personal Narrative," in *WJE* 16: 797. As confirmed by Sereno Edwards Dwight in a moment of family pride, "No other divine has as yet appeared, who has studied the Scriptures more thoroughly. . . . His knowledge of the Bible . . . is probably unrivalled." Sereno E. Dwight, "Memoirs of Jonathan Edwards, A.M.," most widely available in *The Works of Jonathan Edwards*, ed. Edward Hickman (1834; Edinburgh: Banner of Truth Trust, 1974), clxxxvii–clxxxix.

3. Jonathan Edwards, "The Importance and Advantage of a Thorough Knowledge of Divine Truth (1739)," in *The Sermons of Jonathan Edwards: A Reader*, ed. Wilson H. Kimnach, Kenneth P. Minkema, and Douglas A. Sweeney (New Haven: Yale University Press, 1999), 35–36.

4. Ibid., 35, 38, 40, 43.

5. "Notes on Scripture," the "Blank Bible," "Notes on the Apocaplypse," and the typological writings are included in *WJE*. See Jonathan Edwards, *Notes on Scripture*, in *WJE* 15; Jonathan Edwards, *The Blank Bible*, in *WJE* 24; Jonathan Edwards, "Notes on the Apocalypse," in *WJE*5; and Jonathan Edwards, *Typological Writings, WJE* 11. "Hebrew Idioms" is located in manuscript form in folder 1211, box 16, Jonathan Edwards Collection, Beinecke Rare Book and Manuscript Library, Yale University (hereafter Beinecke). "Defense of the Authenticity of the Pentateuch as a Work of Moses and the Historicity of the Old Testament Narratives" is located in folder 1204, box 15, Beinecke. The best example of Edwards's manuscript reflections on assorted Bible doctrines is found in Edwards, *Writings on the Trinity, Grace, and Faith, WJE* 21. On the extent and significance of Edwards's exegesis, see Douglas A. Sweeney, "Jonathan Edwards," in *Historical Handbook of Major Biblical Interpreters*, ed. Donald K. McKim (Downers Grove, IL: InterVarsity, 1998), 309–12.

6. Jonathan Edwards to the trustees of the College of New Jersey, October 19, 1757, in *WJE* 16: 725–30 (quotation from 727–28).

7. Sixteen years after he died, Edwards's sermon series was published with the help of his son, Jonathan Edwards Jr., as *A History of the Work of Redemption: Containing, The Outlines of a Body of Divinity, in a Method Entirely New* (Edinburgh: W. Gray, J. Buckland, and G. Keith, 1774). Frequently reprinted, it is available today in *WJE* 9. For Edwards's notes toward the turning of these sermons into a treatise, see the books in folders 1212–14, box 16, Beinecke.

8. Edwards to the trustees of the College of New Jersey, October 19, 1757, in *WJE* 16: 728–29. For more on this second, unfinished work, see Kenneth P. Minkema, "The Other Unfinished 'Great Work': Jonathan Edwards, Messianic Prophecy, and 'The Harmony of the Old and New Testament,'" in *Jonathan Edwards's Writings: Text, Context, Interpretation*, ed. Stephen J. Stein (Bloomington: Indiana University Press, 1996), 52–65.

9. Sadly, these entries, Nos. 891, 922, 1067, and 1068, are the only "Miscellanies" not included in *The Works of Jonathan Edwards*.

10. See "Types of the Messiah," in *WJE* 11: 191–324.

11. The "Harmony" notebook, nearly two hundred pages in manuscript, did not find its way into the letterpress edition of *The Works of Jonathan Edwards*. See "The Harmony of the Genius, Spirit, Doctrines, & Rules of the Old Testament & the New," folder 1210, box 15, Beinecke.

12. Jonathan Edwards, sermon on Matthew 24:35, L. 2r., folder 502, box 7, Beinecke; Edwards, *WJE* 9: 290–91; Jonathan Edwards, *Freedom of the Will, WJE* 1: 438; Jonathan Edwards, "Heading the Word, and Losing It," in *WJE* 19: 46; and Jonathan Edwards, sermon on I Peter 2:2–3, L. 5r., L. 2v., folder 855, box 11, Beinecke. I have adapted some material in the following five paragraphs from Douglas A. Sweeney, " 'Longing for More and More of It'? The Strange Career of Jonathan Edwards's Exegetical Exertions," in *Jonathan Edwards at 300: Essays on the Tercentenary of His Birth,* ed. Harry S. Stout, Kenneth P. Minkema, and Caleb J. D. Maskell (Lanham, MD: University Press of America, 2005), 25–37.

13. Edwards, "Personal Narrative," in *WJE* 16: 801; Jonathan Edwards, "Life Through Christ Alone," in *WJE* 10: 526; Jonathan Edwards, "The Way of Holiness," in *WJE* 10: 477; Jonathan Edwards, "Divine Love Alone Lasts Eternally," in *WJE* 8: 363; Jonathan Edwards, sermon on Psalm 119:162, L. 1r., folder 189, box 3, Beinecke; Edwards, "The Importance and Advantage of a Thorough Knowledge of Divine Truth," 38, 35; Jonathan Edwards, "Profitable Hearers of the Word," in *WJE* 14: 265–66; Jonathan Edwards, sermon on I Corinthians 2:11–13, L. 3v., folder 719, box 10, Beinecke; Jonathan Edwards, sermon on Matthew 13:23, L. 22r., folder 473, box 6, Beinecke; Jonathan Edwards, *Religious Affections, WJE* 2: 438; Jonathan Edwards, "Stupid as Stones," in *WJE* 17: 180; Jonathan Edwards, sermon on Luke 10:38–42, L. 6v., folder 560, box 7, Beinecke; and Jonathan Edwards, *The "Miscellanies," a-500, WJE* 13: 202.

14. Edwards, sermon on Luke 10:38–42, L. 3r.; Edwards, "Profitable Hearers of the Word," 266; Edwards, "Heeding the Word, and Losing It," 47; Edwards, "Images of Divine Things," in *WJE* 11: 93; and Jonathan Edwards, sermon on Hebrews 6: 7, L. 17r., folder 820, box 11, Beinecke.

15. Perhaps the best known example of this to be found in the Edwards corpus is *Concerning the End for Which God Created the World,* in *WJE* 8: 419–20 (emphasis mine). Many medieval Christians (at least from the twelfth century) also spoke of the need to study both the "book of nature" and Scripture and, like Edwards, interpreted both books theologically. On this, see especially Peter Harrison, *The Bible, Protestantism, and the Rise of Natural Science* (Cambridge, UK: Cambridge University Press, 1998).

16. Jonathan Edwards, *The Distinguishing Marks of a Work of the Spirit of God,* in *WJE* 4: 240; Jonathan Edwards, "Light in a Dark World, a Dark Heart," in *WJE* 19: 720; Edwards, *The "Miscellanies," a-500,* 421 (cf. 422–26, 537; Jonathan Edwards, *The "Miscellanies," 501–832, WJE* 18: 140; and Jonathan Edwards, *The "Miscellanies," 833–1152, WJE* 20: 52–53); and Edwards, *A History of the Work of Redemption,* 520. On Edwards's understanding of the relationship between reason and revelation as it was developed near the end of his life, see the Douglas A. Sweeney, "Editor's Introduction" to Jonathan Edwards, *The "Miscellanies," 1153–1360, WJE* 23: 19–29. On his response to the deists, see especially Gerald R. McDermott, *Jonathan Edwards Confronts the Gods: Christian Theology, Enlightenment Religion, and Non-Christian Faiths* (New York: Oxford University Press, 2000).

17. Edwards, *The "Miscellanies," a-500,* 469–70.

18. Jonathan Edwards, sermon on Luke 11: 27–28, L. IV., L. 6v.-7r., folder 1065, box 14, Beinecke; Jonathan Edwards, "The Pure in Heart Blessed," in *WJE* 17: 65–66; and

Jonathan Edwards, "Treatise on Grace," in *WJE* 21: 178–80. For Edwards on spiritual understanding, see especially *Religious Affections*, 205–6, 225, 266–91, 296–97, 301; *The "Miscellanies," a-500*, 286–87, 297–98, 462–63; *The "Miscellanies," 501–832*, 156–57, 245–48, 452–66; and numerous Edwards sermons, especially "A Divine and Supernatural Light," in *WJE* 17: 405–26; "A Spiritual Understanding of Divine Things Denied to the Unregenerate," in *WJE* 14: 70–96; "False Light and True," in *WJE* 19: 122–42; "Light in a Dark World, a Dark Heart"; "Profitable Hearers of the Word"; and "The Importance and Advantage of a Thorough Knowledge of Divine Truth." For Edwards's notion of biblical power, see also his statement in *The Blank Bible*, at Psalm 29:3 (p. 490): "Lightning and thunder is a very lively image of the word of God upon many accounts. 'Tis exceeding quick, and exceeding piercing, and powerful to break in pieces, and scorch, and dissolve, and is full of majesty"; and also at Hebrews 4:12 (p. 1143), where he makes reference to God's giving of the Law on Mt. Sinai (Ex. 19ff.) "with thunders, and lightnings, and a voice so piercing, awful, and tremendous that the people could not endure it," and compares the Hebrews text, which teaches similarly that "the word in its powerful efficacy . . . does . . . cut the soul asunder."

19. Scholars distinguish "higher" biblical criticism (historical criticism) from "lower" biblical criticism (textual criticism). The former deals with the history behind the biblical texts, interpreting the Bible in its sociocultural contexts. The latter deals with the history of biblical texts themselves, comparing surviving manuscripts for the sake of determining the most reliable variants (those that best resemble what must have been the "original autographs").

20. On Edwards's learned engagement with biblical higher criticism, see Robert E. Brown, *Jonathan Edwards and the Bible* (Bloomington: Indiana University Press, 2002).

21. See, for example, the highly regarded depiction of Stephen J. Stein, "The Quest for the Spiritual Sense: The Biblical Hermeneutics of Jonathan Edwards," *Harvard Theological Review* 70 (1977): 99–113.

22. Origen, *On First Principles* (*De Principiis* in Latin; in Greek, *Periarchon*; c. 230), IV, ii, 4, 9. See the English translation of G. W. Butterworth (1936; Gloucester, MA: Peter Smith, 1973), 275–87. Of course, more orthodox Fathers—Justin, Irenaeus, Clement of Alexandria, as well as a host of other worthies—also employed allegorical and typological methods for interpreting the Bible.

23. Augustine, *De Doctrina Christiana* (*On Christian Doctrine*, completed in 426/7), Book III, sections 84–85. English translation from Augustine, *De Doctrina Christiana*, ed. and trans. R. P. H. Green, Oxford Early Christian Texts (Oxford: Clarendon Press, 1995), 169–71.

24. Academics often distinguish between Origen's "Alexandrian" school of biblical exegesis and the more temperate school of "Antioch," exemplified in textbooks by the likes of Lucian of Antioch, Diodorus of Tarsus, Theodore of Mopsuestia, and John Chrysostom. It is said that Alexandrian exegesis was fanciful, full of allegorical excess, whereas the school of Antioch was much more careful and historical. The difference between these schools is often exaggerated, however. In point of fact, there never was a formal school of Antioch. Further, exegetes in both groups shared a great deal in common. Nevertheless, there were interpreters among the church fathers who opposed

the lofty allegorizing found within the writings of a few of the Alexandrians. Diodorus of Tarsus (in *On the Difference between Theory and Allegory*, only fragments of which remain), Theodore of Mopsuestia (in *Concerning Allegory and History against Origen*, 5 vols., which is no longer extant), and John Chrysostom (in many sermons and commentaries that do survive) distanced their own exegesis from the methods of Origen. Their famous doctrine of *theoria* (θεωρία, a Greek word meaning "vision, insight, or contemplation"), according to which the Hebrew prophets saw and recorded *both* the immediate (historical) and the future (Christological) significance of their prophecies, grounded the spiritual sense of Scripture squarely on the literal sense. It also fixed the correlation between the biblical types and antitypes in the history of redemption. These "Antiochenes" contended that biblical meaning was clearly discernable, not hidden and mysterious, as in Alexandria.

25. Most of the early church fathers made only a broad, generic distinction between the literal and the spiritual sense of Scripture, though some did propose up to seven different senses. John Cassian was the first to promote the fourfold exegesis that became the standard during the Middle Ages. In his *Conferences* (*Collationes*, written during the 420s), 14.8–11, he wrote that on top of the literal sense "there are three kinds of spiritual lore, namely, tropology, allegory, and anagoge.... History embraces the knowledge of things which are past and which are perceptible.... What follows is allegorical, because the things which actually happened are said to have prefigured another mystery.... Anagoge climbs up from spiritual mysteries to the higher and more august secrets of heaven.... Tropology is moral teaching designed for the amendment of life and for instruction in asceticism." English translation from John Cassian, *Conferences*, trans. Colm Luibheid, The Classics of Western Spirituality (New York: Paulist Press, 1985), 159–66.

26. Thomas Aquinas, *Summa Theologiae*, Ia. I, 10. Under Thomas's weighty influence, the three spiritual senses were often said to correspond to the three theological virtues: faith (allegorical), hope (anagogical), and love (tropological).

27. Littera gesta docet, quid credas allegoria,

Moralis quid agas, quo tendas anagogia.

28. This emphasis, of course, had roots in ancient Christianity, as well as in the study of the literal meanings of Scripture initiated in twelfth-century France. See G. R. Evans, *The Language and Logic of the Bible: The Road to Reformation* (Cambridge, UK: Cambridge University Press, 1985).

29. Other Pauline statements cited traditionally as warrants for the spiritual exegesis of the Bible include the following: Romans 15:4; I Corinthians 2:6–7, 3:1–2, 9:9–12, 10:1–4; and II Corinthians 3:6. The book of Hebrews, for Edwards, was a Pauline text as well, one that was full of typological exegesis of the Old Testament.

30. English translation from Martin Luther, *Lectures on Galatians, 1519*, trans. Richard Jungkuntz, in *Luther's Works*, vol. 27, ed. Jaroslav Pelikan and Walter A. Hansen (St. Louis, MO: Concordia Publishing House, 1964), 311. For the original Latin, see *D. Martin Luthers Werke: Kritische Gesamtausgabe* (Weimar: Hermann Böhlaus Nachfolger, 1883–), 2: 550. Whereas for Origen the spiritual senses are given for the mature, for Luther they are mainly for the immature (though Luther himself

made reference to them constantly, confirming his notion that all of us are beggars before the Word).

31. *The Westminster Confession of Faith*, 1.7. I have followed the spelling and punctuation in Joel R. Beeke and Sinclair B. Ferguson, eds., *Reformed Confessions Harmonized* (Grand Rapids: Baker Books, 1999), 15.

32. Edwards, "Types of the Messiah" (*Miscellanies*, No. 1069), in *WJE* 11: 192–95.

33. Edwards, "Images of Divine Things," in *WJE* 11: 114.

34. Edwards, "Types," in *WJE* 11: 148, 151.

35. Edwards, "Images of Divine Things," in *WJE* 11: 59.

36. Edwards, "Types," in *WJE* 11: 152.

37. Jonathan Edwards, "The Excellency of Christ," (1738), in Kimnach, Minkema, and Sweeney, *The Sermons of Jonathan Edwards*, 163, 195–96.

38. Stephen J. Stein, "Jonathan Edwards and the Cultures of Biblical Violence," in Stout, Minkema, and Maskell, *Jonathan Edwards at 300*, 56.

39. Those who want a brief orientation to the scholarly discussion about recovering theological exegesis of the Bible should consult Stephen E. Fowl, ed., *The Theological Interpretation of Scripture: Classic and Contemporary Readings*, Blackwell Readings in Modern Theology (Cambridge, MA: Blackwell, 1997); and Stephen E. Fowl, *Engaging Scripture: A Model for Theological Interpretation*, Challenges in Contemporary Theology (Malden, MA: Blackwell, 1998).

6

Alternative Viewpoint:
Edwards and the Bible

Wolter H. Rose

Professor Sweeney's chapter moves easily between the academy and the church. In my response I will follow that lead, and begin by discussing the ways in which Edwards challenges me as a Bible scholar.

Edwards's Evident Love for the Word of God

Edwards was a passionate man. One of his great passions was the Word of God. Edwards was around twenty years old when he wrote the words quoted by Sweeney about how, when reading Scripture, "oftentimes . . . every word seemed to touch my heart."

It is difficult not to be personally challenged when considering this. At first sight Edwards's words may seem intimidating or off-putting, but the more one is exposed to Edwards's thinking, the more these and similar descriptions of his personal experience can also become an invitation. Edwards will keep me on my toes.

His Vision of the Glory of God
as the Chief End of All Things

Edwards's vision of the glory of God can provide a framework that helps us find coherence in the diversity found in the Bible. A number of Bible scholars have made an effort to identify the theological center of the Old Testament, the New Testament, or both. Some of the themes that have been suggested over the years are *covenant, God's steadfast love, God's holiness, God's sovereignty,* and *God's kingdom.*

It is interesting to note that one recent proposal for a center to biblical theology has been "the glory of God in salvation through judgment"—a theme that sounds familiar to those who know what was at the heart of Edwards's thinking.[1] It comes as no surprise to find in one of the footnotes a reference to Edwards's treatise, *Concerning the End for Which God Created the World.*[2]

Edwards's Desire to Present Christ from All Scripture

If the glory of God provides a framework for a coherent reading of scripture, then the person of Christ may serve as the focal point. As Sweeney has shown, presenting Christ from all Scripture was a major issue for Edwards. Here Edwards exemplifies his own description of the ideal Christian reader of the Bible, sitting at the feet of Jesus, who both challenged his contemporaries to search the Scriptures for their witness to him and taught his apostles, after his resurrection, a new way of reading the Old Testament.

Now I would like to follow up on several other Edwardsian suggestions raised by Sweeney's paper.

On the Usefulness of "Speculative Knowledge"

Edwards makes a distinction between "historical" or "literal" exegesis and spiritual interpretation, and clearly values the latter more. Sweeney has pointed to the importance of spiritual understanding, especially in the context of preaching, and I am in complete agreement here. Yet I hope I will not be seen as preaching to the choir when I look at another segment of readers and preachers of Scripture (including people congenial to Edwards's thinking) who may need to be reminded of the importance of solid historical or literal exegesis. I would argue that it is not an exaggeration to say that historical or literal exegesis can make an important contribution to spiritual understanding. In fact, Edwards himself says something analogous when discussing the relationship between "speculative or natural" knowledge and spiritual knowledge in his sermon "Christian Knowledge": "Spiritual and practical [knowledge] is of the greatest importance; for a speculative without a spiritual knowledge, is to no purpose, but to make our condemnation the greater. Yet a speculative knowledge is also of infinite importance in this respect, that without it we can have no spiritual or practical knowledge."[3]

In 2008 we mark the 250th anniversary of the death of Edwards. Much has happened since 1758, and the area of biblical studies is of course no exception. Edwards was aware of the issues raised by higher criticism, and he sought to address them. One major development, which started only one hundred years after his death, was the exploration of primary sources for the history and culture of the ancient Near East—once archaeological expeditions brought texts and artifacts to the attention of the world and the church. In a recent study on the relationship between ancient Near Eastern thought and the Old Testament, the author laments the slow interaction with this material, particularly "in Protestant circles where the blood of the Reformers flows thick."[4] Whatever one's opinion on the accuracy of this assessment, this area of what certainly belongs to "speculative knowledge" opened up since the middle of the nineteenth century does provide a challenge, in particular for confessional Bible scholars, in whose circles this comparative material has sometimes been perceived as a threat to the uniqueness of God's revelation in the Bible.

One can also look at the relevance of this comparative material from the perspective of the multicultural society in which Europeans increasingly live and in which Americans have lived for a much longer time. Through the awareness of living in a multicultural society, a link can be made with the experience of Israel in the multicultural world of the Old Testament period. Exploring that world can help Christians today see the challenges that the people of Israel were facing and make them reflect on how well they themselves are prepared today to face the challenge of living in a multicultural and multireligious society.

I would submit that, seen from this perspective, this kind of speculative knowledge can be put to good use also in the area of spiritual understanding, when it helps readers of the Bible to appreciate both the similarities and the differences between the Old Testament and surrounding cultures.

On Method in Presenting Christ from All Scriptures

Toward the end of his essay, Sweeney states that "Edwards did things with the Bible that few would do with it today." One area of concern that he mentions is Edwards's "exuberant, canonical, Christological exegesis," which, as he puts it, "was clearly not as controlled as many modern scholars would like." Indeed, at times when reading Edwards, one may feel there is some truth to the charge he expected to be brought against him of being "a man of very fruitful brain and copious fancy." An example here would be the case of the silkworm, mentioned by Sweeney, in which Edwards turns a biblical picture of uselessness and contempt (Psalm 22:6) into a typological image of fruitfulness and glory.

As I have indicated, Edwards's desire to present Christ from all Scripture should be applauded. If, as modern Bible scholars or preachers, we consider Edwards's application of this principle at times somewhat problematic, then we should be very careful not to throw out the baby (Christological interpretation) with the bath water (unconvincing examples of Christological interpretation). In the scope of this response I can make only brief suggestions about how Bible scholars or preachers inspired by Jonathan Edwards might make progress in this area.

First, we should take very seriously Edwards's warnings made in the broader context of typology: presenting Christ from all Scripture should be done in an "exceeding[ly] careful" way. We cannot avoid going beyond the limited number of examples given in the New Testament, but we should be more humble and less insistent when a particular interpretation is not explicitly endorsed in the New Testament, while we can be more confident when our presentation of Christ from an Old Testament passage finds support in the New Testament.

For example, in the translation of the Bible used by Edwards, Genesis 49:10 reads, "The sceptre shall not depart from Judah, nor a lawgiver from between his feet, until Shiloh come; and unto him shall the gathering of the people be" (KJV). The question has to be asked how certain we can be that in this verse Shiloh should be identified with Christ (as Edwards does) when the New Testament gives no clear authority for such an interpretation and the wording and translation of the verse is problematic.[5] The translation "So that tribute shall come to him" [JPS] has more support than the KJV's "until Shiloh come," which would then make Edwards's interpretation far less likely.[6]

A second area in which we can make progress is the terminology we use when presenting Christ from all Scripture. It is not uncommon to find labeled as Messianic any element in the Old Testament that is considered to invite a connection with the person of Christ or his ministry, whatever the precise nature of that element or the connection. This is somewhat remarkable if one takes into account the fact that the Hebrew equivalent of the word *messiah* is not frequently used in the Old Testament, and when it is used, in almost all cases it refers to a king contemporary with the speaker (not to a future model king).

In my view it would be preferable to distinguish where one can point to Christ in different Old Testament passages and label these passages more specifically. "Messianic" would then be merely one of those labels, and not the one label covering all. In this approach Isaiah's portrait of the Suffering Servant

(52:13–53:12) can still be seen as a prophecy of Jesus Christ, even when we decide not to apply the label "Messianic" to it. This will help us understand why Peter found it so objectionable when Jesus told him (Matthew 16:13–23) what kind of Messiah he would be: not simply a triumphant king who would expel the occupying forces—as a number of Jews at that time would expect—but one in whom the very different portraits of the triumphant king and the suffering servant would merge.

This leads to a third suggestion. There are many aspects to the person and the ministry of Christ. Edwards would say that the substitutionary sacrifice of Christ on the cross lies at the heart of what he came to do. Without it, all other aspects of his person and ministry lose their focus. But Edwards has also made it clear that there is more to Christ's person and ministry than his death on the cross. In his famous sermon on "The Excellency of Christ," Edwards wanted his listeners to appreciate the many different aspects of Christ's person and ministry that make him a glorious person.[7]

Using a variety of labels for the different ways we may discover the presence of Christ in all of Scripture may help us to not lose sight of the many different aspects of the person of Christ and his ministry—especially when we study the relation between the two Testaments and how we may know Christ from both. This is necessary if we want to see him as the colorful and multidimensional figure he was and is.

Edwards in Europe

I do not remember finding out about Jonathan Edwards when I studied theology in the Netherlands some twenty years ago. Maybe he was there, somewhere in a footnote, and I missed him. Then, some ten years later, I saw his name coming up in a number of contexts. Some scholars gave him staggering accolades. "Typically American," as continental Europeans would say. The idea that an American minister of the eighteenth century would do theology, let alone creative theology that still deserved our attention more than two hundred years later, seemed preposterous.

One recommendation that I still remember was made by Richards Lints in his book *The Fabric of Theology*:

> He is arguably the most creative and the most orthodox theologian
> that America has yet produced. He was fascinated by the new learn-
> ing of his day, and, although it may seem incompatible to most mod-
> erns, he was also bound by an unparalleled commitment of fidelity

to the Scriptures. Even those who do not agree with his conclusions would be hard pressed to find an individual more driven spiritually and intellectually by a commitment and devotion to God. He stands with Augustine and Luther in the depth of the analysis of religious experience. He stands with Aquinas and Calvin in the breadth of his intellectual grasp of the gospel. He may stand unmatched in his ability to have woven these two strands together effectively.[8]

When I started reading Edwards myself I discovered that these words were not an exaggeration. This match of the intellectual and the experiential—not always easy bedfellows in much of the theology I had studied—is what has attracted me to Edwards ever since. I came to realize that this was a towering figure who made original contributions to theology, who deserved more than a footnote, even in the continental European theological curriculum.

Here is a theologian of the caliber of Augustine and Calvin living in the Age of Enlightenment, who showed a strong interest in the new intellectual mood and made an effort to answer the questions the new thinking raised. At the same time, he laid the groundwork for modern religious psychology in his writings on the nature of religious experience.

As has been noted by a number of scholars, including Sweeney, Edwards's interpretation of Scripture is a topic that has received relatively little investigation in the surge of Edwards scholarship of the past fifty years or so. This would be a most promising area of exploration for a new movement of European Edwards scholars.

Jonathan Edwards is known as "America's theologian." May this book help stimulate an Edwards awakening in Europe in the twenty-first century that continues the momentum generated by the Edwards renaissance in America in the previous century.

NOTES

1. James M. Hamilton Jr., "The Glory of God in Salvation through Judgment: The Centre of Biblical Theology?," *Tyndale Bulletin* 57, no. 1 (2006): 57–84.

2. Ibid., 81 n 90.

3. Jonathan Edwards, "Christian Knowledge," in *The Works of Jonathan Edwards*, ed. Edward Hickman (Edinburgh: Banner of Truth, 1974), 2,157–63; quotation from 158.

4. John H. Walton, *Ancient Near Eastern Thought and the Old Testament: Introducing the Conceptual World of the Hebrew Bible* (Grand Rapids, MI: Baker, 2006), 36.

5. See the extended discussion (with a certain amount of speculative knowledge, if I may say so) by Edwards in his "Notes on Scripture," in the Yale edition of *The Works of Jonathan Edwards* [hereafter *WJE*], 15: 411–2; compare the "Blank Bible," in *WJE* 24: 1, 198–99, and sermon 18 in "A History of the Work of Redemption," in *WJE* 9: 345.

6. *Tanakh: A New Translation of the Holy Scriptures according to the Traditional Hebrew Text* (Philadelphia: Jewish Publication Society, 1985).

7. *WJE* 19: 560–94.

8. Richard Lints, *The Fabric of Theology: A Prolegomenon to Evangelical Theology* (Grand Rapids, MI: Eerdmans, 1993), 172.

7

Edwards and Biblical Typology

Tibor Fabiny

Jonathan Edwards developed a highly original form of biblical typology (or figuralism). Fabiny first defines what biblical typology means, then he shows how Edwards's famous sermon "The Excellency of Christ" is surprisingly similar to what Fabiny wrote about typology in his 1992 book—before he became aware of Edwards's sermon. The author then discusses Edwards's view of beauty, which underlies his typology. In order to show how Edwards's typology was unique, the author outlines the history of typology. Then, after highlighting Edwards's innovations in typology, Fabiny shows how Edwards echoes Luther, Shakespeare, and the metaphysical poets. Finally, Fabiny speaks to the relevance of Edwards's typology for the contemporary reader.

What Is Biblical Typology?

Biblical typology, or "figuralism," is both a principle inherent in the Bible and an interpretation of biblical texts. It is frequently used as a term for the way the Old Testament contains foreshadowings (types) of New Testament events and themes. Typology, or "figural interpretation," as Eric Auerbach called it,

> establishes a connection between two events or persons, the first of which signifies not only itself but also the second, while the second encompasses or fulfils the

first. . . . Both, being real events or figures, are within time, within the stream of historical life. Only the understanding of the two persons or events is a spiritual act, but this spiritual act deals with concrete events whether past, present or future . . . since promise and fulfilment are real historical events, which either have happened . . . or will happen.[1]

The "Lion" and the "Lamb"

In 1992, in *The Lion and the Lamb: Figuralism and Fulfilment in the Bible, Art and Literature*, I suggested that typology may refer to at least nine things: (1) a way of reading the Bible; (2) a principle that unifies the "Old" and the "New" Testaments in the Christian Bible; (3) a principle of exegesis (understanding the meaning of a text from the original language and context); (4) a figure of speech; (5) a mode of thought; (6) a form of rhetoric; (7) a vision of history; (8) a principle of artistic composition; and (9) a manifestation of "intertextuality" (one part referring to another part of a text).[2]

In the conclusion of the book I state, "Reading is testimony." In other words, the choice of the texts we read reveals our commitments. The metaphorical title, *The Lion and the Lamb*, hints in the same direction. The argument is that in the language of the apocalypse, "there is no ego, no argument, nor 'Old' nor 'New' Testament, in which life is not opaque but becomes transparent. It is the appropriation of the surprising final vision of the Seer of Patmos: namely, that the strong, victorious Lion of the tribe of Judah and the weak Lamb pitifully slain, are one."[3]

At the end of the chapter titled "Reading Scripture," a close reading of Revelation 5:2–7 offers the paradoxical vision of the Lion and the Lamb. "In this condensed, poetic language there is no logic or argument. It is intensive, paradoxical. . . . The divine reality of the Apocalypse subverts all human sense of reality."[4]

When writing *The Lion and the Lamb*, I was not familiar with Jonathan Edwards's famous sermon "The Excellency of Christ" (1738). In this great sermon, I learned that Edwards also speaks of Jesus Christ as both the lion and the lamb. His text is also Revelation 5:5–6.[5] Edwards notices that "there is an admirable conjunction of diverse excellencies in Jesus Christ." The word *excellency* means beauty, a union of highest ethical and aesthetic values.[6] The lion excels in strength, the lamb excels in meekness: in Christ there is infinite highness and infinite condescension. Christ, as the highest of highest being, becomes man to expose himself to shame and spitting. "Such a conjunction of infinite highness and low condescension, in the same person, is admirable."[7] The sermon dramatizes the paradoxical nature of the divine mystery: justice and grace, glory and humility, majesty and meekness, reverence and equality, worthiness and patience, authority and obedience, sovereignty and resignation. "Thus is Christ lion in majesty, and a lamb in meekness."[8]

In the first part of his sermon Edwards illustrates "the admirable conjunction of excellencies" in the person of Jesus Christ; in the second part he shows how this "admirable conjunction of excellencies" appears in Christ's works. He discusses Christ's birth, his infancy, and his first miracle in Cana in Galilee. "And though Christ ordinarily appeared without outward glory, and in great obscurity, yet at a certain time he threw off the veil, and appeared in his divine majesty."[9]

Christ's greatest act was his sacrifice, as suggested by Isaiah 53:7 ("He came like a lamb to the slaughter") and 1 Corinthians 5:7 ("Christ our passover is sacrificed for us"): "The greatness of Christ's love . . . appears in nothing so much as its being dying love."[10]

Edwards was aware that in Scripture the lion *in bonam partem* (in the positive sense) is Christ, but *in malam partem* (in the negative sense) is the devil, "the roaring lion." See how he recapitulates the power of the lion/lamb symbolism:

Thus Christ appeared at the same time, and in the same act, as both a lion and a lamb. He appeared as a lamb in the hands of his cruel enemies, as a lamb in the paws and between the devouring jaws of a roaring lion. Yea, he was a lamb actually slain by this lion: and yet at the same time, as the Lion of the tribe of Judah, he conquers and triumphs over Satan, destroying his own devourer, as Samson did the lion that roared upon him, when he rent him as he would a kid. And in nothing has Christ appeared so much as a lion, in glorious strength destroying his enemies, as when he was brought as a lamb to the slaughter. In his greatest weakness he was most strong; and when he suffered most from his enemies, he brought the greatest confusion on his enemies.—Thus this admirable conjunction of diverse excellencies was manifest in Christ, in his offering up himself to God in his last sufferings.[11]

When, several years after writing my book, I read this magisterial sermon, I had mixed feelings: I blushed when I saw how poorly I had written on such a great text, but I also rejoiced that my pale 1992 book had become a shadow—a type!—of Jonathan Edwards's substantial and excellent sermon.

It is appropriate therefore to look for the significance and relevance of Jonathan Edwards's typology. I would suggest that the key can be found in his idea of beauty.

Edwards's Idea of Beauty

Jonathan Edwards, America's theologian, the eighteenth-century descendant of the American Puritans, both the child and the critic of the Enlightenment, was one of those rare Protestant thinkers who resonated to the sense of beauty and even elaborated what we may call today religious aesthetics.[12]

He begins his *Personal Narrative* (1740) by recalling his first impression of the glory of God:

> The first instance that I remember of that sort of inward, sweet delight in God and divine things, that I have lived much in since, was on reading those words, 1 Tim. 1:17: "Now unto the King, eternal, immortal, invisible, the only wise God, be honor and glory forever and ever, Amen." As I read the words, there came into my soul, and was as it were diffused through it, a sense of the glory of the Divine Being; a new sense, quite different from any thing I ever experienced before. . . .
>
> God's excellency, his wisdom, his purity and love, seemed to appear in every thing; in the sun, and moon, and stars; in the clouds and blue sky; in the grass, flowers, trees; in the water, and all nature; which used greatly to fix my mind.[13]

He describes his experience of the holiness of God:

> Holiness, as I then wrote down some of my contemplations on it, appeared to me to be of a sweet, pleasant, charming, serene, calm nature. It seemed to me, it brought an inexpressible purity, brightness, peacefulness and ravishment to the soul: and that it made the soul like a field or garden of God, with all manner of pleasant flowers, that is all pleasant, delightful and undisturbed; enjoying a sweet calm, and the gently vivifying beams of the sun.[14]

In the short essay, *The Beauty of the World* (1725), Edwards is preoccupied with beauty, excellence and the goodness of creation. This short piece begins with these great lines:

> The beauty of the world consists wholly of sweet mutual consents, either within itself, or with the Supreme Being. As to the corporeal

world, though there are many other sorts of consents, yet the sweet-
est and most charming beauty of it is its resemblance of spiritual
beauties. The reason is that spiritual beauties are infinitely the greatest, and bodies being but the shadows of beings, they must be so
much the more charming as they shadow forth spiritual beauties.[15]

Edwards speaks about the suitableness of colors and smells, proportion, harmony, and resemblances of an inferior to a superior cause. The more complex
a beauty is, the more hidden it is.

Edwards's theory of beauty, however, is best elaborated in his *The Nature
of True Virtue*, written in 1757 and published posthumously in 1765. Edwards
starts by suggesting that "True virtue consists in benevolence to Being in general. . . . It is consent, propensity and union of the heart to Being in general."
Edwards calls the "highest," "first" or "primary" beauty "that consent, agreement, or, union of being to being." "Secondary beauty," that can be found in
inanimate things, "consists in a mutual consent and agreement of different
things in form, manner, quantity, and visible end or design, called by the various names of regularity, order, uniformity, symmetry, proportion, harmony,
etc."[16] Secondary beauty is the image of, or God-placed symbol which points
to, primary beauty.

Edwards adds that it pleases God to observe "analogy" in his works:

It has pleased him to establish a law of nature, by virtue of which the
uniformity and mutual correspondence of a beautiful plant, and the
respect which the various parts of a regular building seem to have
one to another, and their agreement and union, and the consent or
concord of the various notes of a melodious tune, should appear
beautiful; because therein is some image of the consent of the mind,
of the different members of a society or system of intelligent beings,
sweetly united in a benevolent agreement of the heart.[17]

Edwards perceives two sorts of agreement or consent of one thing to another:
the first is cordial agreement (union of mind and heart), and the other is union
or agreement where no minds are involved. The first has to do with spiritual or
primary beauty, and the other with natural beauty.

Edwards's theory of beauty and holiness is ultimately Trinitarian. Amy
Plantinga Pauw has shown that "the Trinity was at the heart of Edwards' perception of beauty and excellency." She quotes the *Miscellanies* 117: "One alone
cannot be excellent, inasmuch as, in such case, there can be no consent. Therefore, if God is excellent, there must be a pluralism in God; otherwise, there can
be no consent in him."[18]

True consent, Edwards argued, always requires reciprocal love and delight. His personal experience of holiness as utmost beauty, his idea of beauty as consent of being to being, and his perception of the paradoxical nature of divine beauty in the conjunction of Christ's diverse excellencies can help us understand the roots of Edwards's typological view of reality.

To understand Edwards's use of typology it will be useful to look at some twentieth-century interpretations of typology by biblical scholars and see the historical traditions of this biblical mode of symbolism.

Theories and Traditions of Typology

The word *typology* in biblical studies is of nineteenth-century coinage. It was not used in patristic literature (works written by the Fathers of the church), where we read instead of *tropologia, allegoria,* or *anagogia* (the use of pictures in writing; speaking of one thing under the guise of another; and the mystical sense).

The standard theological work on typology is still Leonard Goppelt's *Typos: Die typologische Deutung des Alten Testaments im Neuen* (1939).[19] Goppelt examined the significant New Testament passages against the background of contemporary Jewish interpretation of Scripture (Paul's contemporary Philo, the great Jewish philosopher) in Hellenistic Judaism. His conclusion was that typology was the dominant form of interpretation for the New Testament use of the Old. One of the most important terms that Goppelt introduced was *Steigerung*. This was translated into English by various authors as "heightening," "escalation," or "enhancement," which means that some persons, events, or things in the New Testament are seen as both analogous to and greater than the persons, events, or things in the Old Testament. It implies that the ministry of Jesus corresponds to that of the prophets of the Old Testament, but that there is "something more" involved in it. Jesus points to his activity as something "greater than Jonah" (Matt 12:6), "greater than Solomon" (Matt 12:42), and "greater than the temple" (Matt 12:6). This implies that his work was neither simply a repetition nor a mere continuation of the prophets, but the "fulfillment," or "re-creation," of their mission.

In 1952, the Old Testament scholar Gerhard von Rad published his programmatic essay, "Typological Interpretation in the Old Testament."[20] In von Rad's view, typology is not a theological device but "an elementary function of all human thought and interpretation."[21] Without this analogical way of thinking, he argued, there would be no poetry, for poetry is also concerned with linking images.

The first great boom in the use of typology to interpret the Bible was in the Patristic period (from the second through the fifth centuries AD). The Fathers, however, did not clearly distinguish their typological method from the allegorism commonly used by the Greeks and their Hellenistic civilization (from Alexander the Great in the fourth century BC until the third century AD). For example, they used the term *allegory* for the Passover, which, for later exegetes, is definitely typology, since typology is concerned with connecting two historical realities. Allegory, on the other hand, suggests hidden and spiritual meanings that are usually unrelated to real events in history.

The Reformation, however, was more aware of the "Hebraic" origins of Christianity. Luther and Calvin endorsed typology, but a more self-conscious and methodologically systematic approach was elaborated by the seventeenth-century Protestant Fathers. If we said that the first "golden age" of typology was in the second century of Catholic Christianity, then it may be added that the new or the "second" golden age of typology is to be found in the second century of Protestant Christianity. Typological thinking became almost a pious vogue among Protestant divines on both sides of the Atlantic. In England it inspired religious poetry, while in New England (the notion of the "new" is itself typological!) it undoubtedly played a decisive role in the formation of American identity.

Typology began to flourish among the seventeenth-century Protestant divines, mainly in conservative and popular circles. This was the century of typological manuals composed in English, meant mainly for practical rather than theoretical purposes.

The author of the first known typological handbook is William Guild (1586–1657), an English divine from Aberdeen. His famous work, *Moses Unveiled: or Figures which Served unto the Pattern and Shadow of Heavenly Things. Pointing out the Messiah Christ Jesus Briefly Explained*, was published in 1620.[22] This booklet discusses fifty-five types of Christ in the Old Testament, beginning with the Tree of Life and ending with Zerubbabel. Another, somewhat more elaborated manual is by Thomas Taylor (1576–1633), *Christ Revealed or the Old Testament Explained, a Treatise of the Types and Shadows of Our Saviour Contained throughout the Whole Scripture. All Opened and Made Useful for the Benefit of the Church*. This book was posthumously published in 1635 by William Jenmat. Taylor was a Puritan divine, formerly a reader of Hebrew in Cambridge, and the first author to treat typology in a "system."

The most significant typological manual was written by Samuel Mather (1626–1671), a distinguished member of a famous dynasty of Puritan divines in New England. He was a son of Richard Mather (1596–1663), the brother of Increase Mather (1639–1723), and the uncle of Cotton Mather (1663–1728). His most famous work, a series of sermons preached for his Dublin congregation, was published posthumously by his brother Nathanael Mather in 1683, *The Figure or Types of the Old Testaments by which Christ and the Heavenly Things of the Gospel Were Preached and Shadowed to the People of God of Old*. In Mather's definition the type is "some outward or sensible thing ordained of God under the Old Testament to represent and hold forth something of Christ in the New," to which he later adds that "there is in a type some outward or sensible thing, that represents an higher spiritual thing, which may be called a sign or a resemblance, a pattern or figure or the like."[23] These sermons forcefully argue that the Gospel is preached already in the Old Testament: the title of each section begins with the word "Gospel," for example, "The Gospel of Circumcision" and "The Gospel of Sacrifices."

The last and almost equally significant treatment of typology was the unique and undeservedly forgotten work of Benjamin Keach (1640–1704) on biblical metaphors, *Tropologia, a Key to Open Scripture Metaphors*, first published in 1682. This book was partly a translation of Solomon Glassius's *Philologia sacra* (1620). Keach was a prolific Baptist minister with some Calvinistic leanings. In his preface he contrasts types to allegories. He says allegories are in the same category as metaphors and parables. "Although metaphors and allegories are useful for mystical purposes," he says, they should not be "taken beyond the analogy of faith."[24] In other words, they must remain within the confines of what Scripture reveals explicitly elsewhere.

Now that we have reviewed the historical background, we can understand how Edwards's use of typology was unique.

Edwards's Innovative Ideas of Typology

Thanks to the recent research of Janice Knight (1991) and Gerald R. McDermott (2000), we have some current assessments of the typological writings of Edwards.[25] Knights's essay was included in Sang Hyun Lee's impressive *Princeton Companion to Jonathan Edwards* (2005).[26] However useful as a critical summary, her essay is limited by the fact that it was written before the appearance of the volume on Edwards's typological writings in the Yale edition of his works.[27] McDermott's comprehensive summary is, therefore, based on more reliable sources.

Jonathan Edwards was obsessed with typology throughout his career. Typology runs as a leitmotif through his sermons, especially in the 1739 sermon series later published as *A History of Redemption*, the series that became the rightly celebrated *Religious Affections* (1746), and even in his endless private notebooks (the *Miscellanies*). In the rest of this chapter I concentrate on the typological works (volume 11) in the Yale edition of *The Works of Jonathan Edwards*. This contains his fragmented and discontinuous notes, *Images and Shadows of Divine Things*, which he began at the age of twenty-five in 1728; his short and substantial pamphlet "Types"; and the long treatise "Types of the Messiah" composed between 1744 and 1749.

In the short pamphlet "Types" Edwards uses the term as a synonym for "parable," "mystery," "figure," "picture," "allegory," "dark saying," "sign," "pledge," and "veil." We are warned to be "exceeding careful" in interpreting types, for "by mysteries is especially meant divine truths wrapped up in shadows and mysterious representations."[28] Nevertheless, he is confident that types are literally all over the world:

> I am not ashamed to own that I believe that the whole universe,
> heaven and earth, air and seas, and divine constitution and history
> of the holy Scriptures, be full of images of divine things, as full as a
> language is of words; and that the multitude of those things that
> I have mentioned are but a very small part of what is really intended
> to be signified and typified by these things: but that there is room for
> persons to be learning more and more of this language and seeing
> more of that which is declared in it to the end of the world without
> discovering all.[29]

However, Edwards departed from his contemporaries by expanding the traditional historical understanding of typology into the natural world. For Edwards, God revealed himself "by his word and works."[30]

> Types are a certain sort of language, as it were, in which God is wont
> to speak to us. And there is, as it were, a certain idiom in that language
> which is to be learnt the same that the idiom of any language is.[31]

Edwards unconsciously echoed Alan of Lille's famous twelfth-century poem:

> Omnis mundi creatura
> quasi liber et pictura
> nobis est et speculum:
> nostrae vitae, nostrae mortis,
> nostri status, nostrae sortis
> fidele signaculum.[32]

This short poem illustrates well the figurative view of reality characteristic of the medieval period and shared by Jonathan Edwards in the eighteenth century. For Edwards, the end of creation was God's communication of himself—

his glory with his creatures.[33] In one of his *Miscellanies* Edwards also notes that "the whole outward creation, which is but the shadows of beings, is so made as to represent spiritual things."[34]

However, McDermott is right in suggesting that "the types do not have power in and for themselves to portray the spiritual world. The typological system is not transparent to all, but only to 'a mind so prepared and exercised.' There is no salvation by the imagination. Salvation is only by Christ and the power of his Spirit, who alone can provide the sense of the heart, which alone can read the types."[35]

Edwards's typology represented a middle-of-the road position between extreme views of typology. He said his aim was "to show how there is a medium between those that cry down all types, and those that are for turning all into nothing but allegory and not having it to be true history; and also the way of the rabbis that find so many mysteries in letters, etc."[36]

Wallace Anderson points out that there were three groups that dismissed the Edwardsian use of typology: first, the rationalists, Lockeans, and deists, for whom typology was illogical; second; the Catholics and high-church Anglicans who wanted to perpetuate old fashions of allegorization; third, Reformed evangelicals of Puritan dissent, who affirmed typology based on the literal sense but would have objected to Edward's expansion of types beyond Scripture into the natural world. "Edwards attempted to free typology from the narrow correspondences of the two testaments without reverting to exaggerated medieval allegory."[37] For example, Moses' lifting up his hands when the Israelites fought with the Amalekites (Exod 17:11) was seen as a type of Jesus' crucifixion. Against a conservative or merely historical idea of typology, Edwards represented a more liberal, ontological view of typology—which means that for Edwards, typology was not limited to two historical events but could link divine events to aspects of the existing world such as things in nature.

Jonathan Edwards's ontological or liberal typology is a logical and organic extension of biblical figurative language. For example, both Jesus' words in John's Gospel and Paul's language are highly figurative. Edwards quotes Jesus' words from John 12:24 about the corn of wheat that falls into the ground and dies, and by dying brings forth much fruit.[38] Edwards's favorite Pauline quote is Ephesians 5:30–32 on "the great mystery" of marriage, which is a type of the union between Christ and the church. Edwards concludes from passages like these that the world is full of types: "It is evident that God hath ordered the state and constitution of the world of mankind . . . that spiritual things might be represented by them."[39]

But who can understand this language of types? Edwards was convinced that it is only by the spiritual perception of the spiritual man, as St. Paul calls it in 1 Corinthians 2:15. In the *Religious Affections* he describes this gift as the first sign of "truly gracious and holy affections." Spiritual persons are the true saints who are sanctified by the spirit of God: "Christians are called spiritual persons because they are born of the Spirit, and because of the indwelling and holy influences of the Spirit of God in them." They then become "creature-partaker[s] of the divine nature." Edwards learned from St. Paul that "natural men have no communion or fellowship with Christ, or participation with him."[40] This is the divine way of knowing that enables the young Jonathan Edwards to see divine mysteries in the phenomena of the natural world. It enables him to see how God created the world with analogy: every inferior being is an imitation or shadow of its superior—as beasts are imitations of human beings, plants are the imitations of animals (*Images,* Numbers 8 and 19), and all this is the "method of God's working" (*Images*, Number 59).

With Gerhard von Rad we have seen that typology is characteristic of poetic imagination. Poets and theologians of highly poetic imagination have also used typology. In what follows we shall see remarkable parallels to Edwards's typology in Shakespeare, Luther, and the metaphysical poets.

Resonances in Edwards's Typology to Shakespeare, Luther, and the Metaphysical Poets

I have written elsewhere on how Shakespeare's language and imagery were indebted to the emblem tradition, which is a special Renaissance genre of combining a motto, a picture, and a text.[41] Edwards himself uses the term *emblem* as a synonym for types, but to this point students of typology have not noticed this connection.

Nor have the other parallels between Edwards and Shakespeare been noticed. When thinking of Edwards's spiritual perception of nature, for example, consider the Duke Senior's words in *As You Like It*:

> And this our life, exempt from public haunt,
> Finds tongues in trees, books in the running brooks,
> Sermons in stones, and good in everything. (Act 2, scene 1,
>   lines 15–17)[42]

Shakespeare's "sermons in stones" is his own signal that he too thought about nature as pointing to the divine. Another Shakespearean image is unconsciously echoed by Edwards when he writes:

> When men stand on very high things, they are ready to grow giddy
> and are in great danger of falling, and the higher they are the more

dreadful is their fall. Which represents the danger men are in, when lifted up on high on the pinnacle of honor and prosperity, of having their eyes dazzle, of being very discomposed and erroneous in their notion of things, especially themselves and their own standing, and the great danger they are in of falling; and how that those that are most highly exalted in pride have the most dreadful fall.[43]

In *Julius Caesar* Brutus says to Cassius:

> We, at the height, are ready to decline
> There is a tide in the affairs of men,
> Which, taken at the flood, leads on to fortune;
> Omitted, all the voyage of their life
> Is bound in shallows and in miseries. (Act 4,
> scene 3, lines 216–18)[44]

According to Edwards, the spiritual person perceives the world christologically, and therefore sees within "the rising and setting of the sun a type of the death and resurrection of Christ" (*Images,* Number 50). Moreover, for him or her "the silkworm is a remarkable type of Christ, which, when it dies, yields us that of which make such glorious clothing. Christ became a worm for our sakes . . . and by his death finished that righteousness with which believers are clothed, and thereby procured that we should be clothed with robes of glory" (*Images,* Number 35; see also Numbers 46 and 142).

This image has antecedents in Luther's commentaries. Luther also associated Christ dying on the cross with the worm (see Psalm 22:6) when he said, "He was not regarded as a godly person but as a venomous worm . . . menace to the entire world. Such was the low esteem in which the world held Him, and His Christians today share this with Him."[45] Commenting on the Genesis story of Sarah's death, Luther remarks, "It has pleased God to raise up from worms, from corruption, from the earth, which is totally putrid and full of stench, a body more beautiful than any flower, than balsam, than the sun itself and the stars."[46]

Another striking similarity in imagery used by both Luther and Edwards concerns spiritual food, or the eucharist. Edwards says:

As wheat is prepared to be our food to refresh and nourish and strengthen us, by being threshed, and ground to powder, and then baked in the oven, whereby it becomes a type of our spiritual food, even Christ, the bread which comes down from heaven, which becomes our food by his sufferings; so the juice of the grape is a type of the blood of Christ, as it is prepared to be our refreshing drink to

exhilarate our spirits and make us glad, by being pressed out in a
wine press. (*Images*, Number 68)

Two hundred years earlier, in his 1518 sermon on "The Blessed Sacrament of
the Holy and True Body and the Brotherhoods," Luther proposed a surprisingly
similar cluster of images:

> For just as the bread is made out of many grains ground and mixed
> together, and out of the bodies of many grains there comes the body
> of one bread, in which each grain loses its form and body and takes
> upon itself the common body of the bread; and just as the drops of
> wine, in losing their own form, become the body of one common
> wine and drink—so it is and should be with us. . . . And through the
> interchange of his blessings and our misfortunes, we become one
> loaf, one bread, one body, one drink, and have all things in common.
>
> Christ appointed these two forms of bread and wine, rather than
> any other, as a further indication of the very union and fellowship
> which is in this sacrament. For there is no more intimate, deep, and
> indivisible union than the union of the food with him who is fed.
> For the food enters into and is assimilated by his very nature, and
> becomes one substance with the person who is fed. . . . Thus in the
> sacrament we too become united with Christ, and are made one body
> with all the saints, so that Christ cares for us and acts in our behalf.[47]

While evoking parallels between Edwards and Shakespeare on the one
hand, and Edwards and Luther on the other, we have linked Edwards to earlier
typological traditions. But Edwards was also fascinated by the created world and
its new discoveries opened by Locke's philosophy and Newton's science. Not
unlike the metaphysical poets (John Donne, George Herbert, Richard Crashaw,
etc.) of a century earlier, Edwards appropriated the physical laws and analytical
sciences for typological purposes. Two examples should suffice, that of gravity
and the telescope:

> The whole material universe is preserved by gravity, or attraction,
> or the mutual tendency of all bodies to each other. One part of the
> universe is hereby beneficial to another. The beauty, the harmony,
> and order, regular progress, life and motion, and in short, all the
> well being of the whole frame, depends on it. This is a type of love or
> charity in the spiritual world. (*Images*, Number 79)

Typology is a future-oriented view of history, presupposing a linear view of
history. Edwards shared this view of the progress of history and therefore

knowledge—a progress that drives humanity toward the approaching millennium. He placed the telescope in this context.

> The late invention of telescopes, whereby heavenly objects are brought so much nearer, and made so much plainer to sight, and such wonderful discoveries have been made in heavens, is a type and forerunner of the great increase in the knowledge of heavenly things that shall be in the approaching glorious times of the Christian church. (*Images,* Number 58)

Edwards's frequently used images of trees (*Images,* Numbers 26, 78, 99, 135) and rivers (Numbers 15, 22, 77) reflect both the successive ages of the world and the dynamism of God's working in history. "The church in different ages is lively represented by the growth and progress of a tree" (Number 99). Other images show the same sense of progress in the history of redemption: "The gradual vanishing of stars when the sun approaches is a type [of] the gradual vanishing of Jewish ordinances as the Gospel dispensation was introduced" (Number 40).

Other graphic images portray the grisly reality of sin. "Death temporal is a shadow of eternal death" (*Images,* Number 1). "The serpent's charming of birds . . . the spider's taking of the fly . . . are lively representations of the devil's catching our souls" (Number 11). "Ravens that with delight feed on carrion seem to be remarkable types of the devils who with delight prey upon the souls of the dead. A dead, filthy, rotten carcass is a lively image of the soul of a wicked man that is spiritually and exceeding filthy and abominable" (Number 61).

Conclusion

Jonathan Edwards was fascinated by the beauty of the created world. In his 1948 edition of *Images and Shadows of Divine Things,* Perry Miller suggested that Edwards's extension of traditional historical typology to nature constituted an "exaltation of nature to a level of authority coequal with [biblical] revelation."[48] However, in a perceptive article on Edwards's spiritual exegesis, Stephen Stein argues that Miller was mistaken not only to place nature on a par with Scripture but also in his attempt to link Edwards with Emerson's naturalism: "Edwards never waffled on the primacy of Scripture as the principal source of divine revelation, nor on the usefulness of biblical typology as an interpretive device."[49] Instead, Edwards was simply trying to gain a "fuller understanding" of the "spirit-given" sense of the text.

Shortly before his untimely and tragic death, Edwards wrote a letter to the trustees of the College of New Jersey in which he revealed his plan to write a "great work" of divinity entitled *History of the Work of Redemption*. In this letter he mentioned his design for "another great work": the *Harmony of the Old and New Testament*. In this latter work he envisaged three parts: the first on prophecies of the Messiah and their fulfillment; the second on the types of the Old Testament and their antitypes in the gospels; the third to highlight the doctrinal and theological harmony of the two Testaments. Apparently Edwards wanted to link traditional ideas about biblical prophecy and doctrine to his new way of doing typology.

Stein illustrates Edwards's view of the doctrinal unity of the testaments by using the Abraham and Isaac story, where the sentence "God will provide himself a lamb" (Gen 22:8), according to Edwards, refers to the sacrifice of Christ, whereby "God would provide the sacrifice by which sins against himself were atoned." Edwards acknowledges that Abraham had not thought of Christ but "the mind of the Holy Ghost had respect to Christ as the sacrifice."[50] Types can be understood only in retrospect after their fulfillment in the cross of Christ.

As Hans Frei has pointed out, the eighteenth century was a time in which "the relationship between the literal meaning of the biblical stories and the historical reality of the events was destroyed."[51] In other words, early critics of the Bible were casting doubt on the historical accuracy of the biblical stories. Pretty soon, the story, historical reality, and theological meaning became three separate things, as the "depicted biblical world" and the "real historical world" were consciously separated in commentaries. Stein concludes that although Edwards was fully aware of this early critical scholarship, his concern was a for a higher and fuller understanding of the spiritual meaning of the whole text—and this he found in his "liberal" typology. Thus "Edwards was not ready to separate word and spirit in the interpretation."[52] He remained within the "precritical" paradigm of biblical interpretation along with Luther and the Reformers of the sixteenth century, for whom the spiritual meaning of the text was to be perceived within the literal meanings, since the spirit was not "above" but "within" the letter. Because of this concern to link the historical with the spiritual—the reading of the whole Bible with each of its parts—one could perhaps use Edwards's sermons, commentaries, and doctrinal works to illustrate what David Steinmetz meant when he spoke of the "superiority of precritical exegesis."[53]

What, then, can we say about the relevance of Edwards's typology for contemporary faith and culture? In an age of modern technology, Edwards helps us open our imaginations in order to apply biblical associations to the world surrounding us. Christian imagination, deeply rooted in the concrete images of the Bible, should be both preserved and renewed. Biblical language should never be permitted to remain a dead fossil as "the language of Canaan" in the midst of contemporary culture. Old words and images wait to be fulfilled and re-created by new substances.

From biblical times onward, typology has been used to understand the "new" in terms of the "old." Thus the dynamism inherent in typology can help the Christian faith remain alive in an always changing world. Jonathan Edwards, with his liberal and highly original adaptation of typology, has a unique and peculiar place in this old tradition.

NOTES

1. Erich Auerbach, "Figura," in *Scenes from the Drama of European Literature*, trans. R. Mannheim (New York: Meridian, 1959), 11–74, quotation on 16.

2. Tibor Fabiny, *The Lion and the Lamb: Figuralism and Fulfilment in the Bible, Art and Literature* (London: Macmillan, 1992), 1–2.

3. Ibid., 44.

4. Ibid., 75.

5. "And one of the elders saith unto me, 'Weep not: behold, the Lion of the tribe of Judah, the Root of David, hath prevailed to open the book, and to loose the seven seals thereof.' And I beheld, and, lo, in the midst of the throne, and of the four beasts, and in the midst of the elders, stood a Lamb as it had been slain" (KJV).

6. See Roland A. Delattre, *Beauty and Sensibility in the Thought of Jonathan Edwards* (New Haven: Yale University Press, 1968), 58–68.

7. Jonathan Edwards, "The Excellency of Christ," in *The Sermons of Jonathan Edwards: A Reader*, ed. Wilson H. Kimnach, Kenneth P. Minkema, and Douglas Sweeney (New Haven: Yale University Press, 1999), 165.

8. Ibid., 168.

9. Ibid., 175.

10. Ibid., 177.

11. Ibid., 181.

12. Robert W. Jenson, *America's Theologian: A Recommendation of Jonathan Edwards* (New York: Oxford University Press, 1988). See Gesa Elisabeth Thiessen, *Theological Aesthetics: A Reader* (Grand Rapids, MI: Eerdmans, 2004), 167–76.

13. Jonathan Edwards, "Personal Narrative," in the Yale edition of *The Works of Jonathan Edwards* [hereafter *WJE*], 16: 792, 794.

14. Ibid., 796.

15. Jonathan Edwards, "The Beauty of the World, " in *A Jonathan Edwards Reader*, ed. John E. Smith, Harry S. Stout, and Kenneth P. Minkema (New Haven: Yale University Press, 1995), 14.

16. "The Nature of True Virtue," in *WJE* 8: 540, 561.

17. Ibid., 565.

18. Amy Plantinga Pauw, "The Trinity," in *The Princeton Companion to Jonathan Edwards*, ed. Sang Hyun Lee (Princeton, NJ: Princeton University Press, 2005), 51, 52.

See also Amy Plantinga Pauw, *The Supreme Harmony of All: The Trinitarian Theology of Jonathan Edwards* (Grand Rapids, MI: Eerdmans, 2002).

19. Leonard Goppelt, *Die typologische Deutung des Alten Testaments in Neuen* (Gütersloh, Germany: Verlag C. Bertelsmann, 1939). The second, enlarged edition was published in 1969. The English translation was published in 1982 as *Typos: The Typological Interpretation of the Old Testament in the New*, trans. D. Madvig (Grand Rapids, MI: Eerdmans, 1982).

20. Gerhard von Rad, "Typologische Auslegung des Alten Testaments," in *Evangelische Theologie* 12 (1952), 17–33. In English: "Typological Interpretation of the Old Testament," in *Old Testament Hermeneutics*, ed. Claus Westermann (Richmond, VA: John Knox Press, 1963), 17–39.

21. Von Rad, "Typological Interpretation," 17.

22. William Guild, *Moses Unveiled* (London, 1620).

23. Quoted by M. I. Lowance in his introduction to Samuel Mather, *The Figures of Types of the Old Testament*, ed. M. I. Lowance Jr. (New York: Johnson Reprint, 1969), xi–xii.

24. See the recent reprint edition of *Tropologia*: Benjamin Keach, *Preaching from the Types and Metaphors of the Bible* (Grand Rapids, MI: Kregel Publications, 1972), xii. See Lowance, 1969, *The Figures of Types of the Old Testament*, 86.

25. Janice Knight, "Learning the Language of God: Jonathan Edwards and the Typology of Nature," *William and Mary Quarterly*, 3d ser., 48 (1991): 531–51; Gerald R. McDermott, *Jonathan Edwards Confronts the Gods: Christian Theology, Enlightemenet Religion, and Non-Christian Faiths* (New York: Oxford University Press, 2000), 110–29.

26. Janice Knight, "Typology," in Lee, *The Princeton Companion to Jonathan Edwards*, 190–209.

27. Jonathan Edwards, *Typological Writings*, *WJE* 11.

28. Ibid., 151.

29. Ibid., 152.

30. Quoted by Knight in Lee, *The Princeton Companion to Jonathan Edwards*, 190.

31. *WJE* 11: 150.

32.   Every created thing of the world
     is like a book or a picture,
     acting to us as a mirror,
     a faithful figure,
     of our life, our death,
     our condition, our lot. (cf. *Patrologia Latina* 210,579a).

33. *WJE* 11: 9; *Miscellanies*, in *WJE* 13: 358–59.

34. *Miscellanies*, in *WJE* 13: 434.

35. McDermott, *Jonathan Edwards Confronts the Gods*, 116.

36. "Types," in *WJE* 11: 151.

37. *WJE* 11: 33.

38. Jonathan Edwards, *Images of Divine Things*, Number 23, in *WJE* 11. Subsequent references are cited parenthetically in the text.

39. *WJE* 11: 67.

40. Jonathan Edwards, *Religious Affections*, in *WJE* 2: 197, 198, 203, 204.

41. Tibor Fabiny, ed., *Shakespeare and the Emblem* (Szeged, Hungary: Attila József University, 1984).

42. William Shakespeare, *As You Like It*, Arden Shakespeare, ed. Agnes Latham (London: Methuen, 1984).

43. *WJE* 11: 91.

44. William Shakespeare, *Julius Caesar*, Arden Shakespeare, ed. T. S. Dorsch (London: Methuen, 1983).

45. *Luther's Works: American Edition* [hereafter *LW*], ed. Jaroslav Pelikan and Helmut T. Lehmann (Philadelphia: Fortress, 1957), 22, 340. Cf. Kenneth Hagen, "The Testament of a Worm: Luther on Testament and Covenant," *Consensus* 8 (1982): 12–20.

46. *LW* 4: 190.

47. *LW* 35: 49–73.

48. Perry Miller, introduction to *Images and Shadows of Divine Things by Jonathan Edwards* (New Haven: Yale University Press, 1948), 28.

49. Stephen J. Stein, "The Spirit and the Word: Jonathan Edwards and Spiritual Exegesis," in *Jonathan Edwards and the American Experience,* ed. Nathan O. Hatch and Harry S. Stout (New York: Oxford University Press, 1988), 125.

50. Ibid., 126.

51. Ibid., 118. See Hans W. Frei, *The Eclipse of Biblical Narrative: A Study in Eighteenth and Nineteenth Century Hermeneutics* (New Haven: Yale University Press, 1974).

52. Stein, "The Spirit and the Word," 128.

53. David C. Steinmetz, "The Superiority of Precritical Exegesis," *Theology Today,* Apr. 1980, 27–38. Robert E. Brown argues that the dichotomy between precritical and critical is too facile and ultimately breaks down, and that Edwards has a foot in both worlds: *Jonathan Edwards and the Bible* (Bloomington: Indiana University Press, 1999), 76–87.

8

Alternative Viewpoint: Edwards and Biblical Typology

Gerald R. McDermott

Principal Insights

Let me first highlight what I take to be Dr. Fabiny's principal insights. He observes initially that in the long history of the tradition, typology has meant at least nine things, and for Edwards at least four: a way of reading the Bible generally, a particular way of linking the Old Testament to the New Testament, a principle of exegesis (taking out of the text what is there, using knowledge of language, history, and culture), and a vision of history.

Then Dr. Fabiny provides for us his own vision of the heart of biblical typology, which we first saw twenty years ago in his book *The Lion and the Lamb,* and which had its own antitype in Edwards's sermon "The Excellency of Christ": Christ is both lion and lamb, and this paradox is illustrated most poignantly in Christ's dying love. The lion becomes a lamb that is led to the slaughter. I would add that for Edwards this is the meaning not only of biblical typology but also the meaning of history and the human person, as the person is joined to Christ.

Dr. Fabiny gives us next his own take on a recurring theme of this book: the distinctively Edwardsian perspective on beauty. As we have seen in previous chapters, Edwards said that primary beauty is the union of being to Being (Edwards's word for God), to which "it pleases God to observe analogy in his works." This means that God places analogies to this beauty throughout his creation. Secondary beauty, which involves different members of a society or system united in conscious or unconscious agreement, is a type or symbol of primary beauty. So the agreement of lines in a beautiful tree is a type or pointer to the spiritual joining of a heart to God. Professor Fabiny observes that all of Edwards's reflections on this are Trinitarian.

We are also given a brief survey of the history of typology, learning that the "second" flowering of typology in the seventeenth century mirrored the first in the second century.

Innovation

Edwards's innovation in this history was to see the entire world full of types. While most of the tradition had said there were types in the Old Testament pointing to New Testament fulfillments, and some had said there are types in nature, Edwards extended this system to history and even the history of religions.

This makes sense of Edwards's view of the creation as a communication of God's glory. If God intended all the creation to glorify his being, then one would expect all the world to be full of signs or pointers to New Testament realities.

Professor Fabiny reminds us that Edwards took what could be called a *via media* (middle road), between the deists on the left who dismissed all types as fanciful, and some medievals on the right who found allegories everywhere—even and especially where the Bible was silent. Yet while Edwards was a moderate in this respect, he was a liberal in his view of typology, for he believed that "God created the world with analogy" and that "every inferior being [is] a shadow of its superior." Among other things, this means that all of being is full of types. You could say that God's fingerprints are everywhere. It also means that reality is hierarchical through and through. We humans may be created equal in human worth, but in most every other way we are unequals. And the rest of nature is chock full of inequality, with diverse hierarchies on display at every turn.

One nice feature of his essay is that Professor Fabiny makes use of his long and deep work in Shakespeare and his more recent exploration of Luther to compare these two great thinkers to Edwards on typology. The result is an interesting confluence of thinking on such subjects as Christ's work on the cross compared to a worm. Our literary scholar also notes that Edwards was not the only one to see types in the emerging new science of Newton and Locke, but that the metaphysical poets saw the same, even paralleling Edwards's vision of gravity as a type of love.

Not Simply "Precritical"

I like Professor Fabiny's conclusion, but I want to add to it. As Fabiny himself notes, Edwards cannot be described as simply "precritical." The distinction between "precritical" and "critical," often used by biblical scholars who subscribe to a certain form of biblical criticism in the twentieth century dominated by Bultmann and his successors, presumes that there is only one sort of critical thinking about the Bible, the kind that adopts form criticism's presuppositions uncritically. Two of those presuppositions are that the gospels do not give us access to eyewitness testimony and that the early church was more interested in its own pastoral and polemical situation than in the historical accuracy of the oral tradition. Richard Bauckham's recent *Jesus and the Eyewitnesses* cogently undermines both of those presuppositions.[1] Robert Brown's *Jonathan Edwards and the Bible* also demonstrates that Edwards was fully aware of emerging biblical criticism, and in fact targeted many of his *Miscellanies* entries to their findings and challenges.[2]

The upshot of this is that Edwards cannot be neatly fit into a simplistic dichotomy of "precritical" versus "critical." Unlike the so-called precritical readers of the Bible, Edwards was quite cognizant of historical and cultural influences on biblical authors, and unlike modern so-called critical readers, Edwards was able to see a theological unity to the Bible while at the same time recognizing diversities of genre and message. Like fundamentalists, historicist readers of Scripture today typically see only one meaning for each passage, identified exclusively by its historical and cultural context. But Edwards, like the Fathers and Reformers, refused to separate letter and spirit, so that the Spirit could infuse the letter with more than one meaning. He acknowledged that the letter was in history, but he also recognized that the spirit or meaning of the letter was not limited to one meaning in that one historical situation. For the spirit was in fact the same Spirit moving history and tradition, and so the letter in one moment of history was informed by the Spirit's work in all the other moments. In this way the letter could point to both its immediate history as a type and to its future history as an antitype, as well as to its past history in the biblical story. In these ways Scripture was infused with layers of meaning, as Scripture pointed to Scripture, and nature and history pointed back to Scripture and its story of Jesus Christ.

Edwards's typology was not only a way to read the Bible but also a way to read all of reality. If the Bible is full of types so that the same passage can point at different levels to different dimensions of the Trinity working in history, and if all of nature and history are full of types, then there is a typological way of looking at reality. In other words, there are ways to look at life in which we see signs of Christ and his redemption showing up everywhere—in the daily routine, in nature, in the course of history, and in nearly every dimension of existence. This is a way of seeing that, I hope, will be more fully explored by theologians who build upon this Edwardsian foundation. They will, I trust, look *through* Edwards's typological model to see even more of the Trinity's footprints in life and history.

NOTES

1. Richard Bauckham, *Jesus and the Eyewitnesses* (Grand Rapids, MI: Eerdmans, 2006).

2. Robert Brown, *Jonathan Edwards and the Bible* (Bloomington: Indiana University Press, 2002).

9

Edwards and Beauty

Sang Hyun Lee

Professor Lee argues that for Edwards, beauty is proportion or consent, and God's consent or love within God's own internal being is the highest and true beauty. God created the world in order to repeat his internal beauty in time and space. The sanctified human mind's imaginative activity of ordering beautiful sense ideas in a beautiful relation, and the mind's delight in that beautiful relation, together constitute the mind's knowing and loving of beauty, or what Edwards calls the "sense of the heart." In and through the saints' knowing and loving God's beauty and the beauty of other beings in relation to God's beauty, God's internal being is repeated in time and space, and God's beauty is enlarged and extended.

Beauty and the perception of beauty are the ideas that play a central role in the philosophy and theology of Jonathan Edwards.[1] The fundamental nature of anything that exists, for Edwards, is beauty, and the most distinctive characteristic of God is his divine beauty. To know and love God, therefore, is to know and love the beauty of God, and to know the ultimate nature of the world is to know and love the world as an image of God's beauty.

What, then, is beautiful? What is the knowing and loving of beauty? How is human life related with God's beauty? How are Christian faith and life related to beauty? In this chapter, we will try to provide Edwards's answers to these questions.

What Is Beauty?

"All beauty consists in similarness or identity of relations," says Edwards.[2] In other words, beauty has to do with similarity between one thing and another. "Proportion," "harmony," and "agreement" are other words Edwards uses to define the basic nature of all that is beautiful. Then he makes some crucial distinctions. A simple "agreement" or "proportion"—for example, the similarity or agreement between two red apples—is a "simple beauty," while a complex proportion or harmony of a beautiful human face is a "complex beauty."

Now a complex presence of relations beauty may contain partial irregularities or disagreement. For example, a beautiful human face may have some partial irregularities. But if the features of the face as a whole make up a proportion, then it is a higher beauty than a simple agreement (6: 334).

The other important distinction Edwards makes is between "primary beauty" and "secondary beauty" (8: 565). The former is the agreement or "consent" between perceiving beings—that is, human beings. Here the word "consent" really means "love." The harmony among nonhuman beings, things in the physical universe, is a "secondary beauty." Edwards tells us that the "primary beauty of love or consent between perceiving beings" is a much higher beauty than "secondary beauty," and also that the "secondary beauty" among physical things is an "image" or "shadow" of the primary beauty (8: 561–68). That is to say, the beauty of trees and rivers mirrors the love between perceiving beings. To apply the distinctions we mentioned earlier, we can say that the love or agreement between two perceiving beings is a "complex beauty" and a "primary beauty" that is a higher beauty than the "secondary or simple beauty" of the agreement between two apples—my apologies to the apples.

The Beauty of God

Edwards said, "God is God, and distinguished from all other beings, and exalted above 'em, chiefly by his divine beauty, which is infinitely diverse from all other beauty" (2: 298). He goes on to say that the divine beauty is "that . . . wherein the truest idea of divinity does consist" (2: 298). And God is not only beautiful but beauty itself and the foundation and fountain of all beauty. God's nature, according to Edwards, is the true beauty, beauty itself, and the criterion of all beauty, and the source or fountain of all beauty (8: 550–60).

In terms of the various distinctions about beauty that Edwards makes (that we discussed above), we could say that God's beauty is the highest form of primary beauty or loving consent and consists of the most complex form of relationality, which as a whole makes up the highest form of proportion. God's beauty as the true beauty is a transcendent beauty "entirely above nature" in that God's beauty is infinitely more beautiful and different in kind from any beauty we normally experience (2: 205).

But God's beauty also has continuity with the beauty within human experience, because God's beauty is still a kind of "proportion" (though entirely above nature), like any other proportions we experience. If this were not true, it would be in principle impossible for human beings ever to experience God's beauty.

We should ask here the question, What does it mean to say that God's beauty is the criterion of all beauty? For Edwards, the answer is that God's beauty is the *true* beauty, and also that all other beautiful relations in the world, as manifested in the loving relations among human beings and the beauties of nature, are really the "images or shadows" of the divine beauty (8: 564–69; 11: 51–135). Therefore, to perceive the beauty in the world in the true way is to perceive that beauty first and then also to perceive its harmony or "fitness" with the beauty of God as embodied in the life of Jesus Christ. So Edwards says, "That which is beautiful . . . with respect to itself and a few things . . . is false beauty and a confined beauty," whereas "that [which] is beautiful with respect to the universality of things has a generally extended excellence, a true beauty" (6: 344). We said earlier that a complex beauty is a higher beauty than a simple beauty. But complexity or extendedness by itself cannot be the true criterion of beauty. A highly extended nexus of relationships, if it is not harmonious with God's beauty as embodied in Christ, is a great deformity and a dissent from God.

Now we must ask the question, what does it mean to say that God is beautiful? We must begin answering the question by noting that, for Jonathan Edwards, God is not only the most beautiful being but in his nature the beautifying being, one who makes other beings beautiful, and thus, as Edwards says, "the fountain" of all beauty. According to Edwards, God is a disposition, a power to communicate his beauty to other beings. God is in his essence a beautifying disposition or power (13: 277–78).

Now this divine disposition to communicate beauty is exercised fully inside the divine being, in God *ad intra*, which is the same thing as saying "within the Trinity." According to Edwards, God's disposition to be beautiful and to communicate beauty is first expressed in the Father. And that same disposition is exercised the second time as the First Person knows and loves and consents to the Son. And the mutual love and consent between the Father and the Son is the Holy Spirit. So within God's internal being, God is actually and infinitely loving and consenting, and is also a perfect repetition or communication of that consenting. So God in his inner life is eternally the infinite fullness of the highest beauty and the communication of that beauty (21: 108–44).

Now, if beauty and its communication are infinitely perfect in God, why does he create the world? As we just saw, God is already fully actual as God.

God has no need to do anything in order for God to be God. The answer to the question "Why creation?" lies in Edwards's dynamic concept of God as the eternal disposition (i.e., abiding tendency or propensity) to communicate beauty. Although God is the full and perfect actuality of the divine beauty, God's essence remains the divine disposition to communicate beauty. In God, actuality and disposition coincide.[3] Although God is perfectly all that God has to be to be God, God now seeks to exercise his disposition to communicate his beauty *ad extra*, that is, outside of himself. The same disposition that was fully exercised within God is what causes God to create the world—true beauty or love that wants to communicate itself. In creating the world, God has to have an aim or a purpose. That aim has to be the highest good, or whatever is the most valuable thing. But the highest good is God himself. If this is the case, then what could be the aim that the perfect God would have in creating the world? Edwards's answer is that God, in creating the world, aims at "an increase, repetition, or multiplication" of his perfect beauty in time and space (8: 433). The idea of "repetition" is important for Edwards, because he wanted to affirm both God's eternal prior actuality (the completeness or perfection of his being) and the creation as God's continuing creative activity.[4]

In creating the world, God becomes more of what he already is eternally. The creation as repetition allows Edwards to affirm God's prior eternal actuality as God, as well as the newness and purposiveness of God's act of creating the world.

So God creates the intelligent beings as well as the physical universe. The purpose in creating the intelligent beings is that they may participate in and promote God's own end (purpose) in creation. As sanctified human beings know and love God's beauty, and practice that beauty by loving other beings, God's internal fullness is repeated in time and space. This process of repeating God's fullness in time and space, Edwards says, will take an everlasting amount of time (8: 443). This is so because God's fullness is infinite and cannot be fully repeated in time and space in a limited period of time. So, according to Edwards, at the eschaton (the end of history as we know it) the sinful world will disappear, but history itself will continue in the "new heaven and the new earth" (9: 348). Heaven includes time and space, and also embodied human beings. The process of God's repeating his eternal fullness in time and space will continue in heaven without ever coming to a temporal end.[5]

We should now ask, If the end for which God created the world is God's own repetition of his beauty in time and space, how is the happiness and salvation of the fallen creation related to that end? God's own end of repeating his beauty outside of himself, according to Edwards, is God's "chief ultimate end" in creation. But the end of the happiness and salvation of the fallen creation is also an ultimate end—an end that is valuable in itself. Yet this end is subordinate to, and comprehended in, God's chief end. God wishes to save and make humanity happy, and this end is valuable in itself. But this end is comprehended in the greater ultimate end—namely, God's own end. So, then, human beings' chief ultimate end should be to pursue God's own in creation. As Edwards puts it, "God has made intelligent creatures capable of being concerned in these effects, as being the willing active subjects, or means; and so they are capable of actively promoting God's glory" (23: 153). Does this subordination of the happiness of humankind to God's end in creation in any way downgrade the dignity of human creatures? Edwards does not think so. For him, human beings have the dignity of participating in God's own life of repeating his beauty in time and space.

The Perception of Beauty

How do we perceive or experience beauty? Edwards's answer is that we perceive beauty when the mind passively receives sense data through sense organs and self-reflection, and then as we actively order those ideas in such a way that their relations become visible to the mind. So the perception of beauty is the result of the cooperation of the mind's passive act receiving sense data and the mind's activity of ordering those ideas in certain ways. So the perception of beauty is not a conceptual or logical process, but an immediate (not discursive or step-by-step) functioning of the mind. This is why Edwards calls the mind's perception of beauty "a sense of the heart."

Edwards read the British empiricist John Locke's *Essay Concerning Human Understanding* very early in his life, probably during his graduate years at the College of New Haven (now Yale). Like Locke, Edwards was convinced that knowledge had to be based on the actual "experience" of the world in order for knowledge to be legitimate knowledge. Using Locke's terminology, Edwards believed that knowledge had to be based on "simple ideas" that are received directly from the world and then introspection into one's own mind.[6] Locke, however, left largely unexplained and unanalyzed how the mind is able to experience the relations among those simple and distinct ideas of sensation. Locke does say that the mind intuits the relation among ideas and combines them into complex ideas, but he did not carry out a detailed analysis of the mechanism of such a combinatory activity of the mind.

At this point Edwards makes an important contribution to Western philosophical understanding of knowledge and the perception of beauty. According to Edwards, knowledge is made possible not only by the passive reception of sense ideas from the world but also by the mind's active ordering of those ideas so that they stand in the mind in certain relationships with each other as they are in the world. It is not that the mind imposes relations on the sense ideas. It is rather that the mind's ordering activity makes explicit in the mind's view the relations in which sense ideas are already ordered when they come into the mind.

So when sense or simple ideas come into the mind through sense organs and introspection, they come in as simple and distinct ideas with a readiness to be related to each other in certain ways. It is then that the mind holds together those ideas so that their relations are visible to it.

Edwards says, "'Tis certain that the human soul can have two ideas and more at the same moment in time; otherwise how could the mind compare ideas and judge between them?" (13: 247). The mind does not apprehend the relations among ideas by abstracting the commonalities among ideas, as in the epistemologies of the scholastics. In other words, for the scholastics, certain things in the world were thought to be the same or similar if they possessed certain identifical qualities considered apart from other differing qualities of particular things. Ideas for Locke and Edwards are simple ideas, however, and there is nothing to abstract from them. They have to be held together in their concreteness if their relations are to be apprehended by the mind.

Now, the big question is, How does the mind know how to order the simple ideas that are passively received through sensation? How does the mind respond correctly to the sense ideas by ordering them in the way the sense ideas themselves tend to be related to each other? Edwards says the mind acquires the habit or disposition to relate certain ideas together through its repeated experiences of seeing them together. He says, further, that the mind is innately (by birth) disposed to order sense ideas into the relationship of contiguity (being next to each other) in time and space, cause and effect, resemblance or harmony (6: 391).

The cause-and-effect relationships, the harmonious relationships, and temporal and spatially contiguous relationships into which the mind is innately disposed to order sense ideas are general in nature. The mind acquires by repeated experiences the more *specific* habit of ordering certain particular ideas into certain particular cause-and-effect and other relationships. For example, by repeated experiences of someone striking a match against a certain surface and the beginning of a flame, the general habit of ordering ideas into cause-and-effect relations becomes the more specific habit of relating the act of striking the match against a particular surface and the beginning of a flame as a cause and an effect. And every time someone strikes a match against a certain surface, the mind thinks of the beginning of a flame. By repeated experiences of apples as resembling each other, the general habit of ordering ideas into relations

of resemblance becomes the specific habit of thinking of apples together in resembling relations. The mind will habitually order apples together as a group.
By repeated experiences of John and Jane being contiguous, the general habit
of ordering ideas into contiguous relationships becomes the specific habit of
thinking of John whenever the mind sees Jane.

The particular disposition to order or habit of ordering ideas in the relationship of divine beauty, however, cannot be acquired by repeated experiences.
The habit of mind does not have the capacity to "recognize" the divine beauty
and order ideas into the divinely beautiful relationship. To put it in a different
way, the mind's general disposition or habit cannot be developed into a specific
disposition to order divinely beautifully related ideas into a divinely beautifully
related relationship. This is so because the finite mind cannot "recognize" the
divinely beautiful kind of resemblance or proportion to learn to begin to order
ideas in such a kind of resemblance and proportion.

According to Edwards, before the Fall of Adam and Eve, human beings
were endowed with this ability to know the divine beauty. But after the Fall, this
ability was lost, and cannot be restored by human effort (3: 380–88).

Now let us return to the question of what is involved in the mind's perception of beauty. The mind's perception of beauty, according to Edwards, is different from conceptual, notional, and abstract knowledge. Edwards calls aesthetic
(related to beauty) perception "a sense of the heart" or a sensible knowledge. It
is an immediate knowledge without involving rationation (logical or conceptual
thinking). Let us clearly list the elements that together make up the mind's
sensing of beauty (18: 452–66).

We'll start with the example of looking at a beautiful tree outside. (1) First,
there are the simple sense ideas, passively received by the mind, of the various
parts of the tree: the simple ideas of the greenness of its leaves, the simple ideas
of the branches, the simple idea of the trunk of the tree, and the simple idea of
the bright sun being reflected off the young leaves on the top of the tree. (2) The
mind by a habit instinctively and without argumentation holds together many
of the received simple ideas of the tree in its view and orders these simple ideas
in such a way that the beauty and proportion of these ideas together are visible
to the mind. (3) Because the habit of mind determines the direction of all the
powers of the self, the mind that has a habit of appreciating beauty will see this
combination of simple ideas and have what Edwards called "lively affections"
for the beauty of the tree. This mind's sensing of the tree's beauty is a heartfelt,
delight-filled sensation of the beauty of the tree. It is what Edwards famously
called "a sense of the heart."

Now, the word "sense" usually refers to one of the sense organs, such as
sight, touch, and so on, through which the sense data or the "simple ideas"

are passively received from the world. If the perception of beauty involves the ordering activity of the mind, how can the perception of beauty be called a sensation received through a sense? For Edwards the answer is that it is precisely through the mind's ordering activity itself that the beauty that is outside the mind can be "received" into the mind. Here passivity and activity coincide. And what is experienced by the mind can be called, as Edwards calls it, "a simple idea" (2: 205). The perception of beauty is like a "sensation" through which the mind receives into itself the objective fact of beauty as it is actually in the world—a fact that is not fabricated by the mind.

At this point, let it be recalled that the imagination is the mind's activity of ordering beautiful ideas in a beautiful way,[7] so that the beauty can be sensed by the mind and heart. Now this imagination of the mind is the function of the disposition or habit of the mind. And the disposition or habit of the mind, according to Edwards, is the direction of the entire human self—including his or her understanding and inclination with its affectional and voluntary expressions. So when a person is sensing beauty, the person's understanding is involved in receiving sense ideas, and his or her affections are also engaged as the mind delights in the perceived beauty. Thus, the entire person becomes, as it were, the sense organ for experiencing beauty or the very act of sensing beauty.

The beauty we have been referring to thus far in this section has been what Edwards called "secondary beauty": the ordinary harmony and proportion that we see in the world. According to Edwards, secondary beauty is an image or shadow of the true beauty, the beauty of God, as embodied in the life of Jesus Christ. Therefore, the true nature of a secondary beauty, the beauty of a flower, for example, is not perceived unless it is perceived as a beautiful image of God's beauty. Indeed, our knowledge of anything is not a true knowledge of that thing unless we perceive it in its relationship with God.

The Perception of the Divine Beauty

As we noted earlier, the human mind does not have the specific habit of mind or disposition to "recognize" the proportion of the divine beauty and, therefore, cannot order and hold in the mind's view the simple ideas of the "divine things" (that is, the ideas of the life of Jesus Christ) in such a way that the transcendent beauty of God can be sensed by the mind. Such a disposition or habit of mind cannot be acquired by the repeated experiences of God's beauty because the habit of mind does not have the capacity to order the ideas of the divine things in a divinely beautiful way even the first time.

How can fallen humans attain the ability to know and delight in God's beauty so that they may further the end for which God created the world and the human beings themselves? At this point, it should be noted, philosophy and theology become one and the same discipline. To know the true beauty (philosophy), in other words, is the same thing as to be redeemed (theology).

To redeem fallen human beings and put them back on track, so to speak, so that they can promote the end for which God created the world, the three persons of the Trinity launch the work of redemption. The Father orders this work, and the Son becomes incarnate and lives a particular kind of life, dies, and is resurrected, perfectly embodying in history the beauty of God's love. In other words, God's transcendent beauty becomes "visible" in time and space to those who have the capacity to see it. Jesus Christ functions as the converted people's "key," so to speak, in their apprehension of God's beauty as reflected and repeated in nature and history. But still fallen humanity does not have the disposition to order the sense ideas of Jesus Christ in a divinely beautiful order. So the third person of the Trinity, the Holy Spirit, according to Edwards, comes into the elect persons, dwells in them, and acts in them "after the manner of a natural principle of habit . . . and as it were settles the soul in a disposition to holy acts" (21: 197). In other words, the Holy Spirit works in and through the converted person's imagination so that his or her the mind can order the ideas of the divine things in a divinely beautiful way.

We must note at this point that for Edwards knowing and being are inseparably related. The essence of a converted person is not a substance, as in medieval theology, but a bundle of human dispositions governed by the indwelling divine disposition. In Edwards, the principle of disposition plays the role that substance played for a long time in Western theology. For Edwards, the ontologically abiding disposition (a tendency that has a reality even when it is not being exercised) constitutes the permanence of an entity. But a disposition is still to be exercised, and then what the disposition is disposed to would become a full actuality. For example, when a Christian's disposition to love his or her neighbor remains only as a disposition, his or her actually loving a neighbor is still "a real possibility." But when this disposition is exercised, his or her loving a neighbor becomes an actuality. Again, a converted person is the divine disposition functioning as a new human disposition. God's life is thereby "repeated" (Edwards's word) in a human life. Now when this person perceives and is delighted by the true beauty of God in Christ and loves his or her neighbor as Christ taught us to do, this person's Christian disposition is exercised, and he or she is for the first time fully actual as a human being. He or she is for the first time actually what God intended him or her to be. At the same time, God's inner-Trinitarian beauty is expressed and repeated through that Christian's action that is governed by the divine disposition.

Now the physical universe, according to Edwards, is created to be so many images of God's beauty. But because the physical universe cannot know or love, how can its being truly be actualized? My reading of Edwards is that the true actuality of the physical universe is achieved through the converted person's perception of it as an image of God's beauty. That is, when a converted person perceives and delights in the beauty of a tree, the full destiny of the tree is truly actualized. This happens in and through the person's converted knowledge and love of the tree as an image of God's beauty.[8]

When a converted person knows and loves God's beauty, and when the physical universe is known and delighted in by a converted person as an image of God's beauty, then God's knowledge and beauty within the Trinity are repeated and enlarged in time and history. The end for which God created the universe (which is to repeat God's inner glory in time and space) is thereby accomplished to that degree. Thus God's external life is to that degree actualized. In short, the human knowing and loving of God's beauty accomplishes the end for which God created the world (at least to that extent), and thereby participates in the project of self-communication and self-enlargement that God himself is engaged in during the time and space of history.

Now the beauty of God within himself which God intends to repeat in time and space is infinite. Therefore the process of God's repeating his glory in time and space will take an everlasting time and will never come to a point in time when it can be said to be finished. The process will continue in the new heaven and new earth for an everlasting time.

Concluding Observations

By way of a conclusion, I would like to lift up two distinctive aspects of Edwards's aesthetics. Edwards is sometimes referred to as a "mystic" in his conception of human knowledge of true beauty. Perhaps the nonconceptual and immediate (direct) character of the perception of the beauty of God, as Edwards conceives it, may create the impression that Edwards is a mystic. However, if the term *mysticism* is used to refer to the kind of knowing that takes the knower away from the concrete and mundane world of the senses and in which the knower is transported to a realm of reality beyond this world, then Edwards is definitely not a mystic. He might be called a mystic only in the sense that he believed in an "immediate" (not logical or conceptual) knowledge of God. For Edwards, knowing God occurs in this mundane world (though made possible by God alone), and the knower remains in this world.

In Edwards's conception of how we see the beauty of God, nothing concrete is left behind, and it happens in space and time. The sense ideas of the "divine things" from the life and teachings of Jesus Christ, or the sense ideas of the physical universe as the images of God's beauty, have to be in the mind's view, related to other ideas in a divinely beautiful manner. In his "Personal Narrative," Edwards describes how he perceived God's beauty in this way:

> After this my sense of divine things gradually increased, and became
> more and more lively, and had more of that inward sweetness. The
> appearance of everything was altered: there seems to be, as it were, a
> calm, sweet cast, or appearance of divine glory, in almost everything.
> God's excellency, his wisdom, his purity and love, seemed to appear
> in everything: in the sun, moon and stars: in the clouds, and blue
> sky; in the grass, flowers, trees; in the water, and all nature; which
> used to fix my mind. I often used to sit and view the moon, for a long
> time, and so in the day time, spend much time in viewing the clouds
> and sky, to behold the sweet glory in these things. (16: 793–94)

Edwards's perception of the beauty of God in nature did not transport him away from the concrete objects in nature in which God's beauty appeared. The sense ideas of the grass, flowers, and trees remained firmly in his mind, and the proportion of beauty he saw in these natural objects (appreciated as the images of the full manifestation and repetition of God's beauty in Jesus Christ) was the very material content of his perception of the beauty of God. Again, nothing is transcended, nor does any abstraction from these concrete things occur. The mind is not taken away from this world into another one, but instead sees the things of this world in a new way.

The end for which God created the world, for Edwards, is to repeat God's beauty in time and space. The converted person's knowing and loving God's beauty repeats God's inner Trinitarian life in time and space. Therefore, real history does matter to Edwards's God. History is the realm in which God's own life is being extended.

Secondly and finally, beauty for Jonathan Edwards is a dynamic, active reality that has practical, ethical, and political consequences. Beauty, according to Edwards, is always an expression of a disposition that is an active tendency that will certainly be exercised whenever a certain type of occasion arises. So Edwards says that the most important sign of the true reality of the conversion of a person's faith is beautiful Christian practice in action. This is so because a Christian is a person in whom the Holy Spirit is present and acts "after the manner of" a new disposition of that person, and the Holy Spirit is the spirit of the beauty of God. So the true virtue, or the truly good act, for Edwards, comes from the active disposition to act in a truly beautiful way—that is to say, to wish for all beings what is harmonious with the true beauty of God as embodied in Jesus Christ. Such a truly virtuous act of the beautiful disposition in a converted person, of course, participates in God's project of repeating God's internal beauty in time and space. Therefore, in the final analysis, the active nature of beauty is rooted in Edwards's dynamic conception of God as essentially the beautiful disposition to communicate beauty.

What are some of the implications of Edwards's aesthetics? First of all, at a time when theologians are not willing to talk about "experiencing" God, Edwards's conception of faith as an actual sensation or apprehension of the beauty of God as embodied in Christ may be helpful in thinking about how one knows God. Second, Edwards's idea of Christian practice as participation in God's activity of enlarging his internal beauty in time and space gives to history an ultimate significance. In the Christian perspective, there is no downgrading of the temporal world. This history is the realm where God's beauty (love) is enlarged and extended. Finally, Edwards's understanding of the physical universe as an image of God's beauty, and of the key role of human knowing and loving of the physical universe as an image of God's beauty, provides contemporary theology with a profound theological foundation for an ecologically responsible view of nature.

NOTES

1. For the most complete and authoritative discussion of Edwards's concept of beauty, see Roland A. Delattre, *Beauty and Sensibility in the Thought of Jonathan Edwards: An Essay in Aesthetics and Theological Ethics* (Eugene, OR: Wipf & Stock, 2006). For a fuller discussion of some of the points presented in this essay, see my *The Philosophical Theology of Jonathan Edwards* (Princeton, NJ: Princeton University Press, 2000). Cf. Jerome Stolnitz, "Beauty: Some Stages in the History of an Idea," *Journal of the History of Ideas* 38 (1961): 185–204.

2. *The Works of Jonathan Edwards*, vol. 6, *Scientific and Philosophical Writings*, ed. Wallace Anderson (New Haven: Yale University Press, 1980), p. 334. (Subsequent references to the Yale edition of Edwards's works are cited parenthetically in the text as the volume and page number.)

3. For a discussion of this point, see Lee, *Philosophical Theology*, 188–93.

4. Karl Barth uses a concept similar to "repetition" in his conception of God's self-revelation in Jesus Christ. See Eberhard Jungel, *The Doctrine of the Trinity: God's Being Is in Becoming* (Grand Rapids, MI: Eerdman, 1976), 100–101, n152.

5. For a discussion of Edwards's view of heaven, see the Yale edition of *The Works of Jonathan Edwards*, 8: 706–38.

6. See John Locke, *An Essay Concerning Human Understanding*, ed. by John W. Yolton (London: J. M. Dent and Sons, 1961), bk. 2, ch. 1; cf. Ernst Cassirer, *The Philosophy of the Enlightenment* (Boston: Beacon Press, 1960), 97–133; C. R. Morris, *Locke-Berkeley-Hume* (London: Oxford University Press, 1963).

7. In Edwards's actual usage, the term "imagination" has a rather narrow meaning. The imagination is, according to Edwards, "that power of the mind, whereby it can have a conception of idea of things of an external or outward nature (that is, of such sort of things as the objects of the outward senses), when those things are not present, and be not perceived by the senses" (2: 210–11) Our contention in this essay is that at work in Edwards's epistemology, there is an implicit but very forward-looking theory of the imagination as the mind's activity of ordering sense ideas in meaningful relations. Edwards's nomenclature, in other words, has not caught up with his theory. Cf. Donald F. Bond, "'Distrust' of the Imagination in English Neo-Classicism," Philological Quarterly 14 (1935), pp. 54–69.

8. The implications of this point for a theology of nature and ecology are discussed in my essay, "Jonathan Edwards in Nature," in *Philosophical Theology*, 243–68.

10

Alternative Viewpoint: Edwards and Beauty

Katalin G. Kállay

One has to take an enormous risk when talking about Edwards and aesthetics. What is at stake is whether this brave and beautiful gesture to address ultimate beauty can perform its own subject, whether by making this gesture one can indeed communicate and thus multiply beauty. It is a question of whether by doing so, one can, in Edwards's words, "actively promote the glory of God" and thereby participate in the work of re-creation.

I believe that it is exactly the focus on divine beauty and aesthetics that makes all the difference between the texts of Jonathan Edwards and other Puritan writers, as well as between Edwards and his eighteenth-century contemporaries. Teaching Edwards in the context of American literature at Károli Gáspár University of the Hungarian Reformed Church, I found that, both in parallel and in contrast with seventeenth-century Puritan writings centered around ethical norms and eighteenth-century texts influenced by thoughts of the Enlightenment, Edwards excels, and attracts students' attention because of his special emphasis on beauty. The gesture of communicating and multiplying beauty is characteristic of his works, so much so that it is not only the basic doctrines of Calvinist faith but the elemental attitude of literary analysis that can become clearer, more accessible, and more understandable through the thorough study of his texts and poetic images. He is a master of creating an aesthetic balance between the logical and the spiritual structure of his sermons. Therefore he becomes an excellent example of a man of letters for present-day students and scholars alike.

My response focuses on four topics. First, I reflect on the term "sense of the heart" with the help of the sense of *smell*. Second, on the basis of Edwards's hierarchy of beauty, I ask what is *necessarily aesthetic*. Third, on the basis of the shift from "substance" to "disposition," I ask about the *vulnerability* of beauty. Finally, on the basis of the tension between passivity and activity, I discuss the experience of *surprise*. I will refer to two sermons by Jonathan Edwards: "A Divine and Supernatural Light" (1734) and a thanksgiving sermon given on November 7 in the same year.[1]

Taste and Smell

In "A Divine and Supernatural Light," Edwards says:

> There is a twofold knowledge of good of which God has made the mind of man capable. The first, which is merely notional, as when a person only speculatively judges that anything is, which, by the agreement of mankind, is called good or excellent, *viz.*, that which is most to general advantage, and between which and a reward there is a suitableness—and the like. And the other is that which consists in the sense of the heart, as when the heart is sensible of pleasure and delight in the presence of the idea of it. In the former is exercised merely the speculative faculty, or the understanding, in distinction from the will or disposition of the soul. In the latter, the will, or inclination, or heart, is mainly concerned.

Edwards makes a distinction between "opinion" and "sense," illustrating it by the "difference between having a rational judgment that honey is sweet, and having a sense of its sweetness." But how can we imagine the human heart as a sense organ? Edwards's example uses the perception of taste. But when the specific sensation of the *heart* is at stake, one almost inevitably gets entangled in a confusion of the senses, very much like Bottom in Shakespeare's *A Midsummer Night's Dream*, when in a parody version of Paul's first epistle to the Corinthians (2:9), he says, "The eye of man hath not heard, the ear of man hath not seen, man's hand is not able to taste, his tongue to conceive, nor his heart to report what my dream was" (act 4, scene 1, lines 209–12). Interestingly enough, both Paul and Shakespeare leave out the olfactory perception from this list (though elsewhere it is of great significance for both authors). I suggest that the sense of smell, being a primary, we could even say primitive, and most of all, irresistible sensation can be brought into a meaningful parallel here with the sense of the heart. Smelling is irresistible: it is impossible to breathe without smelling. Furthermore, the center for smelling in the brain is closest to that of the unconscious and to the center that regulates falling asleep and being awake. It is hard to find words to describe a smell (except for good and bad), similarly to the way we cannot qualify a dream. When relating a dream, we might be able to reconstruct its elements, but the unique blend of impressions and the subtlety of its atmosphere can hardly be specified or measured. As for the heart, it is a fragile and delicate organ. One could say it is the only reliable natural chronometer, marking our entrance into and exit out of time, ticking like a time bomb, since everybody has a finite number of heartbeats. Is the "sense of the heart" irresistible and unavoidable? Can we imagine a "heart lid" which can be shut at will? Or is the sense of the heart instead like a smell that we can't help feeling? Do we have qualifying words for the heart's sensation? I think we must remain in the realm of similes, which can never cover the complexity of the whole experience.

A Hierarchy of Beauty

My second point concerns Edwards's hierarchy of beauty. As we have just read, there is a primary and complex beauty expressed by God, which is different from, but reflected by, the primary and complex beauty of the agreement, consent, or love between human beings. This in turn is reflected in the secondary and simple beauty of nature, as in the similarity between two apples. But is the harmony of complex relations by nature always an aesthetic principle? The answer, according to Professor Lee, Jonathan Edwards, and my own understanding, is no. There may be other, perhaps even harmonious complex relations that are not in harmony with the beauty of God, and therefore are considered to be deformities, expressions of dissent from God. Man might be carried away by his own creation. The beauty of Milton's Satan or the beauty of Machiavelli's argumentation might be brought up here as possible examples. Still, it is not the theme but the attitude that might decide the delicate question. So in both cases, one has to be careful to avoid hasty judgments. But is it then possible to imagine a work of art that is harmonious but expresses dissent from God? What can one say about the undeniably decadent or diabolic beauty expressed in texts of self-destruction? To what extent would Edwards consider works of art, for example, Shakespeare's tragedies, to be dangerous?

But those complex relations that are *in* harmony with the divine beauty are necessarily aesthetic. This can be best observed in the beauty of unselfish

gestures, when human beings wholeheartedly "participate in the work of con-
tinuous creation" or "actively promote the glory of God."

At this point, I would like to call attention to another, equally exciting question of aesthetics that relates to the teaching and studying of literature. The
idea of something (a gesture, a work of art, a text) being necessarily aesthetic
implies a specific certainty in aesthetic quality. In the field of literary analysis,
the notion of quality has long been regarded as completely relative. As John J.
Joughin and Simon Malpas point out in their introduction to *The New Aestheticism,* "The rise of critical theory in disciplines across the humanities during
the 1980s and 1990s has all but swept aesthetics from the map. . . . Theoretical
criticism is in continual danger . . . of throwing out the aesthetic baby with the
humanist bathwater."[2] It is precisely the "aesthetic baby" that the study of Edwards's text helps us to recognize. Being reassured in our sense of beauty, we
might turn to other literary texts with a new openness. This gesture is in line
with the aims of "new aestheticism." Without questioning the importance of
"the unmasking of art's relation to ideology, historical and political context,
self-identification, gender and colonialism," Joughin and Malpas's book offers a
serious shift in critical disposition: "Recognizing the specificity of the aesthetic
requires a significant shift in awareness of the possible modes and practices of
critical enquiry, as well as a reconfiguration of the place of criticism in relation
to philosophy, politics and culture."[3] Thus Edwards's concept of beauty may be
decisively significant in present-day aesthetic discourse.

The Vulnerability of Beauty

The thanksgiving sermon I mentioned earlier juxtaposes the heavenly and the
earthly realms. Edwards's doctrine is that "the work of the saints in heaven
consists in praising God." Whereas here on earth saints labor "in the weari-
some heat of the sun," in heaven they find perfect rest. Life there is full of
action—but without weariness, unpleasantness, self-denial, worries, or grief.
Saints are engaged in blessed employment. The sermon emphasizes the dynamism of praise: though they are at perfect rest, the saints in heaven are
exceedingly active, and their hearts become flames of love. I found a parallel
here with the dynamics of the word *disposition,* which, in Edwards's use, is
the nature or temperament of the soul that determines one's choices, feelings
and thinking. Professor Lee points out the significance for Edwards of the fact
that creation is not a matter of substance but disposition: "In Edwards, the
principle of disposition plays the role that substance played for a long time in
Western theology."

I suggest that the shift from substance to disposition is a shift from some-thing static to something dynamic, a shift from the *what* to the *how*. This shift seems to be more of a gesture than a statement. Therefore it may be more vul-nerable, more exposed to attack or misinterpretation. Gestures are extremely difficult to interpret, and their "truth" can be hardly verified; consequently they are more difficult to defend. According to Professor Lee, "The answer to the question 'Why creation?' lies in Edwards's dynamic concept of God as the eter-nal disposition . . . to communicate beauty." This beauty is embodied in Christ. Since in Christ our human vulnerability is also embodied, the beauty seems to be entirely exposed to danger. God seems to make himself and his beauty vul-nerable by putting it in a divinely human person, Christ, who can be and was, in fact, attacked. God has also made beauty vulnerable by giving his human subjects freedom to destroy that beauty in themselves. The interaction of God's disposition with the human disposition in the converted person is also a very delicate and intimate encounter, based on complete and mutual trust—again, something that might be seen as vulnerable. Beside the ever-flowing emanation of divine beauty, can we sense a touch, a flavor, a sign of vulnerability—which, by the way, might also strengthen that beauty with the beauty of humility?

Surprise

Last but not least, I would like to return to the idea of dynamism in the com-munication of divine beauty, now from the point of view of the tension between the passive and the active human disposition—both of which are necessary and both of which are oriented toward the perception of beauty. Professor Lee describes the case when passivity and activity coincide: "For Edwards . . . it is precisely through the mind's ordering activity itself that the beauty that is out-side the mind can be 'received' into the mind." I think this juxtaposition of activity and passivity can be found in the experience of *surprise*. A surprise is something one cannot count on, cannot be prepared for, cannot guarantee, and cannot avoid. It comes like a sudden scent, odor, or dream: we can't help being surprised. In this sense, passivity is very much a part of being surprised. But the surprise is always an impetus as well: a private, personal and particular momentum that demands immediate response, causing spiritual activity and not passivity.

In the context of teaching literature, for example, texts can constantly be-come surprises, demanding an immediate personal response. Without personal involvement and participation, literary analyses become mechanical, boring, or insignificant. The discussion of Edwards's sermons is always a special occasion in my courses because year after year, Bishop István Szabó comes to my classes to talk about literature and theology, so, surprisingly, the students may come to terms with questions of their own religion (issues like predestination, innate depravity, and salvation only by grace) through studying and recognizing the beauty of Edwards's text.[4] This is indeed a pleasant surprise.

There is, of course, a great risk in welcoming surprises: their unpredictability implies that they may be unpleasant as well. In any case, our reactions are intense and imply spiritual activity. It seems to me that the experience of surprise is part of the Edwardsian perception of beauty. In this way the sudden and irresistible impressions, the necessarily aesthetic unselfish gestures as well as the acknowledgment and appreciation of the upheld vulnerability might all contribute to the ever-pulsating dynamism of the sense of the heart.

NOTES

1. Jonathan Edwards, "Praise, One of the Chief Employments in Heaven," in *The Works of President Edwards, in Ten Volumes*, vol. 8, ed. Sereno E. Dwight (New York, 1829–30), 305–19.

2. John J. Joughin and Simon Malpas, eds., *The New Aestheticism* (Manchester, UK: Manchester University Press, 2003), 1.

3. Ibid., 3, 17.

4. Bishop István Szabó of the Dunamellék District in the Reformed Church of Hungary. He is also a professor of systematic theology at the Reformed Theological Academy, Pápa, Hungary. Professor Szabó has done serious research on the works of Edwards and gives a guest lecture in my course once a year.

II

The Literary Life of Jonathan Edwards

Wilson H. Kimnach

The literary biography of Jonathan Edwards shows him living a frontier life on the western edge of the culture and society from which he derived inspiration. His interests as an aspiring author ranged from natural science to philosophical theology, but it was his life in the church that gave him the essential theater in which he developed his thought and expression. His notebooks and published writings chart the evolution of his career through three major phases as he strove to find an appropriate venue for his philosophical and literary talents.

About twenty-five years ago, Patricia Tracy argued in her brilliant biography, *Jonathan Edwards, Pastor,* that the essential fact of Edwards's pastoral life was that he lived in a time of transition. In one of the early reviews of her book, the historian Edmund S. Morgan gave the book generous praise, but in conclusion qualified its seminal thesis by observing that historians always see antebellum New England as undergoing such radical change, or declension, whatever the particular period under consideration.[1] Both were correct, of course, for we do live in a dynamic system—if system it be—and one of the most significant tests of history is of our perception of the advancing edge of change, especially if we profess to be in some sense leaders.

Jonathan Edwards was a New England Protestant leader who flourished, in the long perspective of history, just halfway between the two peaks of New England Protestant radicalism, Puritanism and Unitarianism. He lived in the Age of the Enlightenment, but before the open questioning of English hegemony in North America and well before Thomas Paine's *Age of Reason*. He lived when the cultural and political leadership of New England was still tenuously clerical and the most radical political activity tended to be reactionary, as when a few Connecticut ministers shocked the public by announcing their desire to join the Church of England and thus assume an ecclesiastical and cultural stance in opposition to the whole history of the Puritan revolution. Inasmuch as two of these rebels were college instructors of Edwards, we might well suspect that he was early made keenly aware of the cultural instability of the society in which he lived.

Even as a child, Jonathan Edwards must have been aware of living on the edge, for his home in East Windsor, Connecticut, was then near the western frontier of the New England settlements. Both his parents were likewise from the Connecticut River Valley, where a sense of danger from intermittent battles with the French and Indians sharpened the atmosphere. His Father, the Reverend Timothy Edwards, had returned from his years at Harvard with a small library of books, many of which reflected his taste for the conservative Puritanism of the Mathers. His mother, Esther, on the other hand, was the daughter of the Reverend Solomon Stoddard of Northampton, one of the more radical opponents of the Mathers and a friend of liberal reformers of Harvard such as Benjamin Colman, Nathanael Appleton, and Benjamin Wadsworth. Although his mother was a spiritual leader among the local ladies, there is no record of theological debates between Edwards's parents. It is revealing of the literary tenor of his childhood home that an elder sister, Esther, penned a theological joke, once attributed to Edwards himself, regarding the nature of the soul.[2] The "soul paper" mocks the theory of the soul's being material, but beyond that it seems implicitly to mock the entire enterprise of esoteric theological speculation. That a bright young minister's daughter should feel comfortable in penning such a piece and making it known to the family—where it was carefully preserved—suggests a level of appreciation for wit and even irreverence not to be expected in pious eighteenth-century clerical families. But then, the Edwards family may have been more than usually prone to edginess.

Youthful Aspiration

As the only son among ten sisters, Jonathan was the outrider of family aspiration, a privilege and a responsibility. His father was widely respected as a teacher who prepared the sons of the local elite for college, and he clearly devoted extra care to the preparation of his own son. Thus Jonathan was able to enter the new Yale College at the tender age of twelve (though that was not as remarkable then as it would be today).³ Trained in the classics and a good Latinist, the young Edwards rose to be an outstanding college student and served as valedictorian of his class, but no sooner had he completed his formal education than he laid plans for success in a much larger literary theater. Shorthand notes he made in the mid-1720s indicate an ambition even greater than that of the young Benjamin Franklin. It appears that Edwards, product of a country village, did not look to Franklin's Boston but beyond to London as the literary center he wished to impress with his writing; however, as he jotted on the cover of his earliest notebook, "Before I venture to publish in London, to make some experiment in my own country; to play at small games first, that I may gain some experience in writing."⁴ Significantly, the notebook on which he made his memorandum was devoted to "natural philosophy," not theology, and it was in the literature of science that Jonathan Edwards was first inclined to make his mark. Living in the age of Locke and Newton, whose thought he was able to explore in the new Dummer collection of books in the college library, Edwards was inspired to attempt certain demonstrations in print that would "put every man clean out of conceit with his imagination."⁵ In other words, in this pre-Romantic era when the "imagination" was identified with popular misconceptions and fantasy, Edwards conceived of himself as the medium of a surprising new awareness, as Newton had been when he analyzed the function of light or identified the power of gravitation. The natural philosopher would introduce his readers to a new reality—such as that the true substance of the world is spiritual, whereas matter is mere shadow—that would fly in the face of conventional reality and yet could be established as a "higher" or more rational reality through conclusive demonstration.

While Edwards's first efforts were thus directed to what we would now call the "natural sciences," and his earliest work to be submitted for publication reported observations of the flying spider, his speculation soon turned to the mental world. An "idealist" heavily influenced by Cambridge Platonists, such as Henry More, to believe that the world must be perceived in order to exist, Edwards began compiling a second notebook in anticipation of a treatise on the mind, or "The Natural History of the Mental World," as he tentatively entitled it. This treatise was to complement one on the natural (or external) world of natural philosophy, although his notes indicate that he increasingly considered the internal mental world to be "in many respects the most important."⁶ Indeed, he made entries in his notebook on natural philosophy only until 1732, but continued to return to his notebook on the mind until 1756 or 1757. However, the scientific treatises, which at first were conceived as comprising a complete system of natural philosophy, were never written, despite his keen interest and his extensive notebook speculations. Apparently he felt that his mathematical training was inadequate to what was in fact theoretical physics, and even in the area of "mental philosophy," or psychology, he was painfully aware of his situation: "The world will expect more modesty because of my circumstances—in America, young, etc. . . . Mankind are by nature proud and exceeding envious, and ever jealous of such upstarts; and it exceedingly irritates and affronts 'em to see 'em appear in print."[7] Whether the would-be author of scientific masterpieces was stymied by self-doubt or realistic caution, it was the first of a series of critical setbacks he would suffer just as major phases of his literary life were seemingly on the verge of fulfillment.

Whether or not he would ever have made a great scientist, Edwards must not have felt his time was wasted in compiling his scientific notebooks, for he confidently believed that all learning culminates in theology, and thus any deep understanding of the nature of things is in a real sense divinity. Of his various scientific notes, those he kept on the mind are most obviously related to his later writing, particularly the definitions of certain key words, such as *excellency* and *the will*. Such terms, developed through related entries in Edwards's notebook on the mind, provided an essential vocabulary for many later sermons and treatises. Perhaps as important as the invention of such verbal resources, however, was the habit of disciplined observation and inductive speculation that Edwards acquired during his early immersion in the literature of science.

His Call to the Church

Seemingly on the edge of a scientific or academic career, Edwards suddenly turned to the church, the default profession for eighteenth-century English intellectuals, whether in England or North America. Of course, he came from a clerical family, and his grandfather the Reverend Solomon Stoddard had achieved eminence as a religious and political leader in the Connecticut River Valley. After trial pulpits in New York and Connecticut, as well as a stint as a Yale College tutor, Edwards was appointed Stoddard's colleague, and after two years he became the sole occupant of the Northampton pulpit upon Stoddard's death. His literary life mirrored his professional life in that he now, in 1730, shifted the focus of his writing to the subject of religion. Edwards composed two early treatises, on the Trinity and faith, though neither was published in his lifetime. His real literary work became mastery of the sermon.

As we observe Edwards settling into the ministerial career for which he is known, it may be helpful to take a moment to consider his relation to the contemporary literary world. His early exposure to scientific and philosophical writings at Yale College was an opportunity he eagerly seized upon, but after making a lifelong commitment to the defense of seventeenth-century Reformed theology, one might anticipate that his relation to the transatlantic literary community would become tangential at best. However, it seems that Edwards accepted the Calvinist tradition primarily as a theological matrix: not an orthodoxy to rest uncritically within but rather a foundation on which he could build in such dimensions and at such times as he saw fit. He had some basic sources, such as Peter van Mastricht's *Theoretico-Practica Theologia* (1699) and Francis Turretin's *Institutio Theologicae Elencticae* (1688), to serve as theological authorities on the foundational structure, and he owned or had access to many additional texts of Reformed theology; however, he constantly pursued the latest books on the controversies of his own day, such as the duel between Arminians and Calvinists, the onslaught of deism and secular rationalism, and the tensions between pietism and moralism. But beyond all those concerns Edwards clearly hankered for knowledge of the learned world in general, nor was he oblivious to the latest trends in education and polite letters. He started to keep an inventory of his books in college, but this list, which he named his "Catalogue," soon became more of a wish list than a list of possessions. In it one sees the intense questing of the virtual autodidact, as he notes every reference he can find to a wide variety of the best books and journals. Edwards also cultivated friendships with other ministers who lived nearer urban centers on both sides of the Atlantic and thus were able to keep him in touch with the latest learning; indeed, some of his Scottish friends regularly sent him packages of books. In the final analysis, Edwards's appetite for reading was almost unlimited, for he believed in reading the writings of his enemies as well as those of his friends, the bad books as well as the good ones.

Among the kinds of books one might not expect Edwards to be consulting in a serious way is *The Ladies Library*, first published by Richard Steele in 1714. Perhaps growing up in a household with ten bright sisters and a brilliant mother, Edwards was ready to consider women's culture seriously, or perhaps this is an example of the provincial's deference to advice from the cosmopolitan world. In any event, one of his earliest references to a work of polite literature is to a set of six rules for effective argument published in *The Ladies Library*.[8] Jotted on the cover of his notebook on "Natural Philosophy" along with the two other notes quoted above, this reference cautions him to consider the reader's limitations and to argue as recommended by the rules in *The Ladies Library*, rules that offer shrewd advice on first mastering one's own thought in order to write effective argument. Indeed, like most of the rest of the advice offered in the three portly octavo volumes of *The Ladies Library*, the material is neither simplistic nor aimed at callow minds, and most of it was selected from the pages of great English divines. The editor notes in passing that, though many of the pieces included are clearly addressed to men, "the Women always understood too; there being but few or no Virtues or Vices which do not alike concern them both."⁹ Edwards not only took advice from the work in his youth but kept the work by him throughout his life. In fact, according to the account book in which he kept a record of books he loaned or borrowed, volumes from *The Ladies Library* are among those he loaned most frequently to friends and colleagues, women and men, laypersons and fellow clerics. The detailed conduct guide or moral Baedeker that he eschewed in his sermons is embodied handily in this secular work, and that was probably as Edwards thought it should be.

Not only did Edwards enjoy advice offered by the great English journalist Richard Steele, he also approved the novels of Samuel Richardson, perhaps for himself as well as for his wife and grown children. Cotton Mather went to his grave inveighing against time wasted in reading novels, the new cultural diversion of the literate, but Edwards clearly liked Richardson's sentimental novels, and he probably recognized in Richardson the kindred spirit of a Christian with a distinctly pietistic sensibility.¹⁰ Edwards possessed copies of both *Pamela* and *Clarissa*, epistolary novels in which the narrative voice dramatizes a divided mind struggling with pernicious social conventions and personal temptation while seeking love and fulfillment. These dramatizations, which he probably read in the 1750s, must have reminded Edwards of his own studies of Phebe Bartlett and Abigail Hutchinson in *A Faithful Narrative* (1737), and perhaps even of his later presentation of Sarah Edwards in *Some Thoughts Concerning the Revival* (1742). However restricted his focus, when compared with the life studies of the most widely praised novelist of his age, Edwards must have felt artistic kinship as he read Richardson's close observations of the workings of the human heart. Both authors had advanced far beyond most of their eighteenth-century peers in deconstructing the relation between reason and affection in the most poignant of life's experiences, and if their doctrines differed at all, their sense of the theater of experience was clearly shared.

The Sermon

As Edwards turned, then, to what would become his particular genre of expression, it was not a choice made in ignorance of alternative modes of expression. He was familiar with the literary cutting edge of his day, whether in journalism, science, history, philosophy, or theology. Between 1720, when he composed his earliest extant sermon, and the fall of 1726, when he joined his grandfather Stoddard in the Northampton church, Edwards perfected a basic sermon form while preaching for brief periods in various pulpits. His sermon is the traditional

Puritan sermon taught him by his father, but Edwards simplified its structure so that the basic divisions of text, doctrine, and application have only a few numbered subdivisions each, whereas his father's sermons comprised as many as sixty or more numbered heads. What Edwards accomplished by this simplification was to move from the seventeenth-century argumentative form, in which the sermon note-taker was given a maximum of "points" to weigh in the argument, to a more open structure that permitted more development of each point and thus more power of specification, illustration, and affective appeal. Perhaps the study of argumentation in *The Ladies Library* had convinced Edwards that a series of logically connected points does not make an argument.

In any case, the early sermons Edwards composed during the years before Northampton reflect the growth of his personal understanding of the essential heart of religion rather than the doctrinal formulae of John Calvin or any other such authority. The next few years show Edwards's rapid intellectual growth as he composes longer and more complicated sermons. His emphasis is still on the positive dimension of faith, but the sermons present more psychological nuance, such as differentiating between truth and reality as degrees of awareness, defining religion as an experience, and mediating between the divine and a decorum of rationality. These early sermons exemplify Edwards's personal literary taste and style, and they articulate many terms and concepts that he would build on throughout his career. If anything, Edwards emerges in these sermons as a Christian "flower child," a devotee of the good and the beautiful that can be realized only through the abandonment of the self and entire submission to the divine. It is the old way of perfection recognized by medieval monks and saints.

But in 1726 Edwards made his first move westward as he became an assistant to his grandfather, the redoubtable Solomon Stoddard of Northampton. There, for two years, he sat under one of the greatest Connecticut Valley preachers in the tradition of Thomas Hooker. Stoddard was not only a superb writer of sermons and treatises, he was a critic of preaching who published sermons on homiletics and, characteristically, had little patience with those who were timid about invoking a God of terrible power. Indeed, Stoddard was known as an awakening preacher who fully appreciated that most people are more readily motivated by fear than by love or hope. "The Pretense that they make . . . is, that they are afraid there is no Hope for them . . . but the true Reason is not that they want Hope, but they want Fears," Stoddard declared.[11] He insisted that good preachers must be "Sons of Thunder" and that their congregations "need to be terrified and have the arrows of the Almighty in them that they may be Converted."[12] Edwards, scholarly, sentimental, and, more than that, skinny and possessing only a small speaking voice, must have been mortified; however, being Edwards he soon took up the art of hellfire homiletics.

He made rapid progress in the two years that he assisted Stoddard, for he preached half of each sabbath service and gave the weekly lecture—all under Stoddard's critical eye. Apparently he pleased his grandfather with his words, if not with his voice and gesture, and contemporary laypersons who knew the eighteenth-century pulpit said Edwards was a "deep preacher." But hardly had he begun to master a more minatory technique when his grandfather died, leaving him, at the age of twenty-five, with sole charge of one of the most important pulpits outside of Boston. Moreover, Stoddard had grumbled in his last days that Northampton had not had a good "harvest" (awakening) in twenty years, throwing down the gauntlet before his aspiring grandson.

Perhaps the first thing that struck Edwards after Stoddard's death was just how taxing the literary production of a full-time minister could be. He had re-preached all the sermons that he had written in his earlier brief pastorates, and now he must produce new ones, two for the sabbath service and one for the lecture each week. Moreover, he now found himself at the head of a community, and thus he had to preach, like all settled pastors, a full cycle of sermons addressing all the needs and occasions of his parish. Edwards had always labored over expression in his sermons, but his efforts were now more complicated as he attempted to extract the maximum use from every page of sermon material. Often he took one of his early efforts and revised the language, improving awkward expressions and eliminating what he now took to be unsuitable colloquialisms so that the sermon would sound like his current preaching. However, he sometimes saw a new way of handling the whole subject and would rewrite sections of a sermon until it was thoroughly "recast," virtually a new sermon despite having the original identifying text and statement of doctrine. In other cases he would literally cut out whole sections of an old sermon to be ingested in a new sermon, a kind of literary cannibalism in which the old sermon was destroyed as its best parts were made part of a new sermon. Occasionally, he even carried two sermons into the pulpit and preached part of each, perhaps the text and doctrine of one with the application of the other, preserving the original sermon manuscripts intact while creating a new, evanescent oral sermon. Thus Edwards's homiletical art was industrialized for greater efficiency, though he did not take preaching lightly and continued to labor over the minutiae of expression in every sermon.

From week to week, Edwards strove to touch his congregation, not only through application of the rhetorical lash but philosophically as well. While there was little immediate result, his reputation as a remarkable preacher apparently reached Boston, and the ministerial association invited him to preach before them at a public lecture. Edwards began what would be his invariable practice (except for some very specific occasional performances) of selecting a sermon he had preached to his congregation and revising it, in this case by sharpening its polemical edge. The result was "God Glorified in the Work of Redemption, by the Greatness of Man's Dependence upon Him in the Whole of It," preached in July 1731. The ministers appreciated his homiletical skill and perhaps his courage, though a good many may not have agreed with the sermon's emphasis. In any event they had it published, and Edwards appeared at last in print—not as a shocking scientist but as an aggressive Calvinist (or theological conservative) confronting the enlightened metropolis of New England. West had marched east and declared itself quite happy to be without the latest imported "improvements": the gesture was archetypal, but it was also essentially Edwards.

Events in Northampton unfolded apace, and in just a little over three years Edwards's awakening efforts yielded a harvest that might have pleased Stoddard himself. Edwards reported it to the only minister in Boston who seemed to be on good terms with everyone, including ministers in London, the Reverend Benjamin Colman. Colman communicated the news to friends in England, Isaac Watts and John Guyse, and before long Edwards's narrative of the Connecticut Valley awakenings, including those of Abigail Hutchinson and Phebe Bartlett, was internationally known. Edwards had again realized an early dream, of making a mark in London, though the genre of A Faithful Narrative (1737) was not exactly the kind of scientific reportage he had originally envisioned. Nevertheless, it involved precise observation and drew international attention to Edwards's current locus of intellectual activity, pastoral preaching. Indeed, the emphasis on the impact of his preaching in the narrative doubtless occasioned the publication of his Discourses on Various Important Subjects in 1738, the only collection of sermons Edwards was ever to publish.

This modest volume of five "discourses" included his first published treatise, Justification by Faith Alone, a sermon he had extensively reworked and hugely enlarged for print. If such an exploitation of the memorial volume of sermons might seem high-handed, Edwards's preface is even more provocative from a strictly literary standpoint. Couched in the ritual humility of the eighteenth century, the language of the preface is nevertheless defiant. Not only does Edwards defend his opposition to the Arminian drift of his contemporaries—a posture sustained from his Quaestio for the master's degree (1723) through "God Glorified"—but he explicitly differentiates himself as a preacher from the "modish" and "polite" preachers of his day. Edwards invokes traditional Puritan preaching's "plain style" and the concomitant Ramistic analytical method as his chosen medium, in contradistinction to the easy generalities and elegant fluency of the Tillotsonian moralists. Positively, he asserts the necessity for intellectual rigor in approaching Scripture, in particular, and religion in general. All in all, the brief preface is the most explicit public statement Edwards ever made assessing his preaching and its relation to his pastoral role in the church.

The World of Print

If the publications attending the awakenings of the 1730s made Edwards known to the world as a preacher, they also serve in retrospect to mark the culmination of his career as a pastoral preacher. Of course, he preached another decade in Northampton and most of a decade in Stockbridge, and the fact that he would not preach "Sinners in the Hands of an Angry God" until 1741 might seem to belie this assertion; however, it is evident that he was becoming "homiletically restive" by the end of the 1730s. In 1738 and 1739 he preached serial sermons, the most notable of which is the thirty-sermon series later printed as *A History of the Work of Redemption*. While these series were masterful, they interrupted the necessary cycle of pastoral preaching, and they became increasingly obvious as treatises smuggled into the pulpit, pieces wherein Edwards preached to the town but wrote for the world. The world was an exciting place for writers during the mid-eighteenth century, for in England and even in North America printing presses were rapidly increasing in number and thus influence.

During the early 1740s the Great Awakening might have been seen as a resuscitation of old-fashioned preaching, and certainly a number of revivalists became noted for their oral performances, but the leader, the Reverend George Whitefield of England, was nothing loath to publish in print, and he kept his publisher Benjamin Franklin very busy. While Edwards participated in the revivals of the 1740s, and may have had "Sinners" printed himself to advertise his continued involvement, his role increasingly became that of interpreter and critic. *The Distinguishing Marks of a Work of the Spirit of God* (1741), *Some Thoughts Concerning the Present Revival of Religion in New England* (1742), and *A Treatise Concerning Religious Affections* (1746), two of which were preached at least in part, delineate Edwards's evolving role as a leader in the world beyond his local parish through the medium of print.

Meanwhile, in the Northampton pulpit Edwards began outlining his sermons more and more, despite the fact that he was never able to preach without notes and used fully written-out sermon manuscripts to the end of his life when the occasion was significant. Of course, he also had a number of disputes with his people during the 1740s, ranging from family government to their traditional communion practice, but it seems likely that the final rupture between Edwards and his people in 1750 resulted from a sense—perhaps on both sides—that his work in the pastoral ministry was somehow less satisfying than it once had been. At the end of the Great Awakening Edwards had done it all, indeed, better than most, and he had no great embarrassments to cover up or forget. Once again, however, as Edwards had seemed on the verge of a great achievement, this time as a leading evangelical pastor, he turned aside.

When Edwards chose his final role as missionary to Native Americans and pastor to a wild west outpost at Stockbridge, he had rejected opportunities in a number of churches in the colonies, from Connecticut to Virginia, and even a chance to go to Scotland. As his involvement with the international learned community, or the "republic of letters," deepened through correspondence, and as his notebooks grew ever richer and subtler in speculation, Edwards had once again moved west, ever farther from London. If he had moved to the edge of civilization to distance himself from it, Edwards nevertheless continued to pursue the cutting edge of learning through every possible means during the Stockbridge years. And despite working conscientiously to instruct and defend his Native American flock, and preaching to the general satisfaction of his tiny English congregation, it is clear that it was his literary career that evolved most significantly in Stockbridge. Here, he was not distracted by the high pastoral and ecclesiastical demands of Northampton, and he turned increasingly to a venue that he had begun to court during his last years in Northampton, the wide world of print.

Thus Jonathan Edwards returned in the final phase of his life to the dream he had entertained as a youth, for he had long since qualified to play at great games in London. Only three years after his arrival in Stockbridge, the work for which he has been most celebrated, *Freedom of the Will*, issued from the press. Soon he would have another treatise, *Original Sin*, ready for the press, although his sudden death made its publication posthumous. But even more captivating to his mind than these polemic refutations of the new liberalism was his vision of a new theology, "a body of divinity in an entire new method."[13] Apparent pieces of it, his dissertations, *Concerning the End for which God Created the World* and *The Nature of True Virtue*, were also completed in Stockbridge. The great work would synthesize his most imaginative speculations in physics, metaphysics, typology, and theology in a compelling historical narrative: a work that would bring a new reality as well as new doctrinal formulations to its readers. Although Edwards had achieved great stature as a preacher, he confided to the trustees of the college at Princeton in one of his last letters, "So far as I myself am able to judge of what talents I have, for benefiting my fellow creatures by word, I think I can write better than I can speak."[14] Whether in the homiletical literature of the pulpit or in forms suitable only for the medium of print, Jonathan Edwards defined himself by the written word, and those words remain in all their magical power long after the small voice was stilled.

Considering his remarkable literary career as a whole, it is evident that Edwards embodied many traits associated with American civilization in any period. Although he took his cultural bearings from England and Europe, he lived on the frontier, literally and culturally, and he kept moving west. Always open to new opportunities in his life and career, he responded to the rapid expansion of English and colonial printing presses. He might live in the backwoods, but his sense of an international community of print communication often seems to have conditioned his ostensibly local actions. Moreover, his conservative theological allegiance did not constrain his free spirit, and he was eminently capable of radical action, whether in confronting the Boston clergy with views they wished to dismiss, censuring the practices of the church his grandfather Stoddard had erected, or packing off his large and vulnerable family to an Indian mission station. Finally, he was profoundly creative in adapting a European theology to his new world, "humanizing" religion by stressing subjective perception and individual experience as the touchstones of efficacious doctrine.

NOTES

1. *The New York Times Book Review,* July 13, 1980, 13, 38.

2. The text of the paper is printed in the Yale edition of *The Works of Jonathan Edwards* [hereafter, *WJE*], 6: 405–6. Edwards's sister Esther was first identified as the author by Kenneth P. Minkema in "The Authorship of 'The Soul,'" *Yale University Library Gazette* 65 (Oct. 1990): 26–32.

3. Rather than attending a formal high school, college-bound students of Edwards's day were tutored, often by ministers such as the Reverend Timothy Edwards, and sent on whenever the tutor thought them ready. While the average age of college matriculation may have been about fifteen, other students, including Edwards's disciple Joseph Bellamy and his nemesis Charles Chauncy, also entered at about the age of twelve.

4. *WJE* 6: 194.

5. "Of the Prejudices of Imagination," in *WJE* 6: 198.

6. "The Mind," in *WJE* 6: 387.

7. *WJE* 6: 193.

8. The rules have been reproduced in the context of Edwards's notes on writing and style in *WJE* 10: 182–84.

9. *The Ladies Library,* published by Mr. Steele (3 vols., London, 1714), 3: 362.

10. Richardson's distinctive sensibility and his Christian advocacy are ably characterized by John A. Dussinger in "Conscience and the Pattern of Christian Perfection in *Clarissa,*" *PMLA* 81 (1966): 236–45.

11. Solomon Stoddard, *The Benefit of the Gospel, to those that are Wounded in Spirit* (Boston, 1713), 181.

12. Solomon Stoddard, *The Defects of Preachers Reproved* (Boston, 1724), 14.

13. Letter to the trustees of the College of New Jersey, October 19, 1757, in *WJE* 16: 727.

14. *WJE* 16: 729.

12

Alternative Viewpoint: The Literary Life of Jonathan Edwards

Anna Svetlikova

Professor Kimnach has given us an overview of Jonathan Edwards's literary career, tracing Edwards's writing interests from his youthful ventures in science and philosophy, through the climactic years of his preaching ministry, to what he revealingly calls the "dissipation of the sermon form" and Edwards's gradual shift to another medium of literary expression: the treatise. Working from the perspective of a literary historian, Professor Kimnach connects Edwards's writings to the events of his life, his personal characteristics, and the broader context of New England culture in the first half of the eighteenth century. Professor Kinmach thereby reminds us that a literary life involves not only writing but also reading, and the connections between output and input. He also ties together the seemingly loose ends of Edwards's scientific, philosophical, homiletic, and theological writings and points out their interdependence. We are invited to reconsider the very categorization of Edwards's written works, for we see that despite their variety, they all emerge from, and ultimately aim at, "a real sense of divinity."

We might have wished to hear more of the unique features of Edwards's sermons to Native Americans in Stockbridge, or the plain style of his Puritan predecessors, or the representations of Edwards and Edwardsianism in American literature of later years—such as Robert Lowell's famous poems on Jonathan Edwards, or nineteenth-century women's fiction that draws directly on Edwardsian ideas. But for whatever had to remain unsaid because of space and time, we were left with worthy compensation: the irresistible reference to the young Jonathan Edwards as an eighteenth-century "Christian 'flower child.'"

Before I move on to a more general reflection on approaching Edwards from a literary perspective, I would like to pursue briefly Kimnach's provocative comparison of Jonathan Edwards and Samuel Richardson, the author whose works, such as *Pamela* and *Clarissa*, helped to rescue the moral reputation of the novel, then regarded as a medium of dubious entertainment and a likely source of moral and social disorder. Kimnach asserts the basic affinity of Edwards's and Richardson's interest in "deconstructing the relation between reason and affection" and their "artistic kinship." Kimnach's literary historical insights invite a number of theoretical responses. Feminist or deconstructivist (such as follow the emphases of the French philosopher Jacques Derrida) readings of course offer themselves readily. Or the juxtaposition of Edwards and Richardson might lead us to the question of fiction and truth in literature: we accept Richardson's novels as "fiction" and Edwards's accounts as "true," but can the distinction really be made so facilely? For Phebe Bartlet and Abigail Hutchinson do not speak for themselves; their voices come to us through Edwards's editing hand, much like the diary of David Brainerd that we know is really a "diary of David Brainerd written by Jonathan Edwards." Are they Phebe and Abigail, or do they also become Pamela and Clarissa? Perhaps we could consider Edwards's account as *narrative*, as we are used to consider Richardson's. Remember also what we know about Edwards's unfinished project of a "body of divinity in an entire new method," which, as Professor Kimnach just mentioned, was supposed to be written as a "compelling historical narrative" and which Edwards seemed to place special emphasis on. We should inquire into how the narrative form of Edwards's argument impacts our reading of the texts or even co-constitutes our understanding of them. These questions are especially pressing given the disciplines Edwards works in, for we cannot easily draw boundaries between fact and fiction here, if indeed we can ever do so at all.

Because we are approaching Edwards as a literary artist, I would like to address three general questions that arise from this view of Edwards and that might trouble some of you depending on your areas of interest in this author.

The first question is one that tends to bother those who study Edwards for his theology and philosophy: Are Edwards's writings literature? Does that not lead to all kinds of wild interpretations, such as those I just suggested, that often run directly contrary to what Edwards was trying to say?

It is true that sermons, treatises, and notes may not be what first come to mind as "literature." Perry Miller, who might be called the inventor of the twentieth-century Edwards industry, famously described Edwards as "one of

America's five or six major artists, who happened to work with ideas instead of with poems or novels."[1] But if Miller was right to call Edwards an artist, he overlooked the medium of Edwards's artistry. Edwards might not have written poems or novels, but his ideas found expression—and artistic at that—in his often lyrical words. Consider this sentence, a favorite of Kimnach's: to think of nothing is "to think of the same that the sleeping rocks dream of."[2] "If this is not poetry," Professor Kimnach likes to say, "I don't know what is."

If we follow Miller's suggestion concerning Edwards as an artist, we should pay attention to the medium he worked in. Written or spoken language was, after all, the only tool and vehicle and output of Edwards's profession. In this respect, literary readings of Edwards that explore, for instance, the rhetorical aspects of his writings, the play of meaning opened up by his figurative language, or the problems of authority in discourse need not be seen as a threat to his contributions to philosophy and theology but rather as reflections on the role of the medium in which these are expressed.

Second, those who prefer contemporary literary theory to traditional literary history might be dissatisfied with Professor Kimnach's picture of the literary Edwards. Is there nothing in Edwards's writings of relevance to current developments in literary and critical theory? Can European literary theorists, for instance, dismiss Edwards as a historical curiosity of merely parochial interest? There is no reason to do so. Not only European Americanists, but all literary scholars influenced by the debates in European philosophy and literary theory concerning discourse, meaning, and interpretation will find Edwards's writings relevant to the issues that interest them. Take, for instance, the Ricoeur-Derrida debate in French philosophy. Despite the obvious differences, Edwards's theology and epistemology (his theory of how we know), especially where concerned with our knowledge of God through typology in his extended sense, can be meaningfully related to these twentieth-century debates. Professor Kimnach already mentioned Edwards's intellectual openness to other influences, and there is a similar openness in Edwards's understanding of language and divine communication. He considers types to be "a certain sort of language, as it were, in which God is wont to speak to us," believes "the whole universe . . . [to] be full of images of divine things, as full as a language is of words," and asserts that "there is room for persons to be learning more and more of this language . . . *without discovering all.*"[3] Edwards's epistemology holds figurative expressions to be vehicles of divine communication ("symbols and emblems," "types and figures and enigmatical speeches," he calls them)[4] and advocates the use of invention in interpreting them. And when he comes to defining the rules for learning this language, his arguments seem to lack the usual determination, as if there was a very thin shadow of doubt hanging over them.[5]

Fundamentally, Edwards would perhaps agree more with a Ricoeurian emphasis on semantics (that is, the claim that, besides signs, language relies also on the sentence as an irreducible whole and that it is from the sentence that sense proceeds) than with a deconstructivist attack on teleology and logocentrism (which is, briefly, the presupposition of a center of meaning in discourse), yet Derrida's insistence on the impossibility of controlling discourse, for instance, might not be entirely alien to him. Remember, for example, Edwards's frustration with how language imposes itself on ideas: "For where we find that the words may be connected, the ideas being by custom tied with them, we think that the ideas may be connected likewise, and applied everywhere and in every way as the words."[6]

Third, there are those who might think, "I know Edwards can be an inspiration for my spiritual life and faith, and I can learn from Edwards the pastor, Edwards the missionary, Edwards the theologian, and perhaps even from Edwards the philosopher. But what use is Edwards the writer for my spiritual life?" Allow me to relate this issue, somewhat personally, to those of us who live in those parts of Europe that are still recovering from long years of antireligious Communist rule. That rule taught us that religion is nothing but stories and empty metaphors and therefore should be dismissed. But here is someone who is not afraid to take the issue of stories and metaphors in Christianity seriously. Edwards's theory and literary practice, as I suggested, holds that narrative and figurative expressions by no means diminish or subvert spiritual reality, but that they are, on the contrary, an essential operative element in the Christian understanding of the world.

Edwards, ever the proponent of the spiritual over the material, asserts that spiritual things elude our customary categories of thinking about the material. Recall a passage that he wrote as a young man in one of his notebooks: "If we would get a right notion of what is spiritual, we must think of thought or inclination or delight. How large is that thing in the mind which they call thought? Is love square or round? Is the surface of hatred rough or smooth? Is joy an inch, or a foot in diameter? These are spiritual things."[7]

I suggest that if thinking about spiritual things is different from thinking about things external and material, as Edwards tells us, then speaking about spiritual things may also call for a different way, and here is where narrative and figurative language come in. Edwards of course does not divorce scientific or referential language from the realm of the spiritual. But as we know, speculative reasoning by itself does not provide true knowledge in his epistemology. Rather, true knowledge comes as experience, as aesthetic experience. To that end, Edwards is more comfortable with figurative expression than with scientific categories. Perhaps this might be an inspiration to those of us who sometimes wish we could measure the diameter of joy. Listen instead how Edwards measures the beauty of Christ:

> As the sun revives the plants and trees and fruits of the earth, so Christ Jesus by his spiritual light revives the soul and causes it to bring forth fruit. In the winter, the trees are stripped of their leaves and stand naked, cease growing and seem to be dead. . . . But when the sun returns, then all things have the appearance of a resurrection . . . the fields, meadows, and woods seem to rejoice, and the birds sing a welcome to the returning spring.[8]

NOTES

1. Perry Miller, *Jonathan Edwards* (New York: William Sloane, 1949), xii.

2. Jonathan Edwards, "Of Being," in the Yale edition of *The Works of Jonathan Edwards* [hereafter *WJE*], 6: 206.

3. "Types," in *WJE* 11: 150, 152; italics mine.

4. "Types of the Messiah," in *WJE* 11: 193.

5. "Types," in *WJE* 11: 150–151.

6. "The Mind," in *WJE* 6: 345–46.

7. "The Mind," in *WJE* 6: 338.

8. *Christ, the Light of the World,* in *WJE* 10: 541.

13

Edwards and Philosophy

Miklos Vetö

Miklos Vetö explores Jonathan Edwards's work as a philosopher. After discussing what that last phrase means, he reviews the possible sources of Edwards's thought, mainly among certain English philosophers of the seventeenth and eighteenth centuries. Then the author analyzes three major domains in Edwards's philosophy: his ontology (view of being), his theory of knowledge (how we come to know something), and his understanding of the will (what happens when we choose something). First Vetö shows that Edwards's "idealism" (the view that all of reality is related to ideas) can be seen properly only through the prism of his ontology and epistemology. Then he unpacks Edwards's complex doctrine of spiritual knowledge, an intriguing synthesis of aesthetic, ethical, and religious elements. Vetö's explanation of knowledge as committed and morally qualified leads naturally to Edwards's description of the power of the will. Although Edwards has always been considered one of the greatest philosophers of the will, not all the implications of his doctrine have been fully considered. But in this essay, Vetö tries to do justice to some of those. In the last section, he measures Edwards's significance in the history of philosophy.

Theology and Philosophy

Jonathan Edwards, generally considered America's greatest theologian, produced the eighteenth century's most important writings in the English language and was perhaps the greatest theologian of his time. But while he is justly known to posterity as above all a religious figure—one of the founders of the New Divinity school of thought, a renowned preacher and theorist of the Great Awakening—the Connecticut Valley pastor was also the premier American philosopher and, more generally, a profound thinker whose works extend into the domains of metaphysics, ethics, and aesthetics.

Edwards was not a philosopher by profession. As was the case for many of the great medieval thinkers, philosophy was for Edwards *ancilla theologiae* (a handmaiden to theology), though this never prevented him from indulging in purely philosophical reasoning *sui generis* (in its own unique way), on a highly technical level.

Edwards's writing career practically began with his notes on being and thinking entitled "The Mind."[1] And at the end of his life he wrote two major philosophical works, *A Careful and Strict Inquiry into the Prevailing Notions of the Freedom of the Will* (1754) and his treatise on *The Nature of True Virtue.*[2] At the same time, during the more than thirty-year period between "The Mind" and *Freedom of the Will*, he never ceased putting his philosophical reflections to paper. Moreover, while the purely philosophical parts of the vast Edwards corpus are not numerous,[3] many of his writings contain philosophical discussions. Above all, it is in his rereading of Calvinist dogma in his treatises, in the *Miscellanies*, and throughout the immense collection of his sermons that Edwards is found to be unceasingly engaged in philosophical reasoning and integrating strictly philosophical themes into the development of theological arguments.

Protestant theology makes less use of "natural reason" than does Catholic theology, since the latter is driven by ancient thought structures. But knowing the role that such thinkers as the Catholic philosopher-theologian Francisco Suarez (1548–1617) played in the elaboration of Protestant dogma in the seventeenth century, one can discern the persistent influence of scholasticism even in those sectors where it is most strongly denounced: the Reformation asserted the absolute sovereignty of the Word of God as opposed to human speculation, but the conceptual achievement of the Middle Ages was never really abandoned.[4]

As a product of the eighteenth century, a time when even in the faraway region of America the signal fires of the Enlightenment were beginning to shine, Edwards employed philosophical reasoning in a far more profound and systematic way than his predecessors, the Puritan preachers of the foundational period of the New England colonies.[5] Hence, in the study of his philosophy one must constantly come back to his theology and homiletics; at the same time, purely philosophical elements within the religious writings must be identified in relation to those explicitly developed philosophical themes in the works.

The three great themes or domains of Edwards's philosophical thought are being, knowledge, and the will. The first is perhaps the least significant: Edwards never dedicated a separate work to this theme, treating it only in passing in certain notes, developments, and definitions buried within his theological and ethical writings.[6] As for the theme of knowledge, it is the subject of the renowned essay "The Mind," a series of notes that never evolved into a full-blown treatise. Really, the Edwardsian "theory of knowledge," or what and how the human mind can know, must be extracted from the sermons, the *Miscellanies*, and above all from the *Treatise on Religious Affections*, before being reconstructed. Finally, while the notion of the will is present throughout the entire corpus, it was fully elaborated only late in the theologian's life, becoming the most famous of all his writings: the *Inquiry into the Prevailing Notions Concerning the Freedom of the Will* (1754).

Edwards's Sources

Although Edwards can legitimately claim the title of first American philosopher, his works did not appear like a deus ex machina.[7] Indeed, historiographers have been debating the sources of his thought unceasingly for more than a century, a task all the more tantalizing considering the limited access he had to the original texts.[8] And yet, in Edwards's time even philosophers who lived in major European cultural centers didn't necessarily read the texts of their predecessors. Edwards, like his contemporaries, worked mainly with compilations, anthologies, and histories of philosophy. Rather than seeking to acquire the writings of great thinkers of the past, he wished to procure "the best history of the lives of the philosophers."[9] Thus, not having any firsthand knowledge of the main figures of Western philosophy, he ends up designating Cicero, that great compiler of previous thought, as "the greatest and best philosopher that . . . perhaps . . . any nation ever produced."[10] Indeed, Edwards did not read the originals of classical thought; his knowledge of them was based essentially on Theophilus Gale's seventeenth-century compilation.[11] Even Saint Augustine is quoted secondhand.[12] As far as the Middle Ages are concerned, he denounces scholastic thought for its "absurd distinctions" despite his lack of any real knowledge of it, adding only that he would be ready to accept those distinctions "which are clear and rational" (19: 795–96). His approach to Cartesian and post-Cartesian philosophy is no different, even though they constitute an essential component of the same Protestant conception and theology to which Edwards himself adhered: he never read Descartes and cites Leibniz only once (11: 128), but there again the reference is secondhand. As for Malebranche, whom he calls "Malebranch" (23: 233), he does seem to have been a significant influence on Edwards, though it is unlikely that he ever read his works.[13]

As one connoisseur of the Edwards corpus put it, the sources of Edwards's thought are best understood "in terms of milieu rather than direct influences."[14] Still, certain direct influences can be identified. Putting aside *La Logique du Port Royal*, for which American Puritans had such great appreciation, these direct influences come mainly from seventeenth- and eighteenth-century philosophers writing in English. Among them, Edwards mentions Thomas Hobbes but admits never having read him (1: 374). Berkeley, on the other hand, has been a constant source of speculation for Edwards historiography, one reader going so far as to call Edwards "this poor country Berkeley," and indeed Edwardsian "idealism" does have a lot in common with that of the Bishop of Cloyne (Malebranche), who, incidentally, donated a part of his personal library to Yale, where it became accessible to Edwards, a young college teacher at the time.[15] Yet the Edwards corpus contains no reference whatsoever to the writings of Berkeley. As far as the Earl of Shaftsbury is concerned, despite the occasional allusion here and there, his thought seems to have left few traces of influence on Edwards's thinking. Even Hume, the "genius" of whose books the Stockbridge exile claims to have been happy to read (16: 679), makes precious little contribution to the development of his thought. In the end, only three thinkers can truly be said to have exerted a significant influence on Edwards's philosophy: Newton, Locke, and Hutcheson.

Edwards was well-versed in scientific knowledge, and he refers frequently to the authority of Newton in what he calls "natural philosophy," the domain where science and metaphysics overlap.[16] Still, though Newton's presence can be felt throughout the works of Edwards, this influence remains limited and plays almost no role in those areas where Edwards has a claim to having made a contribution to the history of philosophy. Locke and Hutcheson, by contrast, can be found at the very heart of Edwards's thought. Beginning with Perry Miller, much has been written on how the discovery of Locke "liberated" the young Edwards from his subjugation to Protestant scholasticism. Actually, Locke's major role was in the metaphysical reformulation of several important doctrines of Christian dogma. Edwards's creative use of Locke's analysis of human personal identity allowed him to conceptualize the church's teaching on original sin. The way the dogma was constructed created a need for a certain metaphysical continuity between the first man, the original transgressor, and his furthest descendants who inherit his guilt.[17] Edwards also adopts Lockean definitions of freedom to explain how the will can be responsible for its actions while remaining radically subject to sin. And it is Locke's theory of ideas that allows Edwards to develop his profound and subtle distinction between intellectual and spiritual knowledge (between knowledge that remains exterior and is applied to objects separately, and intuitive knowledge, which is global), giving rise to an understanding of parts from the perspective of the whole, a comprehension of all implications based on an immediate impression.

Edwards's near contemporary, the English moralist Francis Hutcheson, discovered the notion of "moral sense," a notion that would be of such immense importance in the rise of Kantian thought.[18] This idea of "moral sense" in Hutcheson's treatises plays a crucial role in both the development of Edwards's theory of spiritual knowledge and his construction of what could be called an aesthetical ethics in *The Nature of True Virtue*.[19]

Being and Understanding

Since the end of the eighteenth century, historians have insisted on Edwards's metaphysical gifts and preoccupations, on his seemingly pantheistic ontology,[20] and on his idealism. Edwards, however, an orthodox Calvinist theologian, always professed "the perfect harmony between the Doctrines of the Christian Religion and human reason,"[21] the ultimate identification of faith with reason. Although it is true that he always intended to pursue his metaphysical investigations, it was only with a view to reformulating the essential themes of revelation in a new conceptual framework. In fact, this conviction of the perfect compatibility between religion and philosophy explains the two principal themes of his metaphysics, namely, that in the strictest ontological sense, God alone is, and that all existence is necessarily of a spiritual nature. In other words, there is nothing else but God, and even matter, if it does exist at all, is finally spiritual.

Unlike Leibniz, Schelling, and Heidegger, Jonathan Edwards never felt the need to question the reason for being. Being simply is, and nothing could be clearer: "Existence in general is necessary" (6: 398). It is rather nonbeing that is impossible.[22] Of course, this does not mean that all beings are necessary. The impossibility of nonexistence and the necessity of existence in general cannot be considered without also thinking about being in general, or God.

Hence being in general is not a general principle, but "this great Being . . . who made and rules the world" (16: 789). Following in the best Western metaphysical tradition, Jonathan Edwards identifies Being with God. Other "beings" have existence only in name; God alone "in metaphysical strictness and propriety is."[23] Everything that is not God does not, strictly speaking, exist; it must be given existence and be kept in existence by that which necessarily exists. The things of this world are, as it were, held above the abyss by "the immediate exercise of the power of God" (6: 214). Finite realities do not exist in themselves; they are so many empty envelopes, which the existential divine power fills.

Edwards was accused of pantheism, even monism, but in fact his ontology has a very different goal.[24] "The Great Being" that is God is undoubtedly "almighty" (16: 789), but above all, he is perfectly intelligible and perfectly intelligent—the supreme intelligibility and the supreme intellect. The degree to which things are, therefore, depends on their intelligibility: they are only to the extent that they are intelligible, a position that is only one step away from asserting that they are only insofar as they are known—and indeed, Edwards does take that final step.

In and of itself, matter is nothing (6: 238), for it is substantial only if it is spiritual (6: 206). This, of course, is idealism—an idealism whose radicalism recalls that of Berkeley, though it is ultimately Augustinian in orientation. According to Augustine, God creates things based on exemplars or ideas within his understanding. Thus, the essence of worldly realities is not to be found in themselves; it is but an idea from the divine intelligence. Edwards, for his part, teaches that true existence is only mental; it is an idea. But if it is directly—one might say, empirically—an idea of a created intelligence (i.e., that of a man), it is still, at a deeper level of reality, an idea of an uncreated intelligence (i.e., of God). Worldly things are only to the extent that they are present in an infinite consciousness. Strictly speaking, their being is only an "infinitely exact . . . and perfectly stable idea in God's mind" (6: 344).

The identification of being with intelligibility paves the way for the theory of purely mental existence, the ideality of things. It surreptitiously leads toward a subjectivist vision of the real that is nonetheless more than a simple Weltanschauung (worldview), but which falls short of a purely metaphysical reading of reality. Edwards, the theoretician of the Awakening, teaches the determining role of the knowing subject within knowledge, the radical dependence of knowledge on the condition of the subject. A moral and religious man does not know in the same way that an individual without grace does, lost as he is in transgression, affected by the grievous consequences of original sin. When the young farmer Hermon Hubbart set out to listen to the evangelist George Whitefield, another central figure of the Great Awakening, he heard someone ask, "What does this man preach? Any thing that is News?" Hubbart responded, "No; nothing [except] what you may read . . . in your Bible."[25] Does this comment mean that both regenerate and natural men perceive the same things, that notwithstanding the essential difference of their respective subjective conditions, men know in the same way?

Yes and no. Without spiritual light, natural man sees things dispersed, whereas one who has been justified grasps their coherence and unity. The one has access only to mental elements, which, because they are separate and fragmentary, lack any relation, link, or affinity to each other, while the other benefits from an intuition that immediately grasps its object, unfolding its structure in successive phases.

Men have always been able to distinguish external knowledge from the kind of knowledge that has direct access to its object. Philosophers differentiate purely theoretical from practical knowledge, the former merely describing and classifying objects of consideration, while the latter assimilates and espouses them. There is a conceptual or speculative understanding, which is limited to "the head," and another sort that penetrates to "the heart."[26] Edwards speaks of a "sense of the heart," which furnishes lively, intense, and far more adequate understanding and information than that which is obtained through speculation.[27] The content or matter of the two forms of comprehension may indeed be the same, but the way they act and their respective results are very different. Writing in the 1740s, Edwards once remarked that the saints know (2: 304), whereas the wicked can only conjecture (2: 374). Using the same noetic correlation,[28] a subject's knowledge may be either direct or indirect, depending on his moral-spiritual condition. Edwards calls direct understanding "spiritual," while indirect knowledge he calls "historical" or "notional." For the Reformed theologian, the historical corresponds to a kind of abstract knowledge—or a merely intellectual faith—through which men "assent to the Gospel History,"[29] without the vivifying influence of the Spirit. As a product of an entirely external vision, this historical knowledge is but the acceptance of truths for which one has no direct perception. These truths are presented to the mind as dispersed images, one after another, full of gaps and shadowy regions. In appearance—but only in appearance—this indirect or notional knowledge is the most precise kind of knowledge, more intellectual than common historia. In reality, however, notional understanding does not benefit from experience, which would be superior to faulty historical knowledge. Such knowledge interprets the world through a conceptual framework, but its own conception has no relation to any immediate vision. It merely traces the universal form based on multiple occurrences—in an abstract manner—without ever perceiving the thing as it is in and of itself.[30]

But Edwards teaches that knowledge, even if almost always doomed to compromise and imperfection through dispersion in discourse, seeks to attain a direct and complete relation to its object. So philosophy must seek a way to know immediately and to conceive of the object in such a way that the totality of its elements is present. In short, it seeks knowledge that, while remaining immediate (intuitive or direct), displays its object throughout the whole of its articulation.

In the eighteenth century, the paradigm of immediate understanding is that of taste. It is the century of taste, the century in which aesthetics developed into a full-blown philosophical discipline.[31] Yet taste, the faculty by which one properly perceives beauty, has a meaning that surpasses mere aesthetics, which is usually understood as simply a philosophy of the arts. To taste amounts to possessing a sense or an immediate understanding that is attained without re-sorting to any "line of reasoning" (2: 281). Honey must be tasted to be known; its taste is different from any idea that can be formed of it (2: 259). By tasting something, one obtains a more direct, more existential understanding than any discursive use of human understanding could provide. Yet this immediate knowledge depends on a "precondition," which is none other than a permanent condition of the knowing subject himself. Tasting may be nothing more than an isolated operation, but it is still the consequence, or better yet, the transla-tion of the subject's state. Taste is what might be called a "totalization": good taste expresses the whole of the subject, his entire mental setup. The various domains in which good taste is exercised relate to faculties, to structural mo-ments of our being. The taste of wine is the business of a well-educated palate; the taste for music, melodies, or sounds depends on having a musical ear.

On the other hand, these totalizing, permanent moments of subjectivity do not function like filters or instruments perceiving from the outside. Taste corresponds to a belonging, a giving up of one's self to the object that fills and possesses one. And most essentially, this comprehension-belonging is simulta-neously an overall perception and comprehension of the contents, a conceptual understanding of the structural moments of the object.

Knowledge—in all of its branches—relates to an idea. Locke, whom the young Edwards read with more pleasure than "the most greedy miser finds, when gathering up handfuls of silver and gold,"[32] distinguishes between sim-ple and complex ideas. A simple idea is a single perception that the mind re-ceives immediately, whereas a complex idea is a plurality of ideas, or better still, an idea with a plural structure that the mind develops indirectly or discursively after reflection.[33] Edwards accepts Locke's theory, but by subsuming the com-plex into the simple, he alters it radically. As his own epistemology is developed within a theological context, he speaks, for instance, of the "simple idea of grace" (1: 205). This simple idea is a "spiritual idea," which, while it is imme-diately impressed upon the mind, is not an isolated entity, but an essence, an eidos implying a multiplicity of moments. Such a multiplicity is not a sort of conglomerate, but a whole whose parts are organically linked. The spiritual idea of God contains a multitude of ideas, which are the attributes of God.[34] Likewise, the recognition of Jesus Christ as Savior implies all of the articles of faith (13: 183).

At first sight, this theory appears relatively banal: what is not apparent is implied in what is apparent. The apprehension of something known leads to the apprehension of unknown things, but these unknown things belong (virtually yet truly) to the known (18: 460). The things of this world may appear dispersed, having no relation to each other, but in reality they are linked and constitute the terms of relations that are hidden but very real. Thoughts or ideas may arise with no apparent order, without any relation among them, but "attentive reflection" reveals their mutual relations (18: 456). In all domains of reality or knowledge, everything subsists in half-hidden, obscure relations. Our thoughts and reasoning, even when they appear to have been improvised, with no real relation to those that precede them and those that follow, are related and correspond to them. Edwards puts forth this thesis most clearly in the context of theological expositions. He speaks of a veritable "concatenation" of diverse graces, which are in "conjunction" and "mutual dependence" with each other: "One is . . . implied in the very nature of the other"; one is "essential to another, and belongs to the essence of it" (8: 328ff). This belonging—this mutual implication of things—recalls Leibniz's "compossibility," and, as with the German philosopher, it does not signify a merely logical connection but ontological interdependence. In his youthful notes, Edwards sets himself the task of showing how "the least atom has an influence" not only for the present, but "in the whole course of things throughout eternity." Yet this "influence" is not merely a case of cause and effect; it is essentially a matter of spiritual-moral finality. Everything in the universe exists, the notes continue, according to a strict order, so that "there is very good philosophical reason to think that the hairs of our head are all numbered." In short, we are forced to admit that "all nature consists in things being precisely according to strict rules of justice and harmony" (6: 231–32).

Going beyond notional understanding in this manner leads to an apprehension of that which had not previously been known. The diverse structural elements of things and the things themselves, which are situated next to each other, are now seen in light of their organic continuity. One idea leads to another; instead of gaps and dark spaces, a light begins to shine, flooding the cognitive landscape, filling the cracks between ideas, linking them up (13: 470). This light, which renews the intensity of our world, is not external; it does not come from without, but from within the knowing subject. The things of the world are illuminated and arranged in accordance with the cognitive process. For Jonathan Edwards, "compossibility" (the interconnection of all things in God) becomes apparent only thanks to a condition of the subject in which the notional is subsumed by the spiritual.[35] At the same time, this subsuming is more than a simple rearrangement of the contents or even a sudden appearance and unveiling of the compossibility. Spiritual knowledge does signify a more "perfect" understanding, but this perfection of understanding is not of a theoretical nature. The components of notional understanding are like chimeras (8: 610) or mere "shadows."[36] Spiritual understanding, by contrast, is an entirely different affair. The true Christian's faith "enlarges his understanding and clarifies the eye of his soul" (10: 572) and makes its ideas appear truly "real" (14: 201–2). Although the Fall resulted in the weakening of human intelligence (19: 141), true spiritual knowledge is strong and intensely brilliant.

Spiritual understanding is more intense and alive than notional understanding, but the difference between these two notions is not only quantitative. Indeed, it pertains to the very nature of their respective aims and ends. He who is disposed to comprehend things through spiritual understanding (8: 542) "discerns and distinguishes between . . . holy and unholy, without being at the trouble of a train of reasoning" (2: 281). But the difference between the holy and the profane is of an essentially different order from that of the content of our thinking. As is the case with describing honey, forming ideas of something is not the same as having a taste for it. Thus, a notional understanding can take stock of the actions of a saint, even describe the disposition of his feelings, yet the saint will never be able to understand what makes a saint holy. Classical theology distinguishes between the natural and the moral attributes of God, his omnipotence and omniscience (natural) and goodness and charity (moral). Through notional understanding one can grasp moral characteristics, see and comprehend all their attributes, all their matter, and yet never understand their beauty or their amiability (2: 264). One can comprehend that sin and transgression provoke the wrath of God and deduce the need for punishment, but this remains a wholly theoretical, "objective" judgment. One never manages to grasp the very odiousness of sin: we understand what transgression is and what should be considered bad, but we cannot understand why the bad is bad. In other words, while notional understanding can determine objectively that an action or feeling is good or bad, it has no true "sense" of what makes the bad bad or the good good; a true understanding of what constitutes the goodness of the good and the evilness of evil remains beyond its reach.

Only a spiritual understanding allows a person to discern the true odiousness of evil and the true sweetness of what is good. In this case, it is not an objective, theoretical perception we are dealing with, but taste, and taste is a matter of approbation or disapprobation. One sees almost naturally that an action or judgment is just, but this is not the same thing as approving of it through love. Wicked men and "the devils know that their hatred of God is unreasonable . . . but yet their hearts don't disrelish and loath it: if they did, it would have no place in their hearts" (21: 317)! Indeed, no real distinction can be made between feeling the truly detestable character of an object and actually hating it (13: 527). In other words, spiritual knowledge is not an entirely neutral discernment of content, but an apprehension or realization that results from consent.

At this stage we have definitively gone beyond "notional" understanding. Perhaps we have even put aside all theoretical knowledge, which insists on the objectivity and neutrality of the knowing subject and disdains any bias toward the object being observed. Spiritual knowledge does not value indifference, but on the contrary advocates the engagement of the subject. The perception or apprehension of the sweetness of good and the odiousness of evil are inseparable from approval or disapproval, each of which expresses the engagement of the whole person and, more important, corresponds to an inclination or disinclination. But inclination or disinclination, strictly speaking, pertain not to the domain of knowledge but to the more practical realm of the will.

The Will

Traditionally speaking, truth is considered to be the object of knowledge, just as goodness is that of the will. The proper object of the will is the good. We always want what is good, even if the good is only partial, fragmentary, or even false. Philosophy investigates the freedom of the will, and moralists have always considered the action of the will to be a measure of its freedom. Good actions undertaken by a nonfree will would be void of any merit; bad actions perpetrated by a nonfree will would not engage the responsibility of the actor. Both the philosopher and the layperson, then, would appear to agree that freedom is the sine qua non condition for moral responsibility. Yet the theologian finds himself obliged to argue for the moral responsibility of a will doomed to ill will! Because of original sin, the heritage of our remotest ancestor, the will has become enslaved: all it can do is sin. That is, it desires evil. At the same time, notwithstanding the innate subjugation of the will, transgression remains inexcusable. Faced with this supreme paradox, this inextricable contradiction, Edwards the theologian argues philosophically. He tries to demonstrate the compatibility of the predetermined condition of the will with its freedom. What is important for the will to be free is not that it is capable of choosing among several options, but that it can effectively do what it chooses.

Philosophers teach that to be free the will should be indifferent toward the object of its choice. The will should be indifferent toward the two objects between which it must choose. But how is it possible to choose—as the thesis of the indifference of the will would require—between two things that appear to be the same, neither of which attracts the will more than the other? In any case, the reasoning of proponents of the freedom of indifference is based on a misunderstanding about the timing of choice. They advocate indetermination, or the indifference of the subject at the very moment of choice. However, one cannot ask the subject to be indifferent at the very moment when he chooses; otherwise, he won't choose at all (1: 207)! The freedom of indifference dooms man not to choose at the exact time when he must choose, or else he is driven to "choose without choosing" (1:198).

The freedom of the will does not consist in its supposed indifference to the choice, but in its aptitude to do effectively what it wants. It means one's power to do what one pleases. Or, in other terms, it designates "being . . . in such a state that he may act his pleasure and do what he will."[37] At the deepest level, the will is entirely engaged when one acts. Its freedom is not a distancing from, or an unlimited, permanent neutrality toward, the object of its choice. In short, it does not consist in the ability to turn away from its own acts, but, as followers of the Augustinian tradition know, it is only in its involvement in such acts that it becomes self-determining.[38]

The discussion about the freedom of the will leads to that of what determines it, or rather how it determines itself. The only act that can really be considered free is one that was previously decided on by the subject. If the will were already determined at the moment of choosing, then the will could not be free. The fallen will is enslaved precisely because the inclination to evil and the attachment to transgression were imposed upon it in the past. Human action appears to be subject to the law of efficient causality. Our present wills are undoubtedly the effects of a prior self-determination, which is their very cause. The investigation into moral action, therefore, amounts to a study of a series of causes and effects: the goodness or evil of an action depends on the goodness or evil of the decision that is its cause. Jonathan Edwards is a veritable virtuoso of moral demonstration, and *The Freedom of the Will* is filled with brilliant logical-dialectical demonstrations. But in his dealing with morals, Edwards rejects all influence of causality: the goodness or evil, the justice or injustice of an action does not depend on its cause but on its nature; actions should not be read in terms of their origins but in terms of their quality. Notwithstanding all the speculation and sophistry of philosophers, everyone agrees that liberty is when "a man acts as he himself chooses . . . without considering how he came to choose as he did." The light of nature teaches that he who commits an error by his own choice "deserves punishment, without inquiring how his choice and his will came to be so bad" (14: 168–69).

After having refuted the errors of the freedom of indifference and that of prior causal determination of the moral nature of the will, Edwards turns to the theory of "moral sincerity." Inspired by the laudable desire to judge the moral value of an act by the intention behind it, some have used the following line of reasoning: in order to judge the quality of the will, one should not consider what a man may effectively accomplish, but rather the spirit in which he acted. One can make mistakes or not be capable of realizing one's plans, but what matters is sincerity. Yet sincerity, Edwards explains, is not the same thing as moral intent; all it really signifies is a vigorous affection or violent desire. One may sincerely desire to eat when one is hungry or to find a well-paying job when one has been reduced to a state of poverty. Such sincerity only indicates the strength of one's inclination; it has nothing to do with moral quality! What's more, one can just as well sincerely aspire to illegal or vicious actions or conditions. A man can sincerely want to join a band of pirates or even desire—once again, with perfect sincerity—the prompt recovery of his neighbor's wife simply in order to be able to resume his adulterous relation with her (1: 315). A heavy ambiguity hovers over this reasoning: it implies a conception of sincerity that "signifies no more than reality of Will and Endeavour, with respect to any thing that is professed or pretended; without any consideration of the nature of the principle or aim, whence this real Will and true Endeavour arises." Our attention is continually directed to the essential importance of the authenticity of sincerity as the only criterion for judgment, whereas what one should be striving for is not the reality of the will, but its goodness.[39] Behind the mask of a respectable theory of personal autonomy, a "physical" conception of the will is found to be hiding, which is, however, utterly inadequate for investigations in moral philosophy. Sincerity undoubtedly expresses a person's commitment, even a complete commitment, but this does not mean that it is ipso facto good.

Analyses based on sincerity reinforce the vision of the will as entirely determined by intention. Yet to understand the essential role that intention plays does not only imply a rupture with all physical theories of the will, but it also sheds light on another form of moralistic sophistry. It is thought that to be responsible one must allow free range to one's intentions. But to be inclined to evil, to be almost irresistibly pushed into transgression, diminishes, if not invalidates, guilt, for how can one be condemned when one is apparently incapable of not seeking evil? There are those who seem to have been inclined toward evil since childhood; an invincible attraction or fatal desire prevents them from resisting temptation and forces the will to do evil. Perhaps they effectively want what is evil, but they cannot *not* want it. So how can they be considered responsible for an offense they could not *not* commit?

Edwards reveals the absurdities behind this argument with perspicacity and brilliance. Some may consider a bad disposition from childhood an excuse. But can the fact of having desired and then done evil for a long time, even from early childhood, excuse the author of that evil?[40] It is indeed a strange way of excusing wickedness to argue that a person is so evil that he is incapable of rejecting his own wickedness (1: 137)! If this is the case, then "wickedness always carries that in it which excuses it" (1: 309). One would be obliged always to excuse men of evil character and to do so precisely because their character is evil. Moreover, sin would not only be excusable, but the more deeply rooted it was in the heart, the more excusable it would be. If the inclination to evil acquitted the transgressor of his responsibility, then the more one is dominated by greed, cruelty, or malice, the more one would be pardoned for being mean and acting cruelly (1: 324). If someone were naturally wicked due to his character, others would have to excuse him when he did them harm precisely because he was predisposed to harming others (18: 540). One whose heart has been hardened is perhaps incapable of acting virtuously, but if by virtue of his evil disposition he must be freed from all reprimand, then all moral judgment might as well be thrown overboard. "Thus the strength of sin, is made the excuse for sin" (1: 468). In short, if this theory rejects moral responsibility because of bad character or the innate propensity for evil, then sin becomes its own excuse, and in fact we become less bad in becoming worse.[41]

Faced with the absurdities that flow from theories seeking to acquit the transgressor in light of and in proportion to the depth of his wickedness, the ordinary conscience plainly sees that the more wicked one's heart is, the guiltier one is. Being entirely given over to wickedness does not excuse sin any more than one's making a habit of being charitable would diminish its praiseworthiness. To dramatize his argument, the theologian asks whether the fact that devils are given over to evil means that they are not guilty, and conversely, whether the Son of God, Jesus Christ, who could not sin, is not therefore without moral goodness. Would not inveterate sinners be innocent and the saints entirely lacking in merit? All this questioning reinforces and completes the Edwardsian doctrine that good and evil are not to be found anywhere else but in the will and entirely within the will. Neither past nor present determination can affect responsibility. A man who seeks evil, regardless of why he does so, is evil, just as one who seeks good, regardless of why he does so, is good.

The Significance of Edwardsian Thought
for the History of Philosophy

The larger figure of Edwards as theologian and preacher has become a veritable "icon of American culture,"[42] but what of Edwards the philosopher? Jonathan Edwards was the first American philosopher, his theory of the will in particular inciting heated debate and giving rise to later analyses. He was admired for the dialectical vigor of his argumentation, and even those who could not accept all its implications had to admire its conceptual quality. Some praise has been of a decidedly dubious nature: George Santayana, for example, called Edwards "the greatest master of a false philosophy."[43] But a consensus has begun to emerge along the lines of Josiah Royce's comment that the Stockbridge missionary was the first "representative" philosopher of America.[44] Yet, while Edwards is studied, admired, and sometimes praised to the skies by his compatriots, and while he has also been appreciated by certain British writers, he has been largely ignored by continental European philosophers and historians of philosophy. In all of nineteenth-century German historiography, apparently one single line has been dedicated to him, explaining that he is the "only American philosopher."[45] French histories of philosophy seem to have begun mentioning his name only recently.[46] Such lacunas may be regrettable, even deplorable, but while historical research on the decidedly incidental "influence" exerted by the author of *The Freedom of the Will* would appear to have yielded only meager results, reflection on the pertinence and perspectives of his thought is an undeniably promising pursuit.

Jonathan Edwards wrote during the eighteenth century, a time when Christian dogma was under assault by naturalism, deism, and the Enlightenment. Yet while writers of that time, from Hutcheson to Rousseau and Lessing, sought, as it were, to naturalize theology, Edwards, for his part, almost managed to integrate philosophy into theology.[47] In the dissertation on *The End for which God Created the World*, the real scriptural developments are preceded by an extraordinary metaphysical exposition of the doctrines of creation and providence. *The Nature of True Virtue*, with only one biblical quotation in the entire text, presents a subtle metaphysical formulation of charity. Jonathan Edwards sought to proclaim "the strict, mysterious, spiritual . . . principles of our forefathers" (16: 546), the Puritan preachers, but more than any other theologian of that ilk he successfully rethought and restated Reformed dogma through philosophical argumentation. It is for this reason that this great Protestant theologian, defender of justification by faith alone, reformulator of the doctrine of original sin, and innovative theoretician of spiritual experience and ecclesiastical affiliation, is more comparable to such metaphysicians as Saint Augustine and Thomas Aquinas than to Calvin or Barth. Or perhaps—and this is the preferred option of the present author—these properly metaphysical teachings should be reexamined in light of the major systems of modern philosophy. Perhaps Edwardsian "idealism" is really only a minor deviation in a speculative line of reasoning that culminates in the works of Berkeley. Yet the case is entirely different concerning his "theory of knowledge," which, at least to a certain extent, bears a striking resemblance to that of Leibniz and Hegel and, above all with regard to his writing on the will, prefigures the key passages of Kant's theories.

Jonathan Edwards asserted that spiritual ideas implied a multiplicity of ideas, organically related to each other—in short, a logical and metaphysical coexistence of ideas: as Leibniz would have it, their "compossibility." Obviously, Edwards had not anticipated Hegel; he does not engage in the effective deduction of ideas, one from another; rather, he simply affirms and reiterates that any given concept logically and metaphysically implies all its predicates. That is, the properties and the qualities of a thing are not accidental but may be understood as its organic, necessary components. However, he goes much further than Hegel, though in a different direction, when he distinguishes between the notional and the spiritual. Where notional knowledge, as the *Miscellanies* inform us, only grasps ideas in dispersion, spiritual knowledge, a form of understanding based on taste, allows them to be perceived in organic connection to each other. Edwards may not always be very clear in his attempt to link the understanding to a compossibility with spiritual understanding. Yet what is absolutely certain is that he presents the idea of an understanding that is parallel to and beyond notional knowledge, an understanding or intellectual perception of content that functions through the consent of the mind.[48] The doctrine that emerges from Edwards's writing seems to be the culmination of the Western philosophical tradition's attempt to comprehend the precise nature of spiritual knowledge, and it foreshadows in its own way the distinction between practical and theoretical reasoning.

And yet there is another domain in which he prefigures even more explicitly and significantly Kant's critical philosophy, namely, that of the will.[49] In his passionate defense of the church's teachings, Edwards unceasingly calls into question the moral theories of his time, but through his brilliant denunciation of the absurdities to which those philosophies lead, the polemicist succeeds in developing a highly consistent and complete doctrine of the will. No one before Kant had so momentously or incisively grasped the radical autarchy of the will, its immanent intelligibility, a specific intelligibility of its own, as had Edwards. He showed, perhaps more than anyone previously, that the will cannot adequately be read in light of its past premises, but only in terms of its present actions. The quality and the sense, the value of our wills cannot be found in the vigor of their movements, but in the direction of their intentions. The moral value of the will does not depend on any supposed determination or indetermination, but on its actual exercise.

Edwardsian argumentation is motivated by religious and theological concerns, but it has a distinctively philosophical goal. For some, challenging the validity of looking for the origins—for its determination in the past—of a choice is a refusal to recognize the truly free nature of the will as a faculty. And yet it is precisely this isolation from causes, and hence premises, that serves to maintain the purity of *voluntas*.[50] The will that exerts itself at any given moment must be read on its own terms, not as a function of something else that comes before it, or based on something that is outside of it. The will cannot be taken in terms of its physical action, but only in terms of its choice: the drunkard's desire to drink is not related to the drink itself, but to the act of drinking (1: 143). The defense of the essential purity of the will—that is to say, of its properly voluntary condition—also propels the forceful critique that Edwards applies to "moral sincerity." The will is not a physico-physiological force, but an intention; it is not a power that is exerted from without, but an action undertaken in the inner realm of the mind. The isolation of what is previous and what is on the outside guarantees the unity, the continuity, the homogeneity of the will. *The Freedom of the Will* rejects all consideration of factors prior or exterior to volition; it seeks to study the will beginning with a faithful description that gets at the essence of the choice. The notion of "moral sincerity" is unacceptable because the truth of the will is revealed only in its exercise.[51]

As a thinker in the domain of spiritual knowledge and as a theoretician of the will, Edwards left to posterity a whole range of magnificent texts. But does that suffice to earn him the title of "important philosopher" or "major thinker of his time"? There can be no simple answer to that question. Although the former Yale student cannot really claim to have added a "footnote to Plato,"[52] he nevertheless presents us with an elaborate reflection aimed at fulfilling the apologetic requirements of Calvinist theology, post-Cartesian metaphysics, and the moral reflection of the eighteenth century. He thereby gave birth to a unique and intriguing synthesis that testifies to the extraordinary potential for philosophy in questions posed by religion. It is a synthesis in which certain themes from classical philosophy are reread in a new light and, most important, that gives new insight into the theses and theories found in more recent systems of thought.

To conclude: most of the Edwardsian arguments and themes do have a direct or indirect bearing on important issues in contemporary philosophy of religion, such as the transcendence of God and the radicality of evil. But it is Edwards's theory of the will that reveals an evident pertinence for the problematics of moral thought in our day. The brilliant and fascinating dialectics of the will displayed in *The Freedom of the Will* can inspire those who struggle to conceptualize and account for the paradoxes of the will in the analytical tradition, prevalent mainly in the Anglo-American world. The appreciation of the will according to its "nature," without regard to causal determination, is exceedingly useful to those in the continental tradition of phenomenology who are working on descriptive studies concerning the essence and life of the will. In both of these worlds of twenty-first-century thought, the ideas and the arguments of this eighteenth-century philosopher can play a significant role.

NOTES

A French version of this text is "Les commencements de la philosophie en Amérique," *Archives de Philosophie* 70 (2007): 179–99.

1. It was thought for many years that this text had been written during Edwards's adolescence while he was a student at Yale. We now know that its composition occurred in 1722–23, when he was about twenty. See W. Anderson, Note on "The Mind," in the Yale edition of *The Works of Jonathan Edwards* [hereafter *WJE* in notes], 6: 324–25. (Subsequent references to the Yale edition of Edwards's works are cited parenthetically in the text as the volume and page number.)

2. This piece, along with its companion text, *The End for Which God Created the World*, both written during the last years of Edwards's life, were published only posthumously.

3. These texts are found in *WJE* 6.

4. Scholasticism is the medieval system of teaching based on the Fathers and using categories devised by Aristotle and later commentators.

5. According to Charles Chauncey, Edwards "made use of more philosophy [in religion] . . . than anyone that I know of." Chauncey, Seasonable Thoughts (Boston, 1743), 384, cited in Norman Fiering, *Jonathan Edwards's Moral Thought and Its British Context* (Chapel Hill, NC: Institute of Early American History and Culture, 1981), 49–50.

6. Note on "Natural Philosophy," Of Being, and Of Atoms—which are, respectively, only eighteen, five, and ten pages long. All are found in *WJE* 6. Although it is a distinctly ontological problem, the question of being and goodness as self-diffusion or overflowing are passed over in the present work due to the particularly deep theological roots of Edwards's thinking on the subject. For a careful analysis of the issue, see M. Vetö, *La Pensée de Jonathan Edwards*, 2nd ed. (Paris: L'Harmattan, 2007), 95–108.

7. On the origins of American philosophy, see Fiering, *Moral Philosophy*.

8. See William S. Morris, *The Young Jonathan Edwards: A Reconstruction* (New Haven: Jonathan Edwards Center, Yale University, 2005). On Edwards's intellectual education, the definitive statement is still Morris's momentous work, *The Young Jonathan Edwards*.

9. Jonathan Edwards, Catalogue of Books, in O. Winslow, Jonathan Edwards (New York, 1940), 121.

10. Miscellanies, Number 979, in *WJE* 20: 291. Ephraim Chambers, the author of a philosophical dictionary, is lauded as "a late great philosopher of our nation," in *Religious Affections*, *WJE* 2: 282.

11. Theophilus Gale, *The Court of the Gentiles*, 4 vols. (London, 1669–77).

12. *Freedom of the Will, WJE* 1: 295; Religious Affections, *WJE* 2: 316 n. 6.

13. Edwards cites Malebranche, but only secondhand, in Miscellanies, Number 1294, in *WJE* 23: 235.

14. Robert E. Brown, *Jonathan Edwards and the Bible* (Bloomington: Indiana University Press, 2002), 64.

15. Robert Lowell, "Jonathan Edwards in Western Massachusetts," a 1964 poem. Again, idealism is the notion that everything that exists goes back to ideas. In Edwards's case, they are God's ideas. So, for example, a tree exists only if and when God thinks the tree, or has an idea of it.

16. Metaphysics means, literally, "things after or beyond nature": the study of questions about the reality of the external world, the existence of other minds, innate knowledge, the nature of sensation, memory and other things.

17. Locke teaches that personal identity is based on the constantly renewed links between successive moments and acts of a human being. Edwards shows that an analogous relationship holds between Adam and his offspring.

18. See, for example, Dieter Henrich's excellent study, "Hutcheson und Kant," *Kant-Studien* 49 (1957–58): 49–69.

19. See Fiering, *Jonathan Edwards' Moral Thought*.

20. Pantheism is the notion that God is the same thing as the world; ontology is the study of being.

21. Edwards's "Catalogue of Reading," entry 238, Beinecke Rare Book and Manuscript Library, Yale University.

22. Of Being, in *WJE* 6: 206. Absolute nothingness is a state for which an adequate idea can be obtained only by thinking about what "the sleeping rocks dream of" (206).

23. The Mind, in *WJE* 6: 364. "God is as it were the only substance" (*WJE* 398).

24 Monism is derived from monos, or one: the idea that all is one. Ontology is a theory of being.

25. Alan Heimert and Perry Miller, eds., *The Great Awakening* (Indianapolis: Bobbs-Merrill, 1967), 638.

26. On the opposition between the "head" and the "heart," see Miscellanies, Number 782, in *WJE* 18: 459; "A Divine and Supernatural Light," in *WJE* 17: 416.

27. See Vetö, *La Pensée de Jonathan Edwards*, 331–33.

28. Noetic means having to do with reason.

29. Calvin, *Institutes*, III. ii. 1 (Paris: Vrin, 1959), 14 (a).

30. On notional and historical knowledge, see Vetö, *La Pensée de Jonathan Edwards*, 336–38.

31. See Alfred Bäumler's classic study, *Das Irrationalitätsproblem in der Aesthetik und Logik des 18. Jahrhunderts bis zur Kritik der Urteilskraft*, 2nd ed. (Tübingen: Wissenschaftliche Buchgesellschaft, 1967).

32. Samuel Hopkins, *The Life and Character of the Late Reverend Mr. Jonathan Edwards*, in *Jonathan Edwards: A Profile*, ed. D. Levin (New York: Hill and Wang, 1969), 5–6.

33. John Locke, *An Essay Concerning Human Understanding*, II.i. 3–4.

34. See Miklos Vetö, "Beauté et compossibilité: L'épistémologie religieuse de Jonathan Edwards," in Vetö, ed., *Le Mal—Essais et études*, (Paris: L'Harmattan, 2006), 166–68.

35. For a more complete discussion of the very complex question of the relation of spiritual understanding and knowledge of compossibility, see Vetö, *La Pensée de Jonathan Edwards*, chapter 8.

36. Jonathan Edwards, *Miscellaneous Observations on Important Theological Subjects* (Edinburgh: Gray, 1793), 394.

37. Miscellanies, Number 657, in *WJE* 18: 197. As Edwards notes in his unfinished treatise on Efficacious Grace, "The liberty of the will consists merely in the power of doing what we will . . . [an] opinion wherein the Calvinists agree with Hobbes" (*WJE* 21: 208).

38. Jonathan Edwards, *Remarks on Important Theological Controversies*, in *Works of President Edwards* (Worcester, MA, 1843), 2: 553–56.

39. Ibid.

40. Samuel Hopkins, *System of Doctrines*, in *The Works of Samuel Hopkins, D.D.*, 3 vols. (Boston, 1853), 1: 233–35. Samuel Hopkins was Edwards's closest disciple.

41. See John Smalley, "The Consistency of the Sinner's Inability to Comply with the Gospel" (Hartford, CT, 1769), 15. John Smalley was one of Edwards's most important followers.

42. Paul Holm and Oliver Crisp, eds., *Jonathan Edwards, Philosophical Theologian* (Aldershot, UK: Ashgate, 2003), xi.

43. George Santayana, *Character and Opinion in the United States* (New York: Scribner's, 1920), 5.

44. Josiah Royce, *Basic Writings* I (New York: Fordham University Press, 1991), 291.

45. I. H. Fichte, *Die philosophischen Lehren von Recht, Staat und Sitte* (Leipzig, 1850), 544.

46. See G. Lyon, *L'idéalisme en Angleterre au XVIIIe siècle* (1888), 2nd ed. (Paris: L'Harmattan, 2007), 406–39.

47. Michael McClymond, *Encounters with God: An Approach to the Theology of Jonathan Edwards* (New York: Oxford UniversityPress, 1998), 51–53.

48. *WJE* 6: 380; *WJE* 8: 561–63.

49. For more on this topic, see Miklos Vetö, *La naissance de la volonté* (Paris: L'Harmattan, 2002), 151–80.

50. Latin for "will."

51. Likewise, the moral quality of wanting is to be searched for in action. If good and evil are not to be found in the moral exercise of the will, then they are not to be found anywhere. *WJE* 1: 337.

52. Alfred North Whitehead famously said, "The safest general characterization of the European philosophical tradition is that it consists of a series of footnotes to Plato." Whitehead, *Process and Reality* (New York: Free Press, 1979), 39.

14

Alternative Viewpoint: Edwards and Philosophy

Magdaléna Ševčíková

My response consists of general observations and questions. Along the way, I will point out how Edwards can contribute to important discussions today.

A theologian cannot avoid being at least a part-time philosopher. It is ironic that even though Protestant theology rejected philosophical approaches to God, it nevertheless used philosophical reasoning in its construction of theological arguments. We can see this in arguments made at the Council of Nicaea in 325. Or we can go even further back to Paul's sermon at the Areopagus in Athens in Acts 17. Of course, the measure, method, and quality of philosophy has changed over the centuries. So Edwards was not really being un-Protestant when he, as Professor Vetö puts it, "employed philosophical reasoning in a far more profound and systematic way than his predecessors."

Vetö notes that Edwards's knowledge of philosophy was not based on firsthand reading of most philosophers, but a more indirect influence. I do not see that as a sign of lower quality but of functional and pragmatic wisdom. If Edwards had read all the sources firsthand, how would he have had time to make all the original contributions that he did? What makes a good philosopher is not the scrupulous quoting of sources and verbatim knowledge of primary texts, but originality of thinking that gets at the intersecting questions of human beings.

There are three major philosophical themes in Edwards: being, knowledge, and will. All three represent challenges to theological and pragmatic positions taken today.

Being

Vetö observes that Edwards doesn't question being because, as he puts it, "being simply is." Nonbeing does not exist. Instead, Edwards argues for the ontological reality of divinity and the essentially spiritual nature of all existence. For only God truly is, and his typical attributes are that he is intelligible and intelligent.

This theory of being is a provocative challenge for post-Communist countries such as mine. Communist ideology imposed radically different propositions on its peoples, without tolerating any intelligent alternative.

God is not a being, we were told. Matter alone has being. Because existence is materialistic, only empirically perceived things truly exist. This tyrannical ideology, utterly heedless of consistent philosophical reasoning, was nevertheless powerful and influential. The sad proof is that people who never adopted its central assertions nonetheless came to believe that what is less visible is less real. Edwards's theory of being, which maintains that the spiritual has more reality than the material, is an exciting alternative to two generations of inbred thinking.

Methodologically, Edwards's theory is more convincing because rather than relying on brute force, it appeals to logic and coherent argument. The result is a vision of reality based on reason and the nature of things. Therefore it has the capacity to overcome our societies' presumed divorce between religion and reason, which was an effect of the materialist, so-called scientific worldview.

The Slovak theologian L'ubomír Batka has recently analyzed the relationship of faith and theology to science. All three, he argues, search for ultimate truth. But conflict has arisen when thinkers have misunderstood the relation between empirical experience and ultimate truth. The result, after two centuries of criticism of religion, is the common European assumption that faith is just an individual matter and therefore merely subjective.[1]

Batka attributes this mind-set to the impact of three European thinkers: René Descartes, Immanuel Kant, and August Comte. Descartes doubted the ability of the senses to reach truth, asserting that only nonempirical logic can show us what is true. Kant excluded metaphysical questions (such as eternity, the immortality of the soul, free will, God's existence, and God's providence) from discussions of what can be proved by human reason. According to Comtean positivism and neopositivism, theological knowledge is useless because it explains the world by appealing to supernatural beings and produces statements that are not verifiable by empirical methods. Such assertions are nonsensical and cannot yield absolute truth. Because science, according to Comte, deals only with real, exact, and useful things, neither philosophy nor theology can be considered scientific.[2]

The result of such presumptions was the conclusion that theology and philosophy do not convey any serious truth. Only natural sciences, with their empirical methods, give us access to reality. Theology, then, cannot be taken seriously as a discussion partner.

Of course, theology cannot and should not accept this series of assumptions. But at the same time it cannot ignore science. Instead, it must redefine and reclarify the place of theology in any search for truth. Batka defines this role as follows. Theology asks questions that aim deeper than what is typically called the "scientific quest for truth." Theology poses fundamental questions about the "truth of the scientist," asking about what makes up the substance of a human being. Its methods provoke thinkers to inquire about categories that cannot be measured in a positivistic (empirical) manner.[3]

Here is the point where Edwards inspires theology and philosophy to reenter the debate with scientists. His philosophy can contribute to discussions between scientists and philosophical theologians by asking questions about what Batka calls the "truth of science" and what Vetö calls Edwards's theory of knowledge.[4]

Knowledge

The second part of Vetö's chapter focuses on this theory of knowledge. He explicates for us Edwards's proposal that the natural man without spiritual light sees things dispersed, while one who has been regenerated grasps the coherence and unity of things. The regenerate is also able to move beyond the indirect knowledge of the unregenerate and attain a direct and complete relation to its object of knowledge.

Therefore, to know something about our world and human existence is to have spiritual light and spiritual knowledge. This gives one the ability to know things directly. But it comes only by being in close relation to the only true Being.

This tells us something about science and faith. To be a good scientist means to be humble, which is to realize that our existence is grounded in the One who has not been grounded in anyone or anything else. All good scientific exploration will be marked by this humility and adoration of the true Being. And a proper relationship of Christian faith to science will want to read the "book of nature" with the assistance of science.

Vetö goes on to assert that it is not possible to know when one does not believe. Faith, or spiritual knowing, brings order to what seems disordered. In this sense, faith is a deeper kind of knowledge.

This theory is of great help apologetically. It helps us see faith as the light that leads to true knowing. It shows us that Christian faith does not steal us away from reality, but engages us more deeply with it.

The Edwardsian theory of knowledge also underlines the need for more dialogue between faith and science. Merely "noetical" or "historical" knowledge does not give us the full picture of reality. Edwards, in fact, would say that both faith and reason are necessary for the fullness of each. Vetö's "attentive reflection," by the help of which he speaks of the "interdependence of creation," is appropriate for faith-and-reason dialogues, since mutual dependence is a proven fact, generally accepted by scientists.

According to Vetö, spiritual knowledge is a kind of taste that can be understood as a giving up of the self to an object that possesses the self. Hence spiritual knowledge is not neutral or objectivizing, but a personal engagement of the subject with its object.

These emphases on taste and the nonneutrality of spiritual knowledge provide wonderful material for Lutheran and evangelical ecumenical dialogues, especially in regard to the nature of faith. The idea that faith involves taste, and therefore a kind of experience, is perhaps an evangelical way to help Lutherans understand the way faith is God's attachment of the believer to Christ. Lutherans have rightly stressed the God-givenness of faith, but here the premier evangelical philosopher can show Lutherans that "experience" is part of the faith dynamic—without succumbing to Arminian belief that the self controls the transaction. Faith is necessarily relationship, and relationship is not possible without the experience of taste. So believers do not simply accept a definition of God when they believe the gospel; they are not receiving his attributes in some neutral way; instead, they are overcome by the object of their faith.

If Edwards can help Lutherans learn something about faith as experience, he can also help evangelicals see something of the Lutheran zeal for sacraments. His conception of a "simple" idea being spiritual, implying a multiplicity of connections and things, and his conviction that what is not apparent is implied by what is apparent, can show evangelicals what Lutherans mean by sacrament: the apprehension of something known that leads to a deeper apprehension of the unknown. The bread and wine are visible signs of invisible realities: the body and blood of Christ. In this way Edwards provides a "dictionary" that can help evangelicals see what Lutherans and other Christians mean by their sacramental theology.

Will

According to Professor Vetö, freedom of the will does not consist in indifference to the object. Nor is the quality of the will decided by its past influences; only its nature and choice when it actually decides are important. Vetö effectively rebuts the theory that a will determined by prior influences cannot be held responsible. The strength of sin, he shows, is thereby made the excuse for sin. If that theory were true, Jesus' freedom from sin—his nature not to sin—would imply he does not have true moral goodness. But the truth of the matter is that good and evil are found in the will, not in prior influences.

Edwards's philosophy of the will, as Vetö has represented it, is a stern challenge to moral relativism. This poisonous philosophy leads to a moral dead-end that renders us incapable of discerning the difference between good and evil. Edwards's philosophy of the will opens up an exit filled with light and clarity.

Luther has shown—and here I sense Edwards would agree—that there is no free will as such, but only a liberated will. In other words, none of us is free apart from grace to serve Jesus. But Christians have been liberated from the bondage of the will to sin by the grace of Christ, in order to serve Christ. Yet the service comes not from the inherent nature of the will but only by grace that enables the will to choose rightly. Edwards helpfully shows that corruption of will is no reason to excuse sin, or to release people from responsibility for their evil decisions.

Finally, Edwards's philosophy encourages public theology. It rejects the position that faith is merely a personal matter. On the contrary, it is logical and coherent to see God in everything. One reason Christianity is facing a crisis in Europe today is that it permitted faith to be restricted to a limited field of mere emotions and personal choice. But for Edwards faith is public and provides a public voice in society. Of course, he didn't mean theocracy or Caesaro-papism.

Good public theology is more complex. It requires consistent study and committed believers who are ready to carry the cross of a patient approach, unwilling to find satisfaction in cheap and easy answers.

NOTES

1. L'ubomír Batka, *Patrí teológii miesto na univerzite? O vedeckosti teológie, teologicko-sti viery a vierohodnosti vedy* (Is there a place for theology at the university? On scientific

theology, theological faith and scientific credibility) (Ružomberok, Slovakia: Faculty of Philosophy, Catholic University, 2008), 1.

2. Ibid., 2–3.
3. Ibid., 5.
4. Ibid.

15

Edwards and the World Religions

Gerald R. McDermott

Until very recently, the vast majority of readers and even scholars of Jonathan Edwards have assumed that the eighteenth-century theologian had little or no interest in religions beyond Judaism and Christianity, and certainly no knowledge of the great traditions beyond Palestine. Recent research, however, has shown that from the very beginning of his career Edwards showed interest in other religions, and that he seemed to become more and more intrigued the older he got. Throughout his career he scoured both New and old England for whatever information he could get about the "heathen," and by his last decade he was busy scribbling into his private notebooks hundreds of pages of data about and ruminations on the relationship between Christ and the gods. In this essay I suggest one major stimulus to Edwards's fascination with the religions (deism), and then outline three approaches he took to them. One goes back to Adam and the sons of Noah (the prisca theologia), one is based on Edwards's conviction that God speaks through all of nature and history (typology), and the third stems from his thinking about whether non-Christians can be saved (his dispositional soteriology).

The Prisca Theologia

The fifteenth- and sixteenth-century explorations of the East and the New World discovered not just spices and trade routes but also "heathen" who were reputed to have better morals than most European

Christians. Seventeenth-century geographers estimated that only one-sixth of the planet had heard the gospel, so, according to seventeenth-century English hyper-Calvinists, at least five-sixths of the world's population was doomed to hell. Beginning with Lord Herbert of Cherbury, deists suggested that the Calvinist god responsible for this scenario was a monster. They (the deists) were better than anyone else at popularizing the disjunction between heathens who were damned but morally good, and Christians who were saved but morally bad.

Edwards, no doubt disturbed by deist use of the religions to attack the Reformed God's goodness and justice, worked hard to learn about the religions. He knew of, tried to get, and perhaps read many of the travelogues, dictionaries, and encyclopedias of religion available in his time. The books cited in his *Catalogue* include George Sale's translation of the Qur'an, reports of the Jesuits in China, an analysis of the Kabbalah, comparative mythology, and a wide range of dictionaries and encyclopedias of religion, from the skeptic Peter Bayle's *Historical and Critical Dictionary* to Daniel Defoe's *Dictionary of All Religions Antient and Modern.*[1]

Many of the writers whom Edwards read understood the religions in terms defined by what was called the *prisca theologia* (ancient theology). This was a tradition in apologetic theology resting on misdated texts (the Hermetica, Chaldean oracles, Orpheia, and Sybilline oracles) that attempted to prove that vestiges of true religion were taught by the Greeks and other non-Christian traditions. Typically it alleged that all human beings were originally given knowledge of true religion (monotheism, the Trinity, *creatio ex nihilo*) by Jews or by tradition going back to Noah's good sons (Shem and Japheth) or people before the Flood such as Enoch or Adam. Then it passed down to Zoroaster, Hermes Trismegistus, Brahmins and Druids, Orpheus, Pythagoras, Plato, and the Sybils.[2]

The prisca theologia was developed first by Philo, Justin Martyr, Clement of Alexandria, Origen, Lactantius, and Eusebius to show that the greatest philosophers had stolen from the Chosen People, and then in the Renaissance by Marsilio Ficino and Pico Della Mirandola to synthesize Neoplatonism and Christian dogma.[3] In the seventeenth and eighteenth centuries it was revived by the "Jesuit Figurists," who tried to win acceptance of their mission in China by claiming that China worshipped the true God two thousand years before Christ, and a number of other, mostly Protestant thinkers. Four of these were read carefully and taken seriously by Edwards. First was the Scotsman Chevalier Ramsay (1686–1743), who found trinitarian monotheism among the ancient Egyptians, Persians, Greeks, and Chinese. Ramsay tried to prove that God gave complete revelation of the essential Christian doctrines to the earliest patriarchs, so that most pagan religions teach a trinity similar to the Neoplatonic triad. Edwards also used extensively the work of Philip Skelton (1707–1787), a Church of Ireland divine who wrote the two-volume antideist *Deism Revealed* (London, 1751).

Theophilus Gale (1628–1678) and Ralph Cudworth (1617–1688) are two earlier proponents of the prisca theologia who influenced Edwards. Gale's magnum opus, *The Court of the Gentiles* (1677), was a massive four-volume work dedicated to the proposition that all ancient languages and learning, particularly philosophical, were derived from the Jews. As Numenius of Apamea put it in a line noted by Edwards, "What is Plato but Moses speaking in the Attick language?" (*Misc.*, 1355).[4] Cudworth, the great Cambridge Platonist philosopher, used much of his *True Intellectual System of the Universe* (1678) to show that the wiser pagans were trinitarian monotheists, not unacquainted with the true (Christian) God.

Edwards was clearly impressed by these proponents of the prisca theologia.[5] He copied enormous extracts from their works into his private notebooks, but not slavishly. As Diderot said, imitation is continual invention. From his marginal notes and recapitulation of the tradition in other private notebooks, it is clear that Edwards was selectively and creatively refashioning the tradition to serve his own polemical needs. His principal purpose was to show, against the deists, that nearly all humans have received revelation, and therefore all knowledge of true religion among the heathen is from revelation rather than the light of natural reason. Perhaps more important, five-sixths of the world had *not* been deprived of the basic truths of the gospel.

Edwards went to great lengths detailing in his notebooks the religious truths possessed by the heathen. From Grotius he learned that the Greeks said that the Spirit moved on the waters at the beginning and knew that one can commit adultery in the heart but must forgive and love one's enemies (*Misc.*, 1012, 1023). Virgil, Seneca, Juvenal, and Ovid, Edwards noted, confessed that our original nature was corrupt (*Misc.*, 1073). Ramsay taught him that the Hindu *Vedas* and the Chinese *I Ching* contain stories about a hero who expiates crimes by his own sufferings, and that many heathen from different traditions acknowledged a divine incarnation and realized that virtue comes only by an infusion of grace (*Misc.*, 1351, 1355). Edwards noted in his Blank Bible that heathen stories about gods and goddesses were actually distortions of Hebrew counterparts.[6] Saturn, for example, is a transformation of Adam, Noah, and Abraham; Hercules is a Greek rendition of Joshua, Bacchus of Nimrod, Moses, and the Hebrew deity; Apis and Serapis are Egyptian retellings of the Joseph story.

In his own appropriation of the prisca theologia, Edwards said that the heathen learned these truths by what could be called a trickle-down process of revelation. In the "first ages" of the world the fathers of the nations received revelation of the great religious truths, directly or indirectly, from God himself.[7]

These truths were then passed down, by tradition, from one generation to the next. Unfortunately, there is also a religious law of entropy at work. Human finitude and corruption inevitably cause the revelation to be distorted, resulting in superstition and idolatry.

From Ramsay Edwards learned that the breakdown was caused in part by a problem of language. All original peoples, even the Gauls, Germans, and Britons, shared hieroglyphs with the Egyptians to represent divine things taught by Noah. Over the course of time, pagans dissociated the symbol from its referent. "Men attached themselves to the letter and the signs without understanding the spirit and the thing signified" (*Misc.*, 1255). This accounted for idols and "vile superstitions" (*Misc.*, 1255). It also accounted for the similarity between stories of Christ's sufferings and legends of pagan heroes: the heathen took the symbols of Christ's sufferings and applied them to their own champions. By this mechanism and others the original purity of divine truth was continually breaking down, corrupted by profane and demonic mixture (*Misc.*, 986). God used the Jews to retard the process of degeneration by periodically acting on their behalf with miracles, which reminded the heathen of the traditions they had once learned from their fathers but subsequently forgot (*Misc.*, 350).

In his private commentary on selected biblical passages Edwards recapitulated this drama.[8] "The knowledge of true religion was for some time kept up in the world by tradition. And there were soon great corruptions and apostasies crept in, and much darkness overwhelmed great part of the world." By the time of Moses, most of the truth that had previously been taught by tradition was now lost. So "God took care that there might be something new, [which] should be very public, and of great fame, and much taken notice of abroad, in the world heard, that might be sufficient to lead sincere inquirers to the true God." Hence the heathen nations in the ancient Near East heard about the exodus of the Jews from Egypt, the miracles God performed for them in the wilderness, Joshua's conquests of the Canaanites, and the sun standing still. The defeated Canaanites fled to Africa, Asia, Europe, and the isles of the sea "to carry the tidings of those things . . . so that, in a manner, the whole world heard of these great things."[9]

After these wondrous acts of God, knowledge of true religion was maintained for several generations. But by the time of David, much had been forgotten and distorted. So God acted once more, this time for David and Solomon, "to make his people Israel, who had the true religion, [be] taken notice of among the heathens." The diaspora after the Babylonian captivity spread knowledge of the true God even further abroad, so that "the nations of the world, if their heart had been well disposed to seek after the truth, might have had some means to have led 'em in their sincere and diligent inquiries to the knowledge of the true God and his ways."

And if it wasn't enough for God to send out news of these great events, he saw to it that heathen philosophers came looking for news. Heathen "wise men" and "philosophers" obtained "scraps of light and truth . . . by travelling from one countrey to another," especially Judea, Greece, and Phoenicia.[10] Edwards noted that Plato, for instance, had come to Egypt to learn what he could of the Jewish religion.

The New England pastor was always quick to note that heathen religion and philosophy contained "many absurdities" (e.g., *Misc.*, 1350). But he learned from the prisca theologia that among the absurdities there were enough "scraps of truth" to show the way to salvation (*Misc.*, 1297; NS no. 387). Edwards found one way, then, to respond to the scandal of particularity that reports from the East had posed. He agreed with the deists that the problem could not be ignored, and disagreed with earlier Reformed scholastics who saw nothing beyond knowledge of God the Creator in non-Christian religions.[11] God's justice and goodness were not sufficiently protected by the received tradition, so Edwards appropriated an old tradition to make Reformed history anew. In Edwards's new history God was still good and just, in the context of the new knowledge of pluralism, because knowledge of God the Redeemer had been available from the beginning.

Typology

Eighteenth-century deists imagined they had deflated the overweening pretensions of Christian theology. John Toland (1670–1722), Thomas Chubb (1679–1746), and Matthew Tindal (1657–1733) figured they had exposed traditional Christianity's universal claims as in fact restricted to a small corner of the planet and shown the volumes of Calvinist thought to have been the product of fanciful imaginations. The deists' challenge to orthodoxy was a formidable one: the God of orthodoxy, they avowed, had not revealed himself in history and the Bible. The true God whose will was enshrined in a few simple moral dictates could be discovered by the human mind. But the God of Calvin and Edwards was nowhere to be found in the real world because his supposed revelations were in fact mythical. To put it charitably, he was silent.

The deists had thrown down the gauntlet. Jonathan Edwards eagerly picked it up and threw it back in the form of his typological system—that is, God's system of pointers throughout things he makes and permits. God's nature, Edwards declared, is to communicate itself through this system, that is, to flow out and diffuse itself throughout the creation so that its creatures can come to know its perfections.[12] Therefore God is constantly communicating

Reformed truths wherever the eye can see and the ear can hear. As the psalmist proclaimed, "There is no speech nor language, where their voice is not heard. Their line is gone out through all the earth, and their words to the end of the world" (Ps. 19:3–4 KJV). Types, the New England seer pronounced, "are a certain sort of language, as it were, in which God is wont to speak to us."[13] These types are words in persons, places, and things, and they are found in every part of the creation. Hence there are sermons in the stones, flowers, and stars. God also speaks in history, both sacred and profane. He even speaks in the history of religions, heathen included.

For example, God had planted types of true religion in religious systems that were finally false. God outwitted the devil, Edwards suggested, by using diabolically deceptive religion to teach what is true. In an early entry in the *Miscellanies*, Edwards suggested that the heathen practice of human sacrifice was the result of the devil's mimicry of the animal sacrifice that God had instituted after the Fall.

Sacrifice was taught not by the light of nature but by God's express commandment immediately after he revealed the covenant of grace in Genesis 3:15 ("And I will put enmity between thee and the woman, and between thy seed and her seed; it shall bruise thy head, and thou shalt bruise his heel" [KJV]). The skins with which God clothed the first couple in verse 21 were taken from animals sacrificed by God, who taught them thereby that only the righteousness of Christ won by his sacrifice could cover their sins.[14]

Edwards insisted that animal sacrifice, the main type of Christ in the Old Testament but revealed to all the heathen, taught the necessity of propitiatory sacrifice (sacrifice trying to appease) to atone for sin. Imitating this divine type, the devil led the heathen to sacrifice human beings, even their own sons. Satan believed he had "promote[d] his own interests," outsmarting God, but God outflanked the devil. He permitted this diabolical deception because through it "the devil prepared the Gentile world for receiving . . . this human sacrifice, Jesus Christ." Similarly, the devil induced human beings to worship idols and think that the heathen deities were united to their images. But God used this deception as well for his own purposes, to prepare the Gentile mind for the concept of incarnation, perfectly realized in Christ: "And so indeed was [the] heathenish doctrines of deities' being united to images and the heathenish fables of heroes being begotten [by] gods, a preparation for their receiving the doctrine of the incarnation, of the Deity's dwelling in a human [body], and the Son of God's being conceived in the womb of a virgin by the power of the Spirit of [God]" (*Misc.*, 307).

Twice, then, in the history of religions, God used false religion to teach the true. In each case the devil's machinations were overruled, ironically, by divine wisdom. Practices considered by all Jews and Christians to be abominable—human sacrifice and idol worship—were transformed by a divine plan into teaching devices to prepare the heathen for true religion. In both cases God used non-Christian religions typologically to point to Christian truths.

Far more than incarnation and propitiatory sacrifice, however, was taught by sacrifices. They also showed the heathen that God would not pardon without satisfaction being made, that sin "must be suffered for." They demonstrated God's jealousy and hatred for sin, indicated the need for fear of God and respect for the glory of his holiness, and suggested to sinners that they must trust in God's mercy (*Misc.*, 326).

At the beginning of his career, when he was pastoring in New York in the spring of 1723, Edwards told his congregation that the heathen did not understand the purpose of the sacrifices. Then, and throughout the rest of his career, Edwards made it clear that only those with a regenerate (spiritually awakened) "sense of the heart" were able to read the types in the creation and, we can now add, in the history of religions. He suggested at times that there were some heathen who might have taken advantage of the light they had been given through the Jews and from their own forefathers, and with the light of the Holy Spirit been able to understand the types. But his conviction that most of the heathen would probably never understand did not keep him from noting the wealth of religious knowledge that could be known in non-Christian religions.[15]

There were several reasons the religions abounded with types of the true. The first was that, as we have already seen, most religions shared a common linguistic source. Edwards followed Chevalier Ramsay in believing that both Christian and heathen religions could be traced back to a universal language of hieroglyphics which represented "the divine mysteries of our holy religion, which the first heathens had learned from the antient tradition of the Noevian patriarchs" (*Misc.*, 1255). Over time the meaning of the signs was forgotten.

This was also a reason for the prevalence of "types, figures and enigmatical speeches" in the religions. The fathers of the nations received their wisdom chiefly by tradition from wise men of the church of God, to whom divine instructions had been given in the form of "symbols and emblems." The holy men "in all nations" imitated this manner of representing divine things in "parables" and "types," so they delivered their own wisdom in "allegories, enigmas, [and] symbolic representations." This was why "it became so universally the custom among all ancient nations for their priests, prophets and wise men to utter their auguries and to deliver their knowledge and wisdom, in their writings and speeches, in allegories and enigmas, and under symbolic representations." And this was why the Egyptians and others used "hieroglyphics to represent divine things or things appertaining to their gods and their religion" ("TM," 193–94).

It is striking that Edwards linked Egyptian sacred writings with "holy men [who] were led by the Spirit of God." Even if, as he makes clear elsewhere, he regarded most of Egyptian religion as abominable, nevertheless he clearly believed that there were significant formal similarities between Christianity and other religions of the East. The relationship between these religions was not one of complete discontinuity, but of continuity along several lines. They shared common mythical structures, common linguistic origins, and a common typical form of representation.

There was also continuity in content. As we saw above, Edwards believed that the heathen were given (by the devil!) elementary understanding of propitiatory sacrifice and incarnation. Edwards filled his private notebooks with hundreds of pages recording the doctrines that the heathen shared with Reformed Christians, from the Trinity and a "middle" God who expiates sins to eternal punishment and the notion that "all things owed their beginning and production to love."[16] All of these heathen notions were slightly distorted or incomplete versions of the full truth. But to the extent that they pointed to the work of redemption, in all of its intricately woven parts, they were types as much as human sacrifice was a type of Christ's oblation.

Therefore one could rummage through the religions to find traces of the drama of redemption through the Jews and the Christ. One could discover, for example, that Saturn in heathen myths was a distorted refashioning of Noah, or in fact a "shadow" of Noah. And that Bacchus was a heathen conflation of the stories about Nimrod, Moses, and the Hebrew God. For the "blind heathen" had heard Moses' exploits attributed to God, whom they called Bacchus. One could determine that Hercules was really Joshua, Neptune actually Japheth, and Fohi, the legendary father of the Chinese, in fact Noah, who settled after the flood near Ararat (NS nos. 400–410, 455).

Hence for Edwards the Christian faith could now be seen not as a completely different category, entirely separated in quality from the other religions, but as one end of a long continuum that included religious others. It was at the end because it alone pointed unambiguously to the true reality (antitype), Christ's work of redemption. But it, like other religions, only pointed. Like other types, it was not the actual thing. It could never replace the substance, and like every other religion it came to us through language, which, as Edwards often complained, so imperfectly represented the divine. The New England theologian thus held in tension the divine incomprehensibility and the fact of revelation. God was finally beyond understanding, yet this same God had stooped down to represent himself through broken language. Given the nature of types and the limitations of language, on the one hand, and the deist denial of revelation, on the other, this was a tension Edwards could live with.

Dispositional Soteriology

The third approach Edwards used was what I call dispositional soteriology. Let me explain. For Edwards, the essence of what it means to be a human being is to have a certain "disposition" that can be seen in one or more "habits." Drawing on a tradition that originated with Aristotle and then developed through Thomas Aquinas and Reformed Protestant thinkers, he believed that a habit is an active and real tendency that moves a person to be and do what he or she is and does. This tendency is still there even when there is no opportunity for it to be used, and it will always show itself when it has an opportunity. So when Edwards spoke of a "holy disposition," that is, the disposition of the regenerate, he meant "an active and causal power" that, if it has an opportunity to be exercised, will certainly produce holy effects. As Edwards put it, "All habits [are] a law that God has fixed, that such actions upon such occasions should be exerted" (*Misc.*, 241).

What are these actions or effects? In other words, what does a regenerate disposition look like? Very early in his career Edwards answered this question, and he never diverged from its basic outline in the years following. In *Miscellanies* 39 he declared what he thought to be common to Christians, Old Testament Jews, and all other true religionists "from the beginning of the world": "a sense of the dangerousness of sin, and of the dreadfulness of God's anger . . . [such a conviction of] their wickedness, that they trusted to nothing but the mere mercy of God, and then bitterly lamented and mourned for their sins."

Just a short time earlier Edwards had written that it is this inner religious consciousness (disposition) that is the only thing necessary for salvation. No particular act, even the act of receiving Christ, is necessary: "The disposition is all that can be said to be absolutely necessary. The act [of receiving Christ] cannot be proved to be absolutely necessary. . . . 'Tis the disposition or principle is the thing God looks at."

For an illustration of this point Edwards used the Old Testament Jews. They did not receive Christ in any conscious or explicit manner, but they had the proper disposition, which alone is necessary for salvation:

> It need not be doubted but that many of the ancient Jews before
> Christ were saved without the sensible exertions of those acts in that
> manner which is represented as necessary by some divines, because
> they had not those occasions nor were under circumstances that
> would draw them out; though without doubt *they had the disposition,
> which alone is absolutely necessary now, and at all times, and in all cir-
> cumstances is equally necessary.* (*Misc.*, 27b; emphasis added)

Edwards's subject in this passage is "conversion," and he begins by stating that for salvation there must be "reception of Christ" and "a believing of what we are taught in the gospel concerning him." But his use of Old Testament saints who did not and could not believe precisely what the gospel teaches illustrates his point that in conversion the most essential ingredient is a certain disposition, so that the manner of expressing that disposition by receiving Christ is secondary. Only the disposition is primary. In other words, confessing Jesus as Lord while a person is still alive would not be absolutely essential if that person had never heard that Jesus is Lord.

Edwards used the illustration of a man who dies suddenly, "not in the actual exercise of faith." This man is still saved nevertheless, because "'tis his disposition that saves him." This entry reveals an important structure in Edwards's thinking about salvation: faith is less important than disposition.

Seven years later Edwards made it clear that the disposition is more important than religious and moral behavior. For while the character of a saving disposition is constant, religious and moral expectations differ according to the degree of revelation available. God could overlook ungodly behavior in his saints at various times as long as their disposition was pleasing.[17]

God also overlooked faulty religious knowledge. Early in his pastorate at Northampton Edwards conceded privately that the Jewish saints of the Old Testament did not know about love for enemies, universal love for all humanity, monogamy, or loving one another as Christ has loved us (*Misc.*, 343). Yet they were saved. In Edwards's last decade he became convinced that some heathens had more religious knowledge and even virtue than many Old Testament saints. Greek and Roman moralists, for example, knew that we ought to love and forgive our enemies, return good for evil, and be monogamous (*Misc.*, 1023). Other pagan philosophers knew about infused grace, the necessity of grace for virtue, the Trinity and Incarnation, and redemption by the suffering of a middle god (*Misc.*, 1355). "Socrates, that great Gentile philosopher, . . . worshipped the true God, as he was led by the light of nature," and Seneca "had in many respects right notions of the divine perfections and providence" (*An Humble Inquiry*, 300). Even the (Muslim) Persians and Turks knew true humility and disinterested love for God (*Misc.*, 1257). In the margins of an extract describing Plato's vision of God's beauty, Edwards scribbled, "Right notions of God and religion." At the end of an extract detailing many pagan ideas, he added, "All the chief philosophers have right views of virtue and religion."[18]

These reflections on the religious knowledge and virtue of the heathen may have caused Edwards to rethink, or at least refine, his thinking on justification (God's declaring a sinner to be righteous) and regeneration (the new birth). In a *Miscellanies* entry from the mid-1730s, he began to think about justification and regeneration as phased and, in one respect, life-long processes rather than instantaneous events. Jesus' disciples, he pondered, were "good men *before*" they met Christ, "already in a *disposition* to follow Christ" (*Misc.*, 847; emphasis added). The same was true, Edwards thought, of Zacchaeus and the women of Canaan.[19]

If some are "good" because they have a regenerate disposition before they are outwardly converted to Christ, then perhaps conversion in those cases comes *after* they are already regenerate: "Conversion may still be necessary to salvation in some respect even after he is really a saint." In these cases justification is already a fact in one sense, but in another sense depends on "these after works of the Spirit of God upon the soul" (*Misc.*, 847). That is, the condition of justification still remains to be fulfilled after conversion. Hence saints are still in a state of probation until the end of their lives.[20]

If in a certain sense justification is in stages and finally complete only at death or the end of one's probation on earth, then regeneration can be viewed similarly: "The whole of the saving work of Gods [*sic*] Spirit on the soul in the beginning and progress of it from the very first dawnings of divine light and the first beginnings of divine life until death is in some respect to be looked upon as all one work of regeneration. . . . There is as it were an unregenerate part still in man after the first regeneration that still needs to be regenerated" (*Misc.*, 847).

If regeneration and justification can be considered, at least from one perspective, as processes that unfold in stages, and if one can therefore be a saint before conversion, then theological groundwork has been laid for the position that (some of) the heathen can be saints before they come to Christ if they have the proper dispositions. If their knowledge of Christ is incomplete, it may be because they are still in the initial stages of regeneration and justification, which may be completed in glory, just as it is for infants. Edwards never reached this explicit conclusion, at least in his published writings or private notebooks. But his own theology laid the groundwork for such an interpretation.

More suggestively, Edwards described four types of persons without explicit knowledge of Christ who may nevertheless find salvation. For all four types, disposition is the critical sign of their eternal destiny. Very early in his career Edwards wrote that infants can be regenerated at birth without knowledge of Christ (*Misc.*, 78) and that salvation is based on disposition: "The Infant that has a Disposition in his Heart to believe in Christ if he had a capacity & opportunity is Looked upon and accepted as if he actually believed in Christ and so is entitled to Eternal Life through Christ."[21]

When Edwards asked himself how he was to understand the salvation of Old Testament saints "when yet they had no distinct respect to [Christ]," he reasoned that it was "the second Person in the Trinity" who appeared to them "as the author of temporal salvation and benefits" and whenever God is said to have manifested himself to Israel (*Misc.*, 663). Hence they already believed in Christ in some sense (*Misc.*, 840) and were saved by faith in Christ (*Misc.*, 884, 1283). In an early comment that is fascinatingly relevant to our interests, Edwards wrote that conversions from wickedness to righteousness in the Old Testament era were just as "frequent" as in the New Testament era (*Misc.*, 39). In other words, true faith was plentiful in the Old Testament era among those who did not confess the name of Christ.

New Testament saints followed a similar pattern. "Cornelius did already in some respect believe in X [Christ] even in the manner that the Old Testament saints were wont to do" (*Misc.*, 840). Before he met Peter, that is, Cornelius in some sense believed in a Christ of whom he had not yet heard.²² Edwards said the same about the apostles. Cornelius, Nathaniel, "probably" John's two disciples, and several others were "*good men* before [they met Christ], for they seemed to be found already in a *disposition* to follow [Christ] when [Christ] first appeared to them in his human nature and this seems to have been the case with Zacchaeus and with the women of Canaan" (*Misc.*, 847; emphasis added). Edwards infers from this that "conversion may still be by divine constitution necessary to salvation in some respect even after [a person] is really a saint" (*Misc.*, 847). Once again we see that Edwards is suggesting instances when a person can be regenerate before conversion to an explicit knowledge of Christ. At this point, probably the mid- to late 1730s, Edwards is returning to an inference he had reached very early in his career (1723), that "a man may have the disposition in himself for some time before he can sensibly feel them [the exercises of that disposition], for want of occasion or other reason" (*Misc.*, 27b).

A fourth class of people who enjoyed salvation without explicit knowledge of Christ were those we might call holy pagans. In his 1739 sermons on the history of the work of redemption, Edwards asserted that conversion to true religion, justification, and glorification have occurred in all ages of the world since the Fall, and cited examples of such holy pagans living outside of Israel: Melchizedek, the posterity of Nahor (Job and his family), Job's three friends and Elihu, and Bildad the Shuhite.²³ These were individuals outside the national covenant with Israel and of course without explicit knowledge of Christ who nonetheless seem to have been regenerate.

Late in his career Edwards reflected, tentatively but positively, on the eternal possibilities of the heathen. In *Miscellanies* 1162, after explaining that heathen philosophers had said "such wonderful things concerning the Trinity [and] the Messiah," he asked whether they might have been inspired by the Holy Spirit. Yes, he figured, but then reminded himself that this is not so high "an honour and priviledge as some are ready to think." For "many very bad men have been the subjects of it." Some were idolators such as Balaam. Nebuchadnezzar, "a very wicked man," received a revelation about the Messiah and his future king-dom. Even the devil at the oracle at Delphi was "compelled to confess Christ."

But in any event, of what use were the revelations given to Socrates and Plato "and some others of the wise men of Greece," who were just as inspired as the wise men from the East? These philosophers did not use these revelations to lead their nations toward the truth, so God must have had other intentions. Edwards suggested four: to dispose heathen nations in the future to converse with and learn from the Jews, to prepare the Gentiles for their future reception of the Gospel, to confirm the truths of Christianity, and (in what is one of Edwards's most cryptic comments in the thousands of pages of his private notebooks) to benefit their own souls: "We know not what evidence God might give to the men themselves that were the subjects of these inspirations that they were divine and true . . . and so we know not of how *great benefit* the truths suggested might be to their own souls." Edwards is hesitant and tentative, but he nevertheless clearly opens the possibility that these heathens can use revelation for their own spiritual "great benefit"—a notion that, though not clearly defined, probably includes salvation. When it is recalled that Edwards wrote this entry during a period in which he was frequently quoting from writers who explicitly argued for the salvation of the virtuous heathen, it is difficult to believe that he did not include salvation among the possible "great" benefits to heathen souls.[24]

Near the very end of his life, in a notebook entry arguing against deist views of reason (*Misc.*, 1338), Edwards asserted that reason can confirm many religious truths but cannot discover them on its own. Then he considered the deist objection that most humans have not had the benefit of revelation. There is a "possibility," he replied, of the heathen being "reconciled" to God and thus receiving the benefit of divine revelation, for "the greater part of the heathen world have not [been] left meerly to the light of nature." They had received revelation by tradition from their ancestors and have borrowed from the Jews. Because the means of revelation were available, it was theoretically possible that some could have had a saving disposition and been reconciled to God. But their "extreme blindness [and] delusion" suggested that few had taken advantage of the "benefit of revelation."

We are left with a curious tension in Edwards's thinking about the salvation of the heathen. On the one hand, in most of his explicit commentary on the heathen, he took a negative view characteristic of his Reformed predecessors. While appreciating the religious truth known by the "wiser heathen," he never tired of recording the "absurdities of the worship of the heathen." The later *Miscellanies* contain frequent references to human sacrifice, religious prostitution, fornication, sodomy, castration, and cannibalism.

Edwards was his most uncompromising in his sermons. In an early Northampton sermon he identified immorality and idolatry as characteristically "heathenish."[25] God had forsaken and withdrawn his gracious presence from heathen lands. They were "Lost Nations," and the heathen were the devil's people (30). In a particularly vivid passage, Edwards said, "The devil nurses them [the heathen] up as swine in a pen that he may fill his belly with them in another [world]. . . . They are his prey when they die. That dragon[,] that old serpent[,] then Got 'em into his own den and sucks their blood and feeds upon their bowels and vitals" (30). And there seems no hope, for "those that die heathen he will prey upon and Exert his Cruelty Upon forever" (31).

But that is not the whole picture. Edwards made a series of important theological moves beyond his Reformed predecessors that could have opened the door for a more hopeful view of the salvation of the heathen. The advances he made in typology, the extensive use he made of the prisca theologia, and his development of a dispositional soteriology prepared the theological way for a more expansive view of salvation. He used these developments primarily to argue for a greater knowledge of religious *truth* among the heathen than his favorite Reformed predecessors, Francis Turretin (1623–1687) and Petrus van Mastricht (1630–1706), had allowed.[26] On the question of salvation, he usually conceded only the *possibility* that heathens could be saved and never spoke in the expansively hopeful terms of a Watts, Ramsay, or Skelton, or even a Baxter or Wesley.[27] So, although he built the theological foundations on which a more hopeful doctrine of salvation could quite naturally have been erected, Edwards himself never chose to do so.

For Edwards there was no inconsistency whatsoever between the possibility of reconciliation for the heathen (because of the prisca theologia, God's types in the religions, and a dispositional soteriology) and the probability that only a precious few of the heathen had ever been saved. For this was the testimony of Scripture as he understood it. The sacred authors of the Bible, by the inspiration of the Holy Spirit, portrayed a world in which God had shown himself directly through Jewish history and Jesus Christ. Salvation was available to all, but only through the events of that Jewish-Christian history. News of those events had been heard by most of the world, but few had listened. Hence the world's darkness and delusion were tragic but not unfair. History was a mirror of the human soul: able to perceive cosmic truths but disinclined to appropriate those truths.

Therefore, the fact that God had provided revelation for the majority of the heathen was sufficient to exonerate divine justice. We should be content with that peek into the otherwise inscrutable sanctum of the divine wisdom and trust that the balance of God's administration of the cosmos—though baffling to us much of the time—was finally just. Hence the deist reproach, Edwards reasoned, had been turned back, and God's glory but further magnified.

Relevance for Today's Discussion of the Religions

Edwards is not easily typecast in terms used by current discussions of religious pluralism. Unlike so-called inclusivists today, he never clearly said that some of the heathen were saved. Unlike today's exclusivists (also called restrictivists), at the very least he laid the theological groundwork for the salvation of non-Christians who do not confess Jesus Christ before the moment of death; he may even have meant to suggest this possibility in remarks that are today a bit opaque. Unlike pluralists, he saw Jesus Christ as the only savior, and union with him as the only means to union with God. Unlike most evangelicals, Edwards also envisioned the triune God as not only involved in the history of non-Christian religions but actually revealing truth through them. He may even have been moving, in the months before the smallpox epidemic near Princeton, toward a position that the religions were used providentially by God for the unfolding of the fullness of the work of redemption.

So we are left with the arresting image of a sickly theologian hunched over his desk on the frontier of civilization, greedily devouring scraps of information about non-Christian religions and rethinking received understandings in order to make better sense of new data. In the process he boldly reconceived justification, the extent of revelation, the ministry of Jesus Christ outside the Incarnation, the relationship between regeneration and conversion, and God's redemptive use of demonic religion. If he had survived that smallpox inoculation, there is little doubt that the religions would have played a significant role in the magnum opus he was constructing in his later years.

NOTES

1. He also read or tried to get William Turner's *History of All Religions* (1695), Isaac Watts's *Harmony of All Religions* (1742), Samuel Shuckford's *Sacred and Profane History* (1727), Ephraim Chambers's *Philosophical Dictionary* (1728), Broughton's *Historical Library of Religion Antient and Modern* (1737), and Thomas Dyche's *A New General English Dictionary* (1725), all of which feature articles on non-Christian religions. Edwards, "Catalogue of Reading," Beinecke Library, Yale University.

2. On the prisca theologia, see D. P. Walker, "Orpheus the Theologian and Renaissance Platonists," *Journal of the Wartburg and Courtauld Institutes* 16 (1953): 100–120; Walker, *The Ancient Theology: Studies in Christian Platonism from the Fifteenth to the Eighteenth Centuries* (London: Duckworth, 1972); Walker, *The Decline of Hell: Seventeenth-Century Discussions of Eternal Torment* (London: Routledge, 1964); Frances A. Yates, *Giordano Bruno and the Hermetic Tradition* (Chicago: University of Chicago Press, 1964); Charles B. Schmitt, "Perennial Philosophy: From Agostino Steuco to Leibniz," *Journal of the History of Ideas* 27 (Oct.–Dec. 1966): 505–32; Arthur J. Droze, *Homer or Moses?*

Early Christian Interpretations of the History of Culture (Tubingen: J. C. B. Mohr, 1989); Jean Seznec, *The Survival of the Pagan Gods: The Mythological Tradition and Its Place in Renaissance Humanism and Art* (New York: Bollingen, 1953).

3. Even Augustine seems to have been influenced by this tradition. In his *Retractions* he wrote, "What is now called Christian religion has existed among the ancients, and was not absent from the beginning of the human race, until Christ came in the flesh: from which time true religion, which existed already, began to be called Christian" (1.13).

4. Droze, *Homer or Moses?*, 199; the quote is cited by Edwards in his extract from Ramsey's *Philosophical Principles* on p. 942 of the *Miscellanies* notebook; published in the Yale edition in Jonathan Edwards, *The "Miscellanies" 1153–1360* in *The Works of Jonathan Edwards* [hereafter, *WJE*], ed. Douglas A. Sweeney (New Haven: Yale University Press, 1980), 23: 548. (Subsequent references to the Yale edition are cited parenthetically in the text as volume and page number.)

5. Edwards may have been introduced to the prisca theologia by Samuel Johnson, his tutor at Yale; Norman Fiering, *Moral Philosophy at Seventeenth-Century Harvard* (Williamsburg, VA: Institute of Early American History and Culture, 1981), 15.

6. The Blank Bible was a small copy of the King James Version interleaved with quarto-sized sheets of paper and bound in a large volume; now published in the Yale edition. *WJE* 24, 1: 126–30, 325, 153, 188..

7. *"Miscellanies"* in *WJE* 20: nos. 953, 986, 984. Usually Edwards was ambiguous about the location of the original deposit of revelation. Only occasionally did he pinpoint Adam; in *Misc.* 884 he said that Adam learned the moral law from God and taught it with great clarity to his descendants. In *Original Sin* (*WJE* 3: 170) he wrote that Adam "continued alive near two thirds of the time that passed before the flood," so that most people alive until the flood heard from Adam what "passed between him and his Creator in paradise." Most often, however, he simply referred to the fathers of the nations as identical to or descended from Noah's sons.

8. *Notes on the Scriptures*, Ac. 17: 26–27, no. 387; Edwards Papers, Beinecke Library, Yale University. These are separate notebooks in which he commented on biblical passages, recently published as *Notes on Scripture* [hereafter, *NS*], ed. Stephen J. Stein, vol. 15 of *The Works of Jonathan Edwards* (New Haven: Yale University Press, 1998).

9. This shows that for Edwards there still were, contra Greg Gilbert, opportunities after Moses' time for the heathen to know the true God through the prisca theologia. See Gilbert, "The Nations Will Worship: Jonathan Edwards and the Salvation of the Heathen," *Trinity Journal* 23, NS 1 (spring 2002): 69.

10. "Light in a Dark World, a Dark Heart," *WJE* 19: 713.

11. Following Calvin, they distinguished between knowledge of God the Creator, which is given through nature and conscience but has been distorted by sin, and knowledge of God the Redeemer, which is given through Scripture. Richard Muller, *Post-Reformation Reformed Dogmatics*, vol. 1, *Prolegomena to Theology* (Grand Rapids: Baker Books, 1987), 119–20.

12. *WJE* 8: 430–31, 434–35.

13. "Types," 150. "Types" is one of three notebooks that Edwards devoted exclusively to elaboration of his typological scheme. The other two are "Images of Divine

Things" (hereafter, "Images") and "Types of the Messiah" (hereafter, "TM"). All three are published in *Typological Writings* [hereafter, *TW*], in *WJE* 11. Other notebooks, such as the "Notes on Scripture," the "Blank Bible," and the "Book of Controversies" (Edwards Papers) contain numerous references to typology.

14. *WJE* 9: 134–36.

15. Sermon on Heb. 9:12, in *WJE* 10: 594.

16. See, for example, *Misc.* nos. 151, 326, 1181.

17. *An Humble Inquiry into the Rules of the Word of God, Concerning the Qualifications Requisite to a Complete Standing and Full Communion in the Visible Christian Church,* in *WJE* 12: 281. (Hereafter cited parenthetically in the text.)

18. This note is significant because it comes at the end of *Misc.* 1355, which immediately follows a long series of extracts from Philip Skelton ridiculing pagan notions of God (*Misc.* 1354). This is an illustration of how Edwards took some Reformed polemics against the heathen with a grain of salt. He believed that the heathen were generally lost in darkness but nevertheless was convinced that "the wiser heathen" possessed considerable religious and moral truth.

A similar pattern can be seen in the contrast between *Misc.* 965 (in which Gale scores the spiritual pride of heathen philosophers) and *Misc.* 1357 (an extract from John Brine that criticizes pagan philosophers for their lack of humility and failure to depend on God for virtue), on the one hand, and *Misc.* 986 and 1028, on the other, where Edwards praises Socrates for showing humility by not trusting in himself, and Xenophon, Plato, and Seneca for knowing that virtue is impossible without divine grace.

19. This was simply an application of the principle he articulated in 1729: that "a person according to the gospel may be in a state of salvation, before a distinct and express act of faith in the sufficiency and suitableness of Christ as a Savior" (*Misc.* 393).

20. Edwards also speaks of God justifying, "as it were," a person being received into the visible church on the "presumption" and "supposition" that the person is sincere, which is proved by later "faithfullness" (*Misc.* 689). This "visible covenant" is different from the "covenant of grace," but in each case there is a condition to be fulfilled. In the covenant of grace, however, God covenants "with those that before his allseeing eyes perform that condition of the covenant of grace" (*Misc.* 689).

21. "Book of Controversies" (Edwards Papers), 65 This notebook is published in *WJE* 21. *Misc.* 492 suggests that Edwards considered the state of infants analogous to that of the heathen, since both have less than full knowledge of revelation. In this entry he speculates that without revelation we would not know "who are liable to punishment, whether children, whether heathen."

22. Calvin, in contrast, said that Cornelius was "already illumined by the Spirit of wisdom" and "sanctified by the same Spirit," but stops short of saying that he was regenerate. *Institutes* 3.17.4.

23. *HWR*, 179. Edwards also said in these sermons that after Abraham God rejected all other nations and gave them up to idolatry (*HWR*, 179). That Edwards is speaking of collective groups and not individuals is clear from several discussions in his notebooks, including the one mentioned in the next paragraph of this text.

24. It should also be noted that the Cambridge Platonist Henry More, who, according to Wallace Anderson, had "an early and lasting influence upon Edwards' thought," wrote that the heathen can be saved by grace through "Faithfulness to that Light and Power which God has given them." *WJE* 6: 21; Henry More, *An Explanation of the Grand Mystery of Godliness* (London, 1660), Bk. 10, Chap. 6, 352. Furthermore, the other three purposes of the revelation are related to salvation: to learn from the Jews (who point to Christian salvation), to prepare to receive the gospel, and to confirm the truth of Christian faith (as the way to salvation) for later Christians. None has anything to do with the common grace of moral truth, which is the meaning Gilbert has suggested in "The Nations Will Worship," 63–64. How could information that only condemns be of "great benefit" to heathen souls? In addition, Edwards's use of "soul" commonly is in the context of salvation. Note the following four sermon doctrines:

> ECCL. 12:7: "That when a man dies his soul goes to God who gave it" (n.d.).
> MATT. 5:8: "I. Prop. That it is a thing truly happifying to the soul of man to see God. 2. Prop. That the having a pure heart is the certain and only way to come to the blessedness of seeing God" (n.d.).
> MATT. 16:26: "That the salvation of the soul is a thing of vastly more worth and importance than the whole world" (n.d.).
> MATT. 16:26: "1. The whole world is not a sufficient price to receive to make up for the loss of the soul. 2. When once the soul is lost the whole world would not be a sufficient price to give to recover it" (1734).

25. Sermon on Rev. 3:15 (before 1733), Edwards Papers, 13.

26. Turretin, *Institutes*, 1:9–16; Mastricht, *Theoretica-practica theologia* (Utrecht, 1724), I.i.xxii–xxv.

27. Baxter forthrightly granted salvation to those (outside the "Jewish church") who did not have "knowledge of Christ *incarnate*," and Wesley said pagans just need to live up to the light they are given. Richard Baxter, *The Reasons of the Christian Religion* (London, 1667), 201–2; Wesley, Sermon 68, "The General Spread of the Gospel," in *Works*, 9: 234; see David Pailin, *Attitudes to Other Religions: Comparative Religion in Seventeenth- and Eighteenth-Century Britain* (Manchester, U.K.: Manchester University Press, 1984), 48.

16

Alternative Viewpoint: Edwards and the World Religions

Michal Valco

In my response to McDermott's chapter on the relationship of Jonathan Edwards—an outspoken, well-respected, and influential theologian of the eighteenth century—to the world religions, I will attempt to highlight some of the most interesting points of the lecture, offer an initial critical evaluation, and suggest a few questions for further discussion.

Summary of the Arguments

McDermott opens his presentation with a bold statement about a critical shift in recent research in the area of Edwards's apologetics, including his theodicy. After all, theodicy—either for the sake of his own conscience or for the sake of the critics of Christianity—seems to be the source and focus of Edwards's dealing with non-Christian religions. As McDermott writes, "Edwards, no doubt disturbed by deist use of the religions to attack the Reformed God's goodness and justice, worked hard to learn about the religions."

The attacks of deism, therefore, are identified as "one major stimulus to Edwards's fascination with the religions." This is the first thesis of McDermott's essay. The second one outlines the *prisca theologia*, typology, and dispositional soteriology as three approaches or ways Edwards dealt with the question of the relationship between Christianity and other religions, between the Triune God and the history of non-Christian religious experience.

McDermott presents a competent analysis of the subject, grounded in solid historical research and a careful theological reflection. In his approach, however, he stays a "historical theologian"—more historical than systematic, reluctant to make open theological deductions or suggestions. His essay, nevertheless, is thought-provoking and stimulating. Prisca theologia was a commonly used theological approach in ancient times (especially by early apologists), but it has rarely been connected with Reformed theologians. The same can be said about the interreligious typology described and identified in Edwards's texts. The idea of dispositional soteriology is certainly the most intriguing concept that McDermott chose to emphasize and analyze. This concept is also the one that is most questionable when it comes to its theological value.

The Question of Motivation

Was Edwards "disturbed by deists," or was he truly "fascinated" with other religions? It is an important question to which we do not find a clear answer in McDermott's essay. In other words, was the critique of deism or Edwards's private fascination the "stimulus" for his research on the subject of world religions? McDermott suggests a development in Edwards's thinking on this matter: Edwards was initially "disturbed" by deists, and later on he became "fascinated" with other religions. This question, perhaps, does not seem to possess the critical importance that I am suggesting here, but I would like to suggest that the way we answer this question will significantly influence the way we read Edwards on this topic, as well as the way we integrate Edwards's approaches into our apologetics and interreligious dialogue today.

How could so many respected scholars for such a long time overlook this intriguing feature of Edwards's theology? According to McDermott, "a vast majority" of readers and scholars had had a wrong assumption regarding this issue, seeing Edwards just as an uncompromising defender of Reformed orthodoxy. The reason for this "neglect" by the majority of scholars was the omitting or overlooking of Edwards's marginal notes and some of his sermons, according to McDermott. Still, it seems to me that more research and theological reflection needs to be done to determine, beyond any doubt, if the reason for this "neglect" was merely a "historical" one (in terms of the previous scholarship methods) or a theological one. Could it be that we overemphasize an insignificant theological experiment of Jonathan Edwards, about which he himself was not convinced?

The Influence of the Enlightenment

Edwards, too, was a child of his time. His time was the age of Enlightenment. The underlying characteristic of Enlightenment is an uncritical faith in the objectivity of human reason—in the capacity of reason (a metaphysical, transpersonal category) to explain the world and to teach the human race how to live in it. It would be interesting to investigate how the ideas and methods of the Enlightenment influenced Edwards in his methodology and approaches to theology. Did he feel the need to "rationalize" God's justice and defend God's right to condemn people to hell by explaining that "God had provided revelation for the majority of the heathen," and then maintaining that, because "few had listened," God's justice is exonerated? Did the rationalistic methodology of the Enlightenment make him think that the "prisca theologia, typology, and dispositional soteriology" were the necessary and reasonable tools that will help Christianity become more intelligible to modern man and thus more defensible to the critique of the modern age?

Perhaps the question could be restated as the following: Are we, postmodern interpreters of Edwards, so influenced by the age of reason that we cannot resist the urge to rationalize Christianity, which prompts us to look for respectable archetypes with similar approaches? Although my last words probably are an overstatement of the issue, they reflect a general tendency of much of modern theology to rationalize, psychologize, or historicize some basic teaching of Christianity in order to defend it. The danger is that by so defending Christianity we compromise its very essence.

The Concept of Prisca Theologia Cannot Be Maintained

The line of argument in Dr. McDermott's essay goes as follows: If it can be proved that the heathen had sufficient access to revelation regarding God's redemptive activity—by means of prisca theologia and with the help of interreligious and "natural" typology—God would use that revelation to create an inner disposition in some (although very few) of the heathen, which would enable them to be saved. Many scholars today, however, have far less confidence in the so-called history of the prisca theologia than did early Christians, or Edwards and his contemporaries. The idea of Greek philosophers studying under Hebrew patriarchs or prophets, as well as the idea of a common linguistic root or hieroglyphs shared with the Egyptians, has not been supported by modern archaeological research. If, then, the heathen did not have access to the type of revelation that Edwards suggests, it becomes highly questionable that there was an opportunity for God to create the proper disposition in them in order to save them.

A More "Hopeful" Soteriology

The most thought-provoking part of McDermott's essay is the one on dispositional soteriology. Though one could easily get lost in the scholastic terminology in the beginning of this section (essence, habit, tendency, etc.), it is important to explain the terminology for the sake of the argument that followed. The essence of true religious experience for Christians and non-Christians alike, according to Edwards, is a certain kind of a disposition of the human soul: "a sense of the dangerousness of sin, and of the dreadfulness of God's anger . . . [such a conviction of] their wickedness, that they trusted to nothing but the mere mercy of God, and then bitterly lamented and mourned for their sins." This inner disposition, then, is the only prerequisite to salvation: "The disposition is all that can be said to be absolutely necessary. The act [of receiving Christ] cannot be proved to be absolutely necessary. . . . 'Tis the disposition or principle is the thing God looks at." McDermott's conclusion is that "if one can therefore be a saint before conversion, then theological groundwork has been laid for the position that (some of) the heathen can be saints before they come to Christ if they have the proper dispositions."

Jonathan Edwards, as McDermott rightly pointed out, never drew such a conclusion (as far as we know), but rather remained very critical of heathen idolatry—"lost people" who live in darkness. If it is true that Edwards opened the door for a more "hopeful" or broader soteriology, why did he never choose to follow through? Was he truly fascinated? Did he truly believe in his new approaches? What if he failed building a more hopeful or broader soteriology precisely because he understood the limits of his experiments? What if Edwards was more a theologian of the cross, ready to live with the tension, which our human reason presents when it comes to judgment, condemnation, and salvation? So the question before us is how we should understand this idea of "disposition" and the proposed dynamic relationship between regeneration, conversion, and justification, especially after we seriously take into account the Reformed concept of election as the decisive and ruling factor in human salvation. Dispositional soteriology does not solve the scandal of a God who freely chooses or elects those sinners whom He will graciously regenerate and save! Edwards must have known this!

Historically speaking, because of certain themes in Puritan covenantal theology, regeneration ceased to be understood as a miraculous event bestowed by the Spirit as he wills and came to be understood as a human act of self-determination (as can be seen in many revival movement preachers of the 1740s). Jonathan Edwards opposed this change in meaning, trying to reestablish the miracle of regeneration in the historical event of preaching Christ in the historical community of believers.

According to Edwards, the true question in regeneration is whether we see the true God truly, namely, in Christ who befriends sinners. The cross and resurrection with Christ is the specific way God has redeemed his creatures in order to bring them to communion with himself. In Christ's merciful and victorious love for sinners, revealed in his cross and resurrection, the "loveliness of God" is revealed, which inspires our love. The beauty of God transforms everyone who beholds it. A truly regenerated person, according to Edwards, is one whose love for God has been evoked purely by God's own loveliness rather than by any selfish motive.

Behind the human experience of regeneration is the far more important reality of the divine self-bestowal, which produces this new reality in darkened minds. History is the battleground of the Kingdom of God. But where else can we find this beauty, this marvelous self-bestowal of God through Jesus in the power of the Spirit, but in the midst of the community of the people of God where the Word is preached and God gives himself to us through bread and wine and water according to his promise?

What if we cannot have the right disposition toward God until Christ appears in our field of vision and gives us the God to whom we may have the right disposition—whom we can love? Edwards means very specifically the beauty of the Triune God, the "sweet harmony" of the eternal divine life of the Father and the Son in the Holy Spirit. This and only this type of religious experience, according to Edwards, is life changing, or, to put it in other words: giving the right disposition to sinners on their way to salvation.

The Eastern European Context

The position of the established churches in Eastern Europe has changed dramatically in the post-Communist era. The communication of the Gospel in this new environment has proven to be difficult for churches that were used to a restricted, yet predictable position under Communism. After Communism fell, new religious ideas and sectarian delusions flooded our area of the world. Now Eastern Europe is more multicultural and multireligious than ever, but the churches have fewer tools than their Western brethren have for coping with this new situation. Therefore the study of Christianity's relationship to world religions is of utmost relevance.

The challenge is twofold: Christianity in post-Communist Europe has to "rediscover its face" following a difficult period of oppression, failures, and martyrdom, and it has to deal with a radically new social, political, economic, and religious situation. A faithful Christian witness in this setting needs to start by rediscovering Christianity's own traditions, exploring carefully its own theological roots. Then he or she must try to understand the nature of the changes that have come to the Slovak nation over the past centuries—Reformation and Counter-Reformation in the sixteenth and seventeenth centuries, ethnic tensions in the nineteenth century, the Holocaust during World War II, and four decades of Communism—so that he or she can engage society in a culturally sensitive manner. Only in that process will the churches be able to engage meaningfully in interreligious dialogue.

But at that point it will be all the more pressing to figure out how our Christian faith should understand other religions. Perhaps then we can learn something from Jonathan Edwards—even while recognizing from his own work certain pitfalls that must be avoided.

Conclusion

This is why I believe Professor McDermott's study raises relevant questions in our religiously pluralistic world. As a systematic theologian I regret that we were left with a historical analysis (though a solid one) without clear implications based on a more open theological evaluation of Edwards's ideas. What McDermott did show us through his interpretation of Edwards, though, is the richness of religious experience beyond Christianity and Judaism. He reminded us that Christian "chauvinism" is disrespectful not only to other religions but also to God's greatness, to the richness of his mercy, to the glory of his wisdom. God is greater than our theologies—this is a lesson that we need to remind ourselves constantly. Jonathan Edwards's apologetic experiments did not provide him with ready, infallible solutions. But they did keep him humble in the view of the richness of the life of the Triune God and his amazing and most unexpected involvement in the history of the world for the sake of our salvation. Having said that, the question remains, of course, how far is too far when it comes to our human speculation. Just like Edwards, we have to learn to live with the tension.

Conclusion: Edwards's Relevance Today

Gerald R. McDermott

By now you've seen, I hope, that there's far more to Jonathan Edwards than you ever imagined. He wore more hats than you thought, and though most Americans assumed he was simply a hellfire preacher, you've learned that beauty, not wrath, was at the center of his vision of God.

But perhaps you're also wondering where Edwards and his thinking intersect with your world. The essays in this book have provided some clues. Stout's chapter on revival, for example, has implicitly called into question some of the church's strategies for growth today; Kimnach's essay on literature has demonstrated an alternative to much contemporary preaching; and my essay on world religions has suggested other ways of thinking about rival faiths.

But there is far more to say about the relevance of Edwards's thinking for the church and the world today. In this last essay I add detail to some of the hints above and sketch some additional ways in which Edwards's vision can be of help. I address issues in the Christian church that suggest why Edwards is appealing to more and more Christians, and along the way reflect on how his thinking has resonated even among non-Christians.

Neither Fundamentalist nor Liberal

We have seen over and over again, especially in the essays by Professors Fabiny and Lee, that the heart of Edwards's view of God is *beauty*.

As I mentioned in the introduction, Edwards made beauty more integral to his theology than has anyone else in the history of Christian thought. This is, of course, antithetical to the way Edwards has been portrayed in most history and literature classes, where for decades the "Sinners in the Hands of an Angry God" sermon is all that students read. Despite the fact that the sermon is a rhetorical and literary tour de force, as Professor Stout argued in his essay, most students come away thinking Edwards was a hellfire preacher and nothing more. And that his God is a fearsome ogre.

But the revelation of Edwards's true God, a God of beauty and joy, has brought liberation to many, both conservative and liberal Christians. It also demonstrates that Edwards was neither a fundamentalist nor a liberal, at least as those two words are defined today. He was not a fundamentalist in the sense that he did not preach a God whose essential relation to humanity was a list of do's and don'ts. And he did not base his view of God on a series of disconnected Bible verses. Instead, as Professor Stout has shown, he insisted that the best theology is based on the history of redemption. The story as a whole, not simply words or statements in the story, is most important.

Nor was he a liberal whose religion simply baptized elite culture. Instead, as the essays in this book have suggested, his God challenges early third-millennium Western culture in all sorts of ways, not least of which is its assumption that we are free to define truth as we like. Edwards's God *is* truth, and he shows us the definitive meaning of life. But at the same time, this God is a being of terrible beauty who lures rather than coerces and whose aesthetic magnificence sets the soul free to love truth (and others) by the vision of that beauty.

Nor does Edwards fit into the categories of "precritical" or "modernist." The first word refers to those who did not know, or refused to see, the influence of history and culture on those who wrote the Bible. The second is often used for those who reduce the Bible to something other than what it claims to be (the voice of the living God through the testimony of those whom he inspires)—the experience of people who may or may not be in touch with the divine but are expressing ordinary human desires for meaning and power. Edwards fully accepted the idea that the biblical authors were creatures of time and space, affected by the social and political forces of their times. But he also believed God spoke through their words, even as those words were shaped by contemporary forces.

Another reason that Edwards cannot be labeled either fundamentalist or liberal is that he believed in the authority of both Scripture and reason. His trust in the divine origin of Scripture, in every passage of every book, would make a religious liberal cringe. His refusal to believe that any part of the Bible could contradict another part—for he believed there was ultimately only one author—is repugnant to freethinkers. But his joyful confidence in reason and unblinking use of arguments from opponents and unbelievers would make a religious fundamentalist squirm. As Professor Kimnach shows, Edwards thought science and philosophy can be part of God's (natural) revelation. He believed that although we lack direct access to the truth of either, both Scripture and reason are God-given gifts to help us see the underlying meaning of both (science and philosophy).

Conversion and Spiritual Formation

Edwards has plenty to say to current debates in the church about what it means to convert and how one grows in grace. On conversion, he avoids the dichotomy of head (beliefs as the best test of salvation) versus heart (it's a matter of how you feel about Jesus), saying that the heart of true spirituality is what he called the "affections," which are the basic inclinations of the soul, the root of everything we think, feel, and choose. Conversion comes with a vision of the beauty of God in Jesus Christ and results in transformed affections, which then affect every part of us—our feelings, beliefs, and choices. The best sign of true conversion is Christian practice, which is most reliably seen over the long run. So after the Great Awakening's excesses, Edwards became uncomfortable with declaring that someone was regenerate because of an emotional experience, and he decided that only the test of time, proven by Christian practice, was a reliable sign of true religion.

For spiritual growth, Edwards emphasized a host of practices that don't receive a lot of attention today: fasting and prayer, daily Bible study, intercession for worldwide revival and existing churches and ministers, regular recollection of present and past sins, exhortations and warnings to others, perseverance through times of suffering, and the continual "striving" for holiness and "Christian knowledge" (of the Bible and Christian doctrine).[1] He also emphasized balance in the Christian life. True spirituality, he taught, is balanced between assurance of salvation and fear of God, joy in Christ and mourning for sin, love for God and love for others, love for both friends and strangers, love for neighbor and family, and concern for others' bodies as well as their souls. True spirituality cares about its own sins and not just others', it trusts God for both salvation and financial provision, and it perseveres in faith through both prosperity and trouble. Finally, it is regular at both public worship and secret prayer.[2]

Teacher of Preachers

Most of us are familiar with the "Sinners" sermon. Even if we don't like its threatening message, we can admire Edwards's use of imagery—which was so skillful that, according to note takers present, some of those listening feared the floor would open up beneath them and they'd fall into hell.

But Edwards the fire-breather was also Edwards the Enlightenment rationalist, who looked for the best arguments no matter who made them. He can teach preachers and laity alike that reason is a gift from God, even if it is found on the lips of those who hate God. He can teach thinking Christians today that God pours his rain and shines his sun—and his gifts of truth—on the churched and unchurched alike, both believers and unbelievers. Edwards learned from deists while undermining their system. As the early church put it, he plundered the Egyptians while escaping their clutches. Professor Kimnach shows that he read all the good literature he could get his hands on, and not only literature but also journalism, science, history, philosophy, and theology. He didn't care who wrote as long as they made good use of reason and had something to teach him. He is a model of a Christian mind that fears nothing in the wider world, but joyfully appropriates what is of use to understand that world and its Creator.

Edwards was a model preacher. He didn't have a strong voice and was barely animated in the pulpit. But it is said that his original hearers were often surprised the sermon hour had come to an end so quickly, so captivated were they by the imagery and reasoning they were hearing. What was his secret? Part of it was his incomparable ability to bring to bear upon contemporary problems the depths and riches of the biblical drama. Another part was his skill at making, as Professor Kimnach has put it, what is true become real. Professor Sweeney has told us that Edwards was famous for distinguishing between historical knowledge of the Bible and "spiritual knowledge" of its story of redemption. This would come only when the "divine and supernatural light" shone through the biblical text, and so opened the reader's spiritual eyes that he or she could "see" the vivid reality of "divine things." Today's preachers could learn from this singular determination to not only tell the history of redemption, but to so pray and preach that that story becomes more *real* than any other story.

Preachers can also learn from what Professor Sweeney told us of Edwards's interpretation of the Bible. No part of it could be abstracted from the rest of the canon and its complete story of redemption. Edwards believed, with the Reformers, that Scripture is the best interpreter of Scripture. One can assume a divine unity undergirding the book's whole and should use that conviction to help interpret problem passages. Difficult passages should always be seen in the light of the whole story and its more transparent sections.

Missions

In this day when Christians in Europe and America are surprised to discover the explosion of Christian churches in the global South, some are realizing the long-term impact of missions. Much of this new southern growth has been indigenous, yet even the southern churches acknowledge the important seeds planted by missionaries in previous centuries, largely a result of the eighteenth- and nineteenth-century Protestant missionary movement. One significant part of the story is the role of Edwards. As Chris Chun points out in this volume, Edwards may not have been the father of this movement, but he has rightly been called its grandfather. The main reason for this is the influence of Edwards's books on many of the most important leaders of the modern Protestant missions enterprise. Edwards's *Life of Brainerd*, which was probably the first full missionary biography ever published, provided for many missionaries a portrait of the model missionary. William Carey (1761–1834), an English Baptist missionary to India and the principal founder of Anglo-American missions, drew up a covenant for his missionary band that included the words "Let us often look to Brainerd." According to one of his biographers, Carey so devoured Edwards's life of Brainerd that it became almost a second Bible to him. John Wesley published an abridged version of the *Life* in 1768 (and then seven more separate editions), removing Calvinist passages but writing that preachers with Brainerd's spirit would be invincible. The list of missionaries who have testified to Brainerd's influence is a Who's Who of Anglo-American missions in the past two centuries: Francis Asbury, Thomas Coke, Henry Martyn, Robert Morrison, Samuel Mills, Robert M'Cheyne, David Livingstone, Adoniram Judson, Theodore Dwight Weld, Andrew Murray, and Jim Elliott.

Some of Edwards's other works were also influential in modern missions. Carey used Edwards's *Humble Attempt* (an Edwards treatise urging prayer for worldwide awakenings) to rebut the belief that certain prophecies had to be fulfilled before the "heathen" could be converted. The *Humble Attempt* inspired the founders of the London Missionary Society, the (English) Baptist Missionary Society, and the Scottish Missionary Society, as well as the most celebrated of all Scottish evangelicals, Thomas Chalmers. Edwards's *History of the Work of Redemption*, though not well-received until the nineteenth century, became one of the most popular manuals of Calvinist theology during the Second Great Awakening and excited renewed interest in missionary work both at home and abroad.

What got so many people excited about Edwards on missions? Perhaps it was the paramount role he gave to missions in human history. He argued, as we have seen, that the history of revival is the main story line in the history of humanity, and both are part of what he called the history of redemption. Missions, of which revival is the culmination, is the principal moving force of the history of salvation. Despite the fact that this history never really had a beginning (because "God's electing love and the covenant of redemption never had a beginning") and will have no end, its principal purpose is to repair the damage in time wreaked by the Fall by restoring God's image in humanity (which means its nature and soul) and the world.[3] The history of redemption has four other purposes: to gather together all things into union in one body joined to Christ, to effect the triumph of good over evil, to perfect the beauty of the elect, and to glorify the Trinity.[4] Therefore missions, for Edwards, are the principal means used by God to secure these purposes in history.

Edwards's missiology was innovative in two respects. Although there were others, such as Richard Baxter, who had called for modern missions (and theologians such as Samuel Willard and Cotton Mather who had urged missions to Native Americans), Edwards provided new, high-profile sophistication to the claim that the church should be on missions. The standard theological textbooks of Ames, Wollebius, and Calvin were silent on missions, and no other major work of Protestant dogmatics in the English-speaking world gave missions a prominent place. Many Reformed thinkers since the Reformation, including Edwards's ally Thomas Prince in Boston, believed missions were largely limited to the apostolic age.

By giving such prominent place to the laity's intercession for revival, Edwards was also one of the first Protestant thinkers to apply the Great Commission to all church members and to invest that call with such universal vision. In his *Humble Attempt* Edwards gave first place to the church's intercession and only marginal place to preaching as the stimulus that prompts outpourings of the Holy Spirit upon the earth. His enormous prestige in the century after his death, combined with the extensive reprints of *Humble Attempt*, significantly strengthened nineteenth-century Anglo-American Protestantism's *lay* enthusiasm for foreign missions and the resulting expansion of Christendom to what we now call the third world.

Perhaps Edwards's most productive stimulus to missions was his extraordinary historical optimism and fervent expectation of imminent revival. Beginning in the late 1730s and continuing through the Great Awakening and much beyond, Edwards prophesied that the world was on the verge of massive religious revival. The era was like that of the first century, he wrote: there had just been a quantum leap in learning, and it was a dark time again for religion.

There was nothing in the biblical prophecies that had to be fulfilled before this great outpouring of the Spirit, only prayer and preaching. The revival would bring the "church's prosperity" and at the same time violent opposition because the "great revival" will "mightily rouse the old serpent." The long-term result would be awakening in every nation—among Jews, Muslims, and heathen, and throughout Africa, Asia, and Australia. Repeatedly he projected the conversion of American Indians, as well as the inhabitants of Africa and South Asia: "Many of the Negroes and Indians will be divines, and . . . excellent books will be published in Africa, in Ethiopia, in Turkey."[5]

Here we come full circle to the explosion of Christianity in the global South today. It is intriguing to see that the revival of missions in the two centuries after Edwards led at least indirectly to revival in Africa and Asia, so that African and Asian divines (typically, Anglican archbishops) are now giving religious direction to American Christians and their churches. Edwards's predictions were not too far off the mark. However, it is not his uncanny prophecies that have excited interest in his missiology among many today, but his bold historical optimism and his challenge to all the church to catch the vision of mission.

Catalyst for Renewal?

Many modern Christians have a difficult time cheering Edwards's work in revival and missions. To them, fear plays far too important a role in revival preaching. And if revival is the culmination of mission that drives the engine of history, then fear plays a key role in the work of redemption. But should it? Both revival and fear as a part of it are repellant to the modern mind.

Let's look first at Edwards's claim that revival is the engine of history. Is this credible? Think of the early Christian church, whose rise Edwards called a religious revival. Few would doubt that the rise of Christianity turned the course of the Roman Empire, whose later history in turn shaped the beginning of the Middle Ages. All histories of the high and later Middle Ages show the overwhelming dominance of the church in its culture, much of which was driven by such "revivals" as the Benedictine, Franciscan, and other monastic movements. Arguably, the American Civil War was precipitated by the Second Great Awakening and the abolitionist movement it spawned.

And what about fear? Stout has explained that Edwards believed fear of judgment was an important element in revival preaching. Was he wrong to promote such preaching? Is it always wrong for religion to produce fear? What about slaveholders' fears that God might be angered by their slaveholding? Or the fear of anyone who has abused another human being, that his or her sin might be judged in this life or the next? Anyone who believes that sin matters, and that much human misery is the result of sin, should consider what role religious fear can play in checking social evil. It is probable that down through the ages, many thousands—perhaps millions—have come to faith because of fear. It's also probable that in many cases that fear was later transformed into loving awe before God's beautiful love. Edwards would say that churches that condemn all use of fear in preaching are missing something integral to both faith and human psychology.

If fear can play a role in social and churchly renewal, so can Edwards's distinction between natural and moral ability, which Professor Vetö outlined and we will return to below. Edwards said that we human beings are morally bound to sin because of our sinful nature. But at the same time we have natural ability not to sin. For example, the proud man is bound to tell others about his accomplishments. In a sense, he can't help it. But he also has a mouth that speaks only when his mind tells it to. There is nothing in nature that forces him to speak those words of self-congratulation. So on the one hand, he is bound to praise himself, but on the other, he is responsible for his sin of pride because nothing is *forcing* his lips to form those words. This is why Edwards says he is both bound and free at the same time. Morally he is bound by the pride of his sinful nature, while naturally he is free to choose not to let his lips form those proud words.

As Professor Vetö points out, society risks disintegration if it accepts the principle that moral necessity (a sinner is bound by his or her sinful nature) removes responsibility ("I couldn't help it and so am not to blame"). We've already seen this in cases where criminals are acquitted because they plead that their desires were overwhelming. Vetö points out the absurdity of this reasoning: "Then the more one is dominated by greed, cruelty, or malice, the more one would be pardoned for being mean and acting cruelly." Edwards's remedy to this modern illogic is to use his concept of moral versus natural necessity to show that the criminal with a criminal nature is not thereby absolved of responsibility—for he or she is still *naturally* free to choose against crime.

This principle can also be used for religious renewal. Souls outside of grace who plead that they are helpless to approach God—since Scripture claims the moral inability of the soul to reform itself—can be told there is nothing in nature that is stopping them from going to church or reading the Bible. This is how Calvinist preachers have preached revivals since the Great Awakening, with great success at times. It is also how both individual and church renewal can proceed: we can use our natural abilities to avail ourselves of the means of grace (preaching, fellowship, sacraments, Bible reading), thus, as Edwards put it, building the pile of logs on top of Mount Carmel like Elijah in the hope that

God will send down fire. The fires of revival and renewal have been poured out on countless individuals and churches since, even and especially on those who believed they were morally helpless to change.

The Reformed Tradition

Academic conferences on Edwards are lucky to attract two hundred scholars and students. But in 2003 in Minneapolis twenty-five hundred people thronged a municipal auditorium to listen to three days of talks about America's theologian sponsored by a Reformed megachurch. The cover of the September 2006 issue of *Christianity Today* (this country's largest religious periodical) featured a T-shirt emblazoned with the words "Jonathan Edwards Is My Homeboy." This cover story was about the American churches' resurgence of interest in Reformed theology and its principal theologian, Jonathan Edwards.

What does Edwards contribute to Reformed theology today? Or perhaps more telling, why are so many Reformed Christians drawn to Edwards? In a word, Edwards addresses typical Reformed themes and problems with unique depth and sophistication. For example, a hallmark of Reformed thinking is emphasis on the sovereignty of God. Edwards's *History of the Work of Redemption* weaves together secular and sacred history, suggesting that God has sovereignly superintended both in order to serve the work of redemption. In his private notebooks, as we saw briefly in my essay, he showed the ways God used even the world religions for that same purpose.

One problem that is frequently posed to Reformed Christians is how sovereignty can be squared with human freedom. As it is often put, How can we be free if God controls everything, even our decisions? Edwards didn't shrink from this knotty problem, but instead, as was his custom, attacked it head-on. In four months he wrote the book that set the agenda for philosophical discussions in America until the Civil War: *Freedom of the Will*. In this work he argued that human freedom and divine sovereignty are compatible, and several essays in this book have explained briefly how he thought the two can work together. Not everyone agrees he was successful, but many Reformed readers think this work has yet to be equaled or decisively refuted.

Another problem in the Reformed tradition has been evangelism. If God has already decided who are among the elect, and if God alone can bring conversion, why should we evangelize? Wouldn't that be presuming we can do what God alone does? Many Reformed folks came to that very conclusion and denounced evangelism as unbelief. Edwards stepped into this breach as well. As we have just discussed, he developed the distinction between natural and moral necessity, and one of its chief results was freeing Reformed ministers to preach for conversion with a clear conscience. With this distinction, Reformed Christians could hold to God's sovereignty over the will and yet try to move the will with affective preaching, and still be philosophically consistent. The result was a long history of Reformed revival preaching, which changed the course of both British and American churches and societies.

The Reformed tradition is also well-known for teaching justification by grace through faith and stressing as well a life-long process of sanctification (growth in holiness). Typically, Reformed thinkers have underlined their opposition to Roman Catholicism, arguing that their views of justification and sanctification differ from Rome's. Not infrequently, too, Edwards has been invoked to "demonstrate" those deep differences. After all, "America's theologian" believed the papacy was one of the Antichrists (the other was Islam) and denounced Roman veneration of Mary and the saints, belief in purgatory and indulgences, and its other "superstitions and idolatries" as "contrary to the light of nature."

But recent research shows that Edwards on justification provides in fact a bridge between the two traditions. On the one hand, Edwards maintains Protestant emphases. He denies all human merit in salvation, saying that justification comes only by Christ's work, which becomes ours by virtue of our union with Christ in faith. But he also agrees with Catholic teaching when he says that salvation has "conditions," the beauty of saints is "inherent," grace is "infused," regeneration is (in one sense) lifelong, God's moral goodness becomes ours, and grace acts as a kind of physical influence.[6] This convergence may provide new grist for dialogue between Reformed and Catholic Christians.

The Reformed tradition is also known for its respect for the intellect and its ardent pursuit of holiness. Edwards is a model of both. His efforts to resolve these and other theological puzzles exemplify the first, and his sermons and numerous personal writings illustrate the second. Students of Edwards, especially those in the Reformed tradition, have found great encouragement from America's theologian for both mind and heart.

Ethics and Community

Christians today can also learn from Edwards when thinking about life with others, both inside and outside the church. Two theological principles guided his sense of ethics: the spirit of Christian love and God's relation to his creation. In brief, the spirit of Christian love moves the Christian to concern for the interests of others. The Christian will be concerned not just for the spiritual needs of others, but for their material needs as well. And the Christian will be concerned for the interests of all human beings, regenerate as well as unregenerate. God's relation to his creation, on the other hand, is incarnational. That is, he is present in one's neighbor, and especially in the poor. Therefore the most direct and pleasing way for the Christian to love God is to serve people in society and give to the poor.

Edwards believed the church should work with those outside the church for common moral ends. One basis for this, he said, is a shared image of God in all. All human beings have the same general sense of moral good and evil (an understanding of what philosophers call "natural law") and appreciate many of the same sorts of physical and moral beauty, even if they do not share a common vision of God's beauty. Therefore Christians may share with non-Christians the same moral goals, albeit for different reasons, and can and must sometimes work together in common social projects for the sake of those moral goals.

But Edwards does not have in mind simply the individual working occasionally with other individuals. Both his ethics and his aesthetics pointed to community. All earthly beauty, he said, is based on the concept of "union" and is thereby an image of the union of spiritual beings in the spiritual world. Thus, union of spiritual beings in the spiritual word, to which all earthly beauty is an analogy, consists in "the consent of mind, of the different members of a society or system of intelligent beings, sweetly united in a benevolent agreement of heart."[7]

If all earthly beauty for Edwards is a natural image of a community of minds, all true virtue on this earth (and beyond) creates community. This was the basis for Edwards's social ethics. The essence of virtue is love, and the nature of truly virtuous love is to reach out to being in general (Edwards is speaking philosophically here of all of existence, in God). In reaching out, Edwards asserted, we enlarge ourselves because we are coming into union with "Being in general": God and all his creation. Love's nature, then, is to create community by seeking union with others: "In pure love to others (i.e. love not arising from self-love) there's a union of the heart with others; a kind of enlargement of the mind, whereby it so extends itself as to take others into a man's self: and therefore it implies a disposition to feel, to desire, and to act as though others were one with ourselves."[8]

For Edwards this meant, among other things, working to help the poor. Christians should work with others toward this common moral goal. Besides the philosophical reasons just outlined, the Christian has theological reasons for doing so. First, helping the poor is a measure of true love. Lest love be interpreted by Christians as simply concern for the souls of the unregenerate, Edwards insisted that true love cares for their bodies as well. In *Religious Affections* he wrote that true religion cares for the material as well as spiritual needs of others. He criticized those who "pretend a great love to men's souls, that are not compassionate and charitable towards their bodies. . . . And if the compassion of professing Christians towards others don't work in the same ways [i.e., to their bodies], it is a sign that it is no true Christian compassion."[9]

Helping the poor was also an indispensable sign of one's love for God. While Edwards conceived of the world as re-created by God at every moment and in such a way that even what is created is not a substance but an instance of God's acting, nevertheless Edwards so particularized God's being in the world as to restrict it, for the purpose of this doctrine, to the person of one's neighbor. In the Christian's neighbor God is found. So if Christians want to express love for God, they must serve their neighbors. For one's neighbor is God's "receiver": "We can't express our love to God by doing anything that is profitable to God; God would therefore have us do it in those things that are profitable to our neighbors, whom he has constituted his receivers."[10]

If helping the poor is a necessary sign of love for God, it is also a litmus test for judging religious experience. After the Great Awakening Edwards instructed ministers not to affirm the religious experience of anyone who did not seek to relieve the poor, though "they tell a fair story of illuminations and discoveries." He preached to his church in Northampton, Massachusetts, that charity to the poor is a duty as important for the Christian as prayer or church attendance. No commandment is laid down in stronger terms than the commandment of giving to the poor. It is therefore an all-important test of grace. "And the Scripture is as plain as it is possible it should be, that none are true saints, but those whose true character it is, that they are of a disposition to pity and relieve their fellow creatures, that are poor, indigent and afflicted."[11]

This is an objective standard by which every Christian would be judged. But effort alone was not enough; Edwards judged the sufficiency of Christian charity by the number of poor remaining in a community. Unless there were none in the community "that are proper objects of Charity . . . [suffering] in pinching [want]," Christians in the community had not done enough. "Rich men" were urged by Edwards to establish and support schools "in poor towns and villages" and to support ministerial students from poor families.[12]

Politics and Society

I have described elsewhere how Edwards's public theology was, contrary to earlier scholarly opinion, neither nationalistic nor chauvinist.[13] He did not forecast a millennium centered in America. Nor did he think New England or America was a righteous nation. Both, he thought, were given more privileges than any nation in history, and so were more guilty than any because they had abused those privileges. The older he got, the further the Kingdom of God receded from America in his thinking.

But Edwards did not retreat from engaging his America. He didn't just draw pictures of heaven for his parishioners bound for heaven, but used his pulpit and study to subject eighteenth-century political powers to the judgment of transcendent ideals. He did this in a number of ways. First, he limited the pretensions of society's power brokers by shifting the locus of authority from the social hierarchy ("the authorities must be right") to the inner recesses of the heart (the spiritual authority of those who have seen the divine beauty). Edwards generally defended the structures of colonial society, but he also exposed the spiritual poverty of New England's movers and shakers by pronouncing God's esteem for the ordinary God-fearing Christian. For that reason, he proclaimed, the poor, the black slaves, the uneducated, women, and young people who had found salvation could hold their heads high, for they possessed greater personal worth than their worldly superiors. Edwards never contemplated or advocated a reordering of society, but his ennoblement of the common Christian may have given confidence to those colonials who tried to challenge society's elites. It is no wonder that Edwards's most important theological disciples (Samuel Hopkins, Joseph Bellamy, and Jonathan Edwards Jr.) advocated resistance against Britain after 1760 and trained legions of pastors who "energetically promoted" the patriot cause in the American Revolution.

Second, Edwards limited economic pretensions by teaching that God was found especially in the poor and that God called the poor into his Kingdom more often than he called the rich. The Christian serves God, according to Edwards, by helping the poor. Both the church and the state ought to actively assist the underprivileged.

Third, Edwards defended the poor by denouncing their exploitation in the marketplace. He attacked businessmen for taking advantage of the poor family's desperation in order to make an unreasonable profit. He warned merchants that God would defend the poor and threatened that those who did not contribute to the town's poor collections might be struck dead. He supported the town's welfare system and attacked his own church for preferring the rich in its seating design.[14]

What It Means to Be Human: Beauty, Being, and Understanding

I have just talked about ways Edwards can help Christians understand ethics and life in community. But Edwards has always appealed to people outside the church as well. Years ago, in the mid-twentieth century, Arthur Schlesinger Jr. and others joked about forming an "Atheists for Niebuhr" society. Reinhold Niebuhr was a theologian whose writings on society and politics were deeply attractive to many American intellectuals. Edwards has had similar appeal to a wide variety of intellectuals, especially since atheist Perry Miller, with his 1949 biography of Edwards, started what could be called his "Atheists for Edwards" society. Aestheticists (those interested in the meaning of beauty) and philosophers have found his little *Nature of True Virtue* to be a work of groundbreaking insight into the relation between morality and beauty. Four essays in this volume (by Professors Kimnach, Vetö, Fabiny, and Lee) have admired, each in a different way, the way he describes beauty and its relation to God. Not all of Edwards's admirers believe in God, but most have been intrigued—some inspired—by the way he found beauty to be the central meaning of human experience. For this eighteenth-century New Englander, proportion is at the heart of existence. That means relations and relationships. To the extent that relations are pleasing and fitting, they are beautiful. Natural relations in, say, a beautiful landscape point by analogy to the sweet consents among minds that share common ideals. And if nature is animated by a principle of order and ultimate justice—which some call the Dao and others Brahman, and Christians the Logos—then beauty is the sweet agreement between human minds and that ultimate order. Edwards, of course, called it God and said that all natural proportion in the world is a pointer to or type of the sweet agreements among the three persons of the Trinity. In any event, this idea of beauty as proportion and therefore the meaning of human existence has drawn many minds to its elegant contours.

Professor Vetö shows how Edwards's philosophy has much to say to people, religious and nonreligious, who wonder about being, knowledge, and will. We have already seen that Edwards's distinction between natural and moral ability can help society see that people are still responsible for what they think they can't help—as long as they did what they did voluntarily. Edwards's doctrine of being, which sees all of reality as spiritual because it is the fleshing out, if you will, of God's thinking, will never enthuse atheists. But it will interest the majority of people who believe reality is finally spiritual rather than material and are struck by modern physicists who tell us that matter is energy. It will make theological sense to those theists who wonder what to do with the "butterfly effect," which means that the fluttering wings of one butterfly on one side of the planet will affect things on the other side, thus demonstrating that everything is interdependent. Edwards's doctrine of being helps us understand why things are that way. His answer is that it is because they are all in God's mind, and he is ordering them all toward a final goal.

Edwards's doctrine of understanding (recall Professor Vető's discussion) is primarily about spiritual perception. It describes the quasi-mystical experience of those who say they suddenly came to "see" the beauty of God and all of existence. Their inner eyes were opened and now everything appears in a new light. But it can also be used to help us understand moral experience. For example, why is it that some people really seem to "get it" morally? They see intuitively the "badness" of moral evil and the goodness of moral good without needing it to be explained to them. They seem compelled to pursue the one and fight the other.

Edwards would say, using his doctrine of understanding, that they have been gifted with a "taste" of moral reality. This taste or vision has suddenly opened up to them the organic links between certain actions or states of being and the ultimate categories of Good and Evil. They didn't need a university course in ethics (although this can help refine their taste). No, their moral taste was given from above. And it is an invaluable tool—Edwards would call it the essential vision—for seeing the moral order of things. This is a third way in which Edwards's philosophy—of will, being, and understanding—can be of use to those who don't share his theology, even though this philosophy was his way of rationally unfolding that theology.

Pluralism and Religious Violence

Today many are afraid of religiously inspired violence. More than a few fear the rise of a conservative Christian movement that would impose its religion on a nation or the world, deeming all other religions demonic and lacking any truth. The last essay in this book demonstrates that an Edwardsian view of other religions would fight this tendency. While Edwards believed that Christian faith was God's final revelation (Judaism was also revealed by the true God, but incomplete), he nevertheless believed that Christianity as lived in its first seventeen hundred years was an imperfect incarnation of God's truth, and that God had given truth—even religious truth!—to other religions. Not only had God shown human virtue and supernatural realities to non-Christians (including the atonement and Trinity!), but he had used even devilish pagan rites such as idol worship and human sacrifice to teach religious truths—not to approve of idolatry or murder, of course, but to suggest divine incarnation and God's sacrifice of his own son. The bottom line is not that pagan headhunters were somehow godly (for Edwards, they were still condemned by their sins), but that God was working on non-Christians to reveal his truths, and that somehow the history of other religions might be used for the final redemption of the world.

No one who believes what Edwards taught about the religions could ever join a theocratic movement bent on dominating the world. Edwards showed a way that believers can work for a world in which there is freedom for other religions, have respect for truth in other religions, and at the same time hold the conviction that God has finally and fully revealed himself in Jesus Christ.

Jonathan Edwards could not have imagined the extent to which his own writings have influenced so many minds in so many different disciplines—and now in more and more countries of the world. But he did intend to influence many different kinds of thinkers, not only ordinary people in the churches but also learned minds inside and outside the churches. After all, he wrote his book on virtue without ever quoting the Bible for people on both sides of the Atlantic who had been influenced by deism, which was a movement dedicated to the destruction of Christian orthodoxy.[5] He expected his massive tome on the will to be read by philosophers of all different sorts. At the same time, he preached for Christian believers and wrote biblically centered books on spiritual discernment, original sin, revival, and God's work in history.

If this book has been successful, it has inspired you, dear reader, to explore Edwards's own writings. We hope it has convinced you that he has something to say not only to theologians and philosophers, but to every sort of person who seeks the good, the true, and the beautiful.

NOTES

1. For his recommendations on the spiritual life, see his letter to a young convert: "Letter to Deborah Hatheway, "in the Yale edition of *The Works of Jonathan Edwards* [hereafter, *WJE*], 16: 90–95.

2. For more on Edwards's prescriptions for spiritual formation, see Sam Storms, *Signs of the Spirit: An Interpretation of Jonathan Edwards' Religious Affections* (Wheaton, IL: Crossway Books, 2007), and Gerald R. McDermott, *Seeing God: Jonathan Edwards and Spiritual Discernment* (Vancouver, Canada: Regent College Publishing, 1995).

3. *History of the Work of Redemption*, in *WJE* 9: 119, 123–24.

4. Ibid., 124–25.

5. Ibid., 480.

6. For more on this, see Gerald R. McDermott, "Jonathan Edwards and Justification—More Protestant or Catholic?," *Pro Ecclesia* 17, no. 1 (winter 2008): 92–111.

7. *Nature of True Virtue*, in *WJE* 8: 565.

8. Ibid., 589.

9. *Religious Affections*, in *WJE* 2: 369.

10. *Some Thoughts Concerning the Revival*, in *WJE* 4: 523–24.

11. *Religious Affections*, in *WJE* 2: 335, 355.

12. Sermon on Malachi 3:10–11, July 1743, Edwards Papers, Beinecke Rare Book and Manuscript Library, Yale University; *Some Thoughts Concerning the Revival,* in *WJE* 4: 515.

13. See Gerald R. McDermott, *One Holy and Happy Society: The Public Theology of Jonathan Edwards* (University Park: Pennsylvania State University Press, 1992), especially chapters 1 and 2.

14. For more on Edwards and society, see McDermott, *One Holy and Happy Society.*

15. There are two very indirect allusions, but no explicit citation of the Bible, in *The Nature of True Virtue,* in *WJE* 8: 551, 560.

Further Reading

EDWARDS HIMSELF: SHORT COLLECTIONS

Bailey, Richard A., and Wills, Gregory A., eds. *The Salvation of Souls: Nine Previously Unpublished Sermons on the Call of Ministry and the Gospel by Jonathan Edwards.* Wheaton, IL: Crossway Books, 2002.

Faust, Clarence H., and Johnson, Thomas H. *Jonathan Edwards: Representative Selections.* New York: Hill and Wang, 1935.

Kimnach, Wilson H., Kenneth P. Minkema, and Douglas A. Sweeney, eds. *The Sermons of Jonathan Edwards: A Reader.* London: Yale University Press, 1999.

Simonson, Harold P., ed. *Selected Writings of Jonathan Edwards.* Prospect Heights, IL: Waveland Press, 1970.

Smith, John E., Harry S. Stout, and Kenneth P. Minkema, eds. *A Jonathan Edwards Reader.* New Haven: Yale University Press, 1995.

Winslow, Ola Elizabeth, ed. *Jonathan Edwards: Basic Writings.* New York: Penguin Books, 1966.

EDWARDS HIMSELF: THE YALE EDITION OF *THE WORKS OF JONATHAN EDWARDS*

Vol. 1, *Freedom of the Will*, ed. Paul Ramsey.
Vol. 2, *Religious Affections*, ed. John E. Smith.
Vol. 3, *Original Sin*, ed. Clyde A. Holbrook.
Vol. 4, *The Great Awakening*, ed. C. C. Goen.

> *A Faithful Narrative*
> *The Distinguishing Marks*

Some Thoughts Concerning the Revival
Preface to True Religion by Joseph Bellamy

Vol. 5, *Apocalyptic Writings*, ed. Stephen J. Stein.

Notes on the Apocalypse
An Humble Attempt

Vol. 6, *Scientific and Philosophical Writings*, ed. Wallace E. Anderson.

The "Spider" Papers
Natural Philosophy
The Mind
Short Scientific and Philosophical Papers

Vol. 7, *The Life of David Brainerd*, ed. Norman Petit.
Vol. 8, *Ethical Writings*, ed. Paul Ramsey.

Charity and Its Fruits
Concerning the End for Which God Created the World
The Nature of True Virtue

Vol. 9, *A History of the Work of Redemption*, ed. John F. Wilson.
Vol. 10, *Sermons and Discourses, 1720–1723*, ed. Wilson H. Kimnach.
Vol. 11, *Typological Writings*, ed. Wallace E. Anderson and Mason I. Lowance.

Images of Divine Things
Types
Types of the Messiah

Vol. 12, *Ecclesiastical Writings*, ed. David D. Hall.

A Letter to the Author of an Answer to the Hampshire Narrative
An Humble Inquiry
Misrepresentations Corrected
Narrative of Communion Controversy

Vol. 13, *The "Miscellanies," a–500*, ed. Thomas A. Schafer.
Vol. 14, *Sermons and Discourses, 1723–1729*, ed. Kenneth P. Minkema.
Vol. 15, *Notes on Scripture*, ed. Stephen J. Stein.
Vol. 16, *Letters and Personal Writings*, ed. George S. Claghorn.

Letters
Resolutions
Diary
On Sarah Pierpont
Personal Narrative

Vol. 17, *Sermons and Discourses, 1730–1733*, ed. Mark Valeri.
Vol. 18, *The "Miscellanies," 501–832*, ed. Ava Chamberlin.
Vol. 19, *Sermons and Discourses, 1734–1738*, ed. M. X. Lesser.
Vol. 20, *The "Mescellanies," 833–1152*, ed. Amy Plantinga Pauw.
Vol. 21, *Writings on the Trinity, Grace and Faith*, ed. Sang Hyun Lee.

Discourse on the Trinity
On the Equality of the Persons of the Trinity
Treatise on Grace
Effacious Grace
"Controversies" Notebook
Faith
Signs of Godliness
Christ's Example
Directions for Judging of Persons' Experiences

Vol. 22, *Sermons and Discourses, 1739–1742,* ed. Harry S. Stout and Nathan O. Hatch.

Vol. 23, *The "Miscellanies," 1153–1360,* ed. Douglas A. Sweeney.

Vol. 24, *The "Blank Bible,"* Parts 1 and 2, ed. Stephen J. Stein.

Vol. 25, *Sermons and Discourses, 1743–1758,* ed. Wilson H. Kimnach.

Vol. 26, *Catalogues of Reading,* ed. Peter J. Theusen (forthcoming).

Catalogue of Reading
Account Book

EASY AND BASIC: OVERALL INTRODUCTIONS

Lesser, M. X. *Jonathan Edwards.* Boston: Twayne Publishers, 1988.

Nichols, Stephen J. *Jonathan Edwards: A Guided Tour of His Life and Thought.* Phillipsburg, NJ: Puritan and Reformed, 2001.

Piper, John. *God's Passion for His Glory: Living the Vision of Jonathan Edwards.* Wheaton, IL: Crossway Books, 1998.

Simonson, Harold P. *Jonathan Edwards: Theologian of the Heart.* Macon, GA: Mercer University Press, 1982.

MORE CHALLENGING OVERALL INTRODUCTIONS

Cherry, Conrad. *The Theology of Jonathan Edwards: A Reappraisal.* Bloomington: Indiana University Press, 1966.

Holmes, Stephen R. *God of Grace and God of Glory: An Account of the Theology of Jonathan Edwards.* Grand Rapids, MI: William B. Eerdmans, 2000.

Jenson, Robert W. *America's Theologian: A Recommendation of Jonathan Edwards.* New York: Oxford University Press, 1988.

McClymond, Michael J. *Encounters with God: An Approach to the Theology of Jonathan Edwards.* New York: Oxford University Press, 1998.

Smith, John E. *Jonathan Edwards: Puritan, Preacher, Philosopher.* Notre Dame, IN: University of Notre Dame Press, 1992.

BIOGRAPHIES

Dods, Elisabeth. *Marriage to a Difficult Man: The Uncommon Union of Jonathan and Sarah Edwards.* Laurel, MS: Audubon Press, 2005.

Gura, Philip F. *Jonathan Edwards: America's Evangelical*. New York: Hill and Wang, 2005.

Marsden, George M. *Jonathan Edwards: A Life*. London: Yale University Press, 2003.

Miller, Perry. *Jonathan Edwards*. New York: Meridian Books, 1949.

Murray, Iain H. *Jonathan Edwards: A New Biography*. Carlisle, PA: The Banner of Truth Trust, 1987.

MORE CHALLENGING BOOKS ON SELECTED THEMES

Brown, Robert E. *Jonathan Edwards and the Bible*. Bloomington: Indiana University Press, 2002.

Danaher, William J., Jr. *The Trinitarian Ethics of Jonathan Edwards*. Louisville, KY: Westminster John Knox Press, 2004.

Daniel, Stephen H. *The Philosophy of Jonathan Edwards*. Bloomington: Indiana University Press, 1994.

Fiering, Norman. *Jonathan Edwards: Moral Thought and Its British Context*. Williamsburg, VA: University of North Carolina Press, 1981.

Guelzo, Allen C. *Edwards on the Will: A Century of American Theological Debate*. Middletown, CT: Wesleyan University Press, 1989.

Lee, Sang Hyun. *The Philosophical Theology of Jonathan Edwards*. Princeton, NJ: Princeton University Press, 1988.

McDermott, Gerald R. *Jonathan Edwards Confronts the Gods: Christian Theology, Enlightenment Religion, and Non-Christian Faiths*. New York: Oxford University Press, 2000.

———. *One Holy and Happy Society: The Public Theology of Jonathan Edwards*. University Park: Pennsylvania State University Press, 1992.

———. *Seeing God: Jonathan Edwards and Spiritual Discernment*. Vancouver, Canada: Regent College Publishing, 1995.

Moody, Josh. *Jonathan Edwards and the Enlightenment: Knowing the Presence of God*. Lanham, MD: University Press of America, 2005.

Morimoto, Anri. *Jonathan Edwards and the Catholic Vision of Salvation*. University Park: Pennsylvania State University Press, 1995.

Morris, William Sparks. *The Young Jonathan Edwards*. Brooklyn, NY: Carlson Publishing, 1991.

Pauw, Amy Plantinga. *The Supreme Harmony of All: The Trinitarian Theology of Jonathan Edwards*. Grand Rapids, MI: William B. Eerdmans, 2002.

Sherry, Patrick. *Spirit and Beauty: An Introduction to Theological Aesthetics*. Birmingham, UK: SCM Press, 2002.

Storms, Sam. *Signs of the Spirit: An Interpretation of Jonathan Edwards' Religious Affections*. Wheaton, IL: Crossway Books, 2007.

Tracy, Patricia J. *Jonathan Edwards, Pastor: Religion and Society in Eighteenth-Century Northampton*. New York: Hill and Wang, 1980.

Wilson, Stephen A. *Virtue Reformed: Rereading Jonathan Edwards's Ethics*. Leiden: Brill, 2005.

Zakai, Avihu. *Jonathan Edwards's Philosophy of History: The Reenchantment of the World in the Age of Enlightenment.* Princeton, NJ: Princeton University Press, 2003.

COLLECTIONS OF SCHOLARLY ARTICLES

Hart, D. G., Sean Michael Lucas, and Stephen J. Nichols, eds. *The Legacy of Jonathan Edwards: American Religion and the Evangelical Tradition.* Grand Rapids, MI: Baker, 2003.

Hatch, Nathan O., and Harry S. Stout, eds. *Jonathan Edwards and the American Experience.* New York, Oxford University Press, 1988.

Helm, Paul, and Oliver Crisp, eds. *Jonathan Edwards: Philosophical Theologian.* London: Ashgate, 2003.

Kling, David W., and Douglas A. Sweeney, eds. *Jonathan Edwards at Home and Abroad: Historical Memories, Cultural Movements, Global Horizons.* Columbia: University of South Carolina Press, 2003.

Lee, Sang Hyun, ed. *A Companion to the Theology of Jonathan Edwards.* Princeton, NJ: Princeton University Press, 2005.

Lee, Sang Hyun, and Alan Guelzo, eds. *Edwards in Our Time: Jonathan Edwards and the Shaping of American Religion.* Grand Rapids, MI: Eerdmans, 2000.

Oberg, Barbara O., and Harry S. Stout, eds. *Benjamin Franklin, Jonathan Edwards, and the Representation of American Culture.* New York: Oxford University Press, 1993.

Piper, John, and Justin Taylor, eds. *A God-Entranced Vision of All Things: The Legacy of Jonathan Edwards.* Wheaton, IL: Crossway, 2004.

Stein, Stephen J., ed. *Jonathan Edwards's Writings: Text, Context, Interpretation.* Bloomington: Indian University Press, 1996.

———, ed. *The Cambridge Companion to Jonathan Edwards.* Cambridge, UK: Cambridge University Press, 2006.

OTHER RELEVANT BOOKS AND ARTICLES
BY AUTHORS IN THIS VOLUME

Fabiny, Tibor, *The Lion and the Lamb: Figuralism and Fulfillment in the Bible, Art and Literature.* New York: St. Martin's Press, 1992.

Hatch, Nathan O., and Harry S. Stout, eds. *Jonathan Edwards and the American Experience.* New York: Oxford University Press, 1988.

Kimnach, Wilson H. "General Introduction to the Sermons: Jonathan Edwards' Art of Prophesying." In *The Works of Jonathan Edwards,* vol. 10, *Sermon and Discourses, 1720–1723.* New Haven: Yale University Press, 1992, 3–258.

———. "Jonathan Edwards's Early Sermons: New York, 1722–1723." *Journal of Presbyterian History* 55 (1977): 255–56.

———. "Jonathan Edwards's Sermon Mill." *Early American Literature* 10 (fall 1975): 167–77.

Lee, Sang Hyun. "Editor's Introduction." In *Works of Jonathan Edwards,* vol. 21, *Writings on the Trinity, Grace, and Faith.* New Haven: Yale University Press, 2003, 1–106.

————, ed. *The Princeton Companion to the Theology of Jonathan Edwards*. Princeton, NJ: Princeton University Press, 2005.

Minkema, Kenneth P. "Old Age and Religion in the Life and Writings of Jonathan Edwards." *Church History* 70 (Dec. 2001): 674–704.

Sweeney, Douglas A. *Nathaniel William Taylor, New Haven Theology, and the Legacy of Jonathan Edwards*. New York: Oxford University Press, 2003.

Vetö, Miklós. *La pensée de Jonathan Edwards*. Paris: Éditions due Cerf, 1987.

————. *The Religious Metaphysics of Simone Weil*. Translated by Joan Dargan. Albany: State University of New York Press, 1994.

Index